COMPUTER BOOK SERIES FROM IDG

Visual F... For Du...

MW00436655

Joining Tables in a View

You're joining two tables to form a view. You can use a view the way that you use a table:

✔ The tables must have at least one field in common, which is the field that you'll use to join the tables.

✔ The common field must have the same name, type, and size in both tables.

✔ You use the View Designer dialog box to join tables into a view.

✔ Save the view so that you don't have to go back and join the tables again.

Creating a Database and a Table

To create a database and table:

1. Write down the information that you want to store in the fields of the table.

2. Choose File➪New to display the New dialog box.

3. Select the Database radio button.

4. Click the New file button to display the Database Designer dialog box.

5. Choose File➪New to display the New dialog box again.

6. Select the Table radio button.

7. Click the New file button to display the Database Designer dialog box again.

8. Enter a name for the table.

9. Click Save to open the Table Designer dialog box.

10. Enter the fields (name, type, and size).

11. Click OK to save the table.

12. Choose File➪Close to close the Database Designer.

IDG BOOKS WORLDWIDE

...For Dummies: #1 Computer Book Series for Beginners

Visual FoxPro™ 5 For Dummies®

Cheat Sheet

Viewing Data in a Table

To view data in a table:

1. Choose File⇨Open to display the Open dialog box.

2. Click the database that contains the table that you want to open.

3. Click OK to display the Database Designer dialog box.

4. Double-click the box containing the table that has the data you want to see.

5. Choose File⇨Close to close the Database Designer.

Useful Keyboard Shortcuts

Command	Shortcut
Go away!	Esc
Undo	Ctrl+Z
Cut	Ctrl+X
Copy	Ctrl+C
Paste	Ctrl+V
Add a record	Ctrl+Y
Get help fast	F1
Mark a record for deletion	Ctrl+T
Close the current window	Ctrl+F4

Field Types

Field Type	Description
Character	Anything with letters or numbers; the most common field type
Date	Dates
Numeric	Normal numbers, with or without decimal points
Logical	Yes or no; designed for simple questions
Memo	Long free-form text field, such as for notes
Float	Scientific numbers

...For Dummies: #1 Computer Book Series for Beginners

VISUAL FOXPRO™ 5 FOR DUMMIES®

by Jim Keogh

IDG Books Worldwide, Inc.
An International Data Group Company

Foster City, CA ♦ Chicago, IL ♦ Indianapolis, IN ♦ Southlake, TX

Visual FoxPro™ 5 For Dummies®

Published by
IDG Books Worldwide, Inc.
An International Data Group Company
919 E. Hillsdale Blvd.
Suite 400
Foster City, CA 94404
http://www.idgbooks.com (IDG Books Worldwide Web site)
http://www.dummies.com (Dummies Press Web site)

Library of Congress Catalog Card No.: 97-70367

ISBN: 0-7645-0123-2

Printed in the United States of America

10 9 8 7 6 5 4 3 2 1

1DD/RU/QT/ZX/IN

Distributed in the United States by IDG Books Worldwide, Inc.

Distributed by Macmillan Canada for Canada; by Transworld Publishers Limited in the United Kingdom and Europe; by WoodsLane Pty. Ltd. for Australia; by WoodsLane Enterprises Ltd. for New Zealand; by Longman Singapore Publishers Ltd. for Singapore, Malaysia, Thailand, and Indonesia; by Simron Pty. Ltd. for South Africa; by Toppan Company Ltd. for Japan; by Distribuidora Cuspide for Argentina; by Livraria Cultura for Brazil; by Ediciencia S.A. for Ecuador; by Addison-Wesley Publishing Company for Korea; by Ediciones ZETA S.C.R. Ltda. for Peru; by WS Computer Publishing Company, Inc., for the Philippines; by Unalis Corporation for Taiwan; by Contemporanea de Ediciones for Venezuela. Authorized Sales Agent: Anthony Rudkin Associates for the Middle East and North Africa.

For general information on IDG Books Worldwide's books in the U.S., please call our Consumer Customer Service department at 800-762-2974. For reseller information, including discounts and premium sales, please call our Reseller Customer Service department at 800-434-3422.

For information on where to purchase IDG Books Worldwide's books outside the U.S., please contact our International Sales department at 415-655-3023 or fax 415-655-3299.

For information on foreign language translations, please contact our Foreign & Subsidiary Rights department at 415-655-3021 or fax 415-655-3281.

For sales inquiries and special prices for bulk quantities, please contact our Sales department at 415-655-3200 or write to the address above.

For information on using IDG Books Worldwide's books in the classroom or for ordering examination copies, please contact our Educational Sales department at 800-434-2086 or fax 817-251-8174.

For press review copies, author interviews, or other publicity information, please contact our Public Relations department at 415-655-3000 or fax 415-655-3299.

For authorization to photocopy items for corporate, personal, or educational use, please contact Copyright Clearance Center, 222 Rosewood Drive, Danvers, MA 01923, or fax 508-750-4470.

is a trademark under exclusive license to IDG Books Worldwide, Inc., from International Data Group, Inc.

About the Author

Jim Keogh is a professor of computer science at Saint Peter's College in Jersey City, New Jersey. He has developed FoxPro systems for major Wall Street firms and is the author of more than 30 books on computers, including *UNIX Programming For Dummies*. He is a former columnist and contributing editor of *Popular Electronics* magazine, as well as a former associate editor of *Personal Computing* magazine.

ABOUT IDG BOOKS WORLDWIDE

Welcome to the world of IDG Books Worldwide.

IDG Books Worldwide, Inc., is a subsidiary of International Data Group, the world's largest publisher of computer-related information and the leading global provider of information services on information technology. IDG was founded more than 25 years ago and now employs more than 8,500 people worldwide. IDG publishes more than 275 computer publications in over 75 countries (see listing below). More than 60 million people read one or more IDG publications each month.

Launched in 1990, IDG Books Worldwide is today the #1 publisher of best-selling computer books in the United States. We are proud to have received eight awards from the Computer Press Association in recognition of editorial excellence and three from *Computer Currents'* First Annual Readers' Choice Awards. Our best-selling *...For Dummies*® series has more than 30 million copies in print with translations in 30 languages. IDG Books Worldwide, through a joint venture with IDG's Hi-Tech Beijing, became the first U.S. publisher to publish a computer book in the People's Republic of China. In record time, IDG Books Worldwide has become the first choice for millions of readers around the world who want to learn how to better manage their businesses.

Our mission is simple: Every one of our books is designed to bring extra value and skill-building instructions to the reader. Our books are written by experts who understand and care about our readers. The knowledge base of our editorial staff comes from years of experience in publishing, education, and journalism — experience we use to produce books for the '90s. In short, we care about books, so we attract the best people. We devote special attention to details such as audience, interior design, use of icons, and illustrations. And because we use an efficient process of authoring, editing, and desktop publishing our books electronically, we can spend more time ensuring superior content and spend less time on the technicalities of making books.

You can count on our commitment to deliver high-quality books at competitive prices on topics you want to read about. At IDG Books Worldwide, we continue in the IDG tradition of delivering quality for more than 25 years. You'll find no better book on a subject than one from IDG Books Worldwide.

John J. Kilcullen

John Kilcullen
CEO
IDG Books Worldwide, Inc.

Eighth Annual
Computer Press
Awards ≥1992

Ninth Annual
Computer Press
Awards ≥1993

Tenth Annual
Computer Press
Awards ≥1994

Eleventh Annual
Computer Press
Awards ≥1995

IDG Books Worldwide, Inc., is a subsidiary of International Data Group, the world's largest publisher of computer-related information and the leading global provider of information services on information technology. International Data Group publishes over 275 computer publications in over 75 countries. Sixty million people read one or more International Data Group publications each month. International Data Group's publications include: **ARGENTINA:** Buyer's Guide, Computerworld Argentina, PC World Argentina; **AUSTRALIA:** Australian Macworld, Australian PC World, Australian Reseller News, Computerworld, IT Casebook, Network World, Publish, Webmaster; **AUSTRIA:** Computerwelt Osterreich, Networks Austria, PC Tip Austria; **BANGLADESH:** PC World Bangladesh; **BELARUS:** PC World Belarus; **BELGIUM:** Data News, PC World Belgium; **BRAZIL:** Annuário de Informática, Computerworld, Connections, Macworld, PC Player, PC World, Publish, Reseller News, Supergamepower; **BULGARIA:** Computerworld Bulgaria, Network World Bulgaria, PC & MacWorld Bulgaria; **CANADA:** CIO Canada, Client/Server World, ComputerWorld Canada, InfoWorld Canada, NetworkWorld Canada, WebWorld; **CHILE:** Computerworld Chile, PC World Chile; **COLOMBIA:** Computerworld Colombia, PC World Colombia; **COSTA RICA:** PC World Centro America; **THE CZECH AND SLOVAK REPUBLICS:** Computerworld Czechoslovakia, Macworld Czech Republic, PC World Czechoslovakia; **DENMARK:** Communications World Danmark, Computerworld Danmark, Macworld Danmark, PC World Danmark, Techworld Denmark; **DOMINICAN REPUBLIC:** PC World Republica Dominicana; **ECUADOR:** PC World Ecuador; **EGYPT:** Computerworld Middle East, PC World Middle East; **EL SALVADOR:** PC World Centro America; **FINLAND:** MikroPC, Tietoverkko, Tietoviikko; **FRANCE:** Distributique, Hebdo, Info PC, Le Monde Informatique, Macworld, Reseaux & Telecoms, WebMaster France; **GERMANY:** Computer Partner, Computerwoche, Computerwoche Extra, Computerwoche FOCUS, Global Online, Macwelt, PC Welt; **GREECE:** Amiga Computing, GamePro Greece, Multimedia World; **GUATEMALA:** PC World Centro America; **HONDURAS:** PC World Centro America; **HONG KONG:** Computerworld Hong Kong, PC World Hong Kong, Publish in Asia; **HUNGARY:** ABCD CD-ROM, Computerworld Szamitastechnika, Internetto online Magazine, PC World Hungary, PC-X Magazin Hungary; **ICELAND:** Tolvuheimur PC World Island; **INDIA:** Information Communications World, Information Systems Computerworld, PC World India, Publish in Asia; **INDONESIA:** InfoKomputer PC World, Komputek Computerworld, Publish in Asia; **IRELAND:** ComputerScope, PC Live!; **ISRAEL:** Macworld Israel, People & Computers/Computerworld; **ITALY:** Computerworld Italia, Macworld Italia, Networking Italia, PC World Italia; **JAPAN:** DTP World, Macworld Japan, Nikkei Personal Computing, OS/2 World Japan, SunWorld Japan, Windows NT World, Windows World Japan; **KENYA:** PC World East African; **KOREA:** Hi-Tech Information, Macworld Korea, PC World Korea; **MACEDONIA:** PC World Macedonia; **MALAYSIA:** Computerworld Malaysia, PC World Malaysia, Publish in Asia; **MALTA:** PC World Malta; **MEXICO:** Computerworld Mexico, PC World Mexico; **MYANMAR:** PC World Myanmar; **NETHERLANDS:** Computer! Totaal, LAN Internetworking Magazine, LAN World Buyers Guide, Macworld Netherlands, Net, WebWereld; **NEW ZEALAND:** Absolute Beginners Guide and Plain & Simple Series, Computer Buyer, Computer Industry Directory, Computerworld New Zealand, MTB, Network World, PC World New Zealand; **NICARAGUA:** PC World Centro America; **NORWAY:** Computerworld Norge, CW Rapport, Datamagasinet, Financial Rapport, Kursguide Norge, Macworld Norge, Multimediaworld Norge, PC World Ekspress Norge, PC World Nettverk, PC World Norge, PC World ProduktGuide Norge; **PAKISTAN:** Computerworld Pakistan; **PANAMA:** PC World Panama; **PEOPLE'S REPUBLIC OF CHINA:** China Computer Users, China Computerworld, China InfoWorld, China Telecom World Weekly, Computer & Communication, Electronic Design China, Electronics Today, Electronics Weekly, Game Software, PC World China, Popular Computer Week, Software Weekly, Software World, Telecom World; **PERU:** Computerworld Peru, PC World Profesional Peru, PC World SoHo Peru; **PHILIPPINES:** Click!, Computerworld Philippines, PC World Philippines, Publish in Asia; **POLAND:** Computerworld Poland, Computerworld Special Report Poland, Cyber, Macworld Poland, Networld Poland, PC World Komputer; **PORTUGAL:** Cerebro/PC World, Computerworld/Correio Informático, Dealer World Portugal, Mac*In/PC*In Portugal, Multimedia World; **PUERTO RICO:** PC World Puerto Rico; **ROMANIA:** Computerworld Romania, PC World Romania, Telecom Romania; **RUSSIA:** Computerworld Russia, Mir PK, Publish, Seti; **SINGAPORE:** Computerworld Singapore, PC World Singapore, Publish in Asia; **SLOVENIA:** Monitor; **SOUTH AFRICA:** Computing SA, Network World SA, Software World SA; **SPAIN:** Communicaciones World España, Computerworld España, Dealer World España, Macworld España, PC World España; **SRI LANKA:** Infolink PC World; **SWEDEN:** CAP&Design, Computer Sweden, Corporate Computing Sweden, Internetworld Sweden, it.branschen, Macworld Sweden, MaxiData Sweden, MikroDatorn, Nätverk & Kommunikation, PC World Sweden, PCaktiv, Windows World Sweden; **SWITZERLAND:** Computerworld Schweiz, Macworld Schweiz, PCtip; **TAIWAN:** Computerworld Taiwan, Macworld Taiwan, NEW ViSiON/Publish, PC World Taiwan, Windows World Taiwan; **THAILAND:** Publish in Asia, Thai Computerworld; **TURKEY:** Computerworld Turkiye, Macworld Turkiye, Network World Turkiye, PC World Turkiye; **UKRAINE:** Computerworld Kiev, Multimedia World Ukraine, PC World Ukraine; **UNITED KINGDOM:** Acorn User UK, Amiga Action UK, Amiga Computing UK, Apple Talk UK, Computing, Macworld, Parents and Computers UK, PC Advisor, PC Home, PSX Pro, The WEB; **UNITED STATES:** Cable in the Classroom, CIO Magazine, Computerworld, DOS World, Federal Computer Week, GamePro Magazine, InfoWorld, I-Way, Macworld, Network World, PC Games, PC World, Publish, Video Event, THE WEB Magazine, and WebMaster; online webzines: JavaWorld, NetscapeWorld, and SunWorld Online; **URUGUAY:** InfoWorld Uruguay; **VENEZUELA:** Computerworld Venezuela, PC World Venezuela; and **VIETNAM:** PC World Vietnam. 2/14/97

Dedication

This book is dedicated to Anne, Sandra, and Joanne, without whose help this book wouldn't have been possible.

Author's Acknowledgments

When you read a book, you give most of the credit to the author. In reality, a great many talented professionals devote many long hours taking the author's words and making them into something you're willing to spend money to read. Here are those unsung heros who made this book possible: Kelly Ewing, Kathy Simpson, Debbie Stailey, Linda Boyer, Rachel Garvey, Gary Randolph, and Stephanie Koutek.

Publisher's Acknowledgments

We're proud of this book; please send us your comments about it by using the Reader Response Card at the back of the book or by e-mailing us at feedback/dummies@idgbooks.com. Some of the people who helped bring this book to market include the following:

Acquisitions, Development, and Editorial

Project Editor: Kelly Ewing

Acquisitions Editor: Gareth Hancock

Copy Editors: Kathy Simpson, William A. Barton, Joe Jansen, Tina Sims, Patricia Yuu Pan

Technical Editor: Gary Randolph

Editorial Manager: Seta K. Frantz

Editorial Assistant: Chris H. Collins

Special Help: Stephanie Koutek, Proof Editor

Production

Project Coordinator: Debbie Stailey

Layout and Graphics: Brett Black, Cameron Booker, Valery Bourke, Linda M. Boyer, Dominique DeFelice, Maridee V. Ennis, Angela F. Hunckler, Todd Klemme, Jane Martin, Drew R. Moore, Anna Rohrer, Brent Savage, Kate Snell, Michael A. Sullivan

Proofreaders: Ethel Winslow, Joel K. Draper, Rachel Garvey, Nancy Price, Robert Springer, Karen York

Indexer: Sherry Massey

General and Administrative

IDG Books Worldwide, Inc.: John Kilcullen, CEO; Steven Berkowitz, President and Publisher

IDG Books Technology Publishing: Brenda McLaughlin, Senior Vice President and Group Publisher

Dummies Technology Press and Dummies Editorial: Diane Graves Steele, Vice President and Associate Publisher; Judith A. Taylor, Brand Manager; Kristin A. Cocks, Editorial Director

Dummies Trade Press: Kathleen A. Welton, Vice President and Publisher; Stacy S. Collins, Brand Manager

IDG Books Production for Dummies Press: Beth Jenkins, Production Director; Cindy L. Phipps, Supervisor of Project Coordination, Production Proofreading, and Indexing; Kathie S. Schutte, Supervisor of Page Layout; Shelley Lea, Supervisor of Graphics and Design; Debbie J. Gates, Production Systems Specialist; Tony Augsburger, Supervisor of Reprints and Bluelines; Leslie Popplewell, Media Archive Coordinator

Dummies Packaging and Book Design: Patti Sandez, Packaging Specialist; Lance Kayser, Packaging Assistant; Kavish+Kavish, Cover Design

♦

The publisher would like to give special thanks to Patrick J. McGovern, without whom this book would not have been possible.

♦

Contents at a Glance

Cartoons at a Glance

By Rich Tennant • Fax: 508-546-7747 • E-mail: the5wave@tiac.net

page 99

page 9

page 137

page 249

page 207

page 299

Table of Contents

Introduction

• •

*T*hink back to the day that you first sat behind the steering wheel of a car or whatever else has terrified you on your first try. Driving looked so simple from the passenger's seat, but when the time came for you to take control of the car, frightening thoughts ran rapidly through your mind:

"I can't do this."

"I'm going to kill someone."

With the help of your driving instructor, who sat quietly in the passenger seat, you cautiously overcame the fear of being the cause of a hundred car pileup. The confident voice to your right assured you that everything was going to be okay and that you, too, could become the master of the rolling hunk of metal — and that voice was right!

Visual FoxPro 5 is a lot like driving — you may be terrified at first, but soon you'll be sporting along at a breakneck pace.

In *Visual FoxPro 5 For Dummies,* I'm your driving instructor, and I show you the ropes of mastering Visual FoxPro at a speed that matches your pace. You can get up to speed quickly, and you won't cripple your computer in the process.

About Visual FoxPro 5

You've seen on television and in the movies how someone sits in front of a computer, pounds away at the keyboard, and is able to retrieve all sorts of information within seconds. And you know computers can spit out an enormous amount of information on practically every conceivable topic — including your credit report.

Information just doesn't pop out of a computer. Someone must enter the information into the computer first. Actually, someone enters the information into a database program that runs on a computer. The database program takes in all the information, organizes the information, and responds with just the information you requested.

The person typing on a computer keyboard is likely to be entering information into a database program or asking the database program to recall information to the computer screen.

Visual FoxPro is a database program for your personal computer. After Visual FoxPro is loaded on your computer, you can store and retrieve information in practically the same way as corporations and the government — although the information in your database will be different.

You can use Visual FoxPro to computerize your address book or maintain important information about your business. In fact, you can use Visual FoxPro to create customized computer database programs for business — and make extra money. Of course, don't start spending your newfound wealth until you've mastered Visual FoxPro, which is what I show you how to do throughout this book.

Visual FoxPro is more flexible than specialized programs, such as those that manage your money. You can design your own customized database program to work the way you want rather than be forced to accept the limitations imposed by specialized programs.

What's New about Visual FoxPro

Visual FoxPro is the latest version of a long line of successful FoxPro database programs. Major corporations have been using FoxPro to build small customized database programs for more than a decade.

So, if you're already familiar with previous versions of FoxPro, here's what you have to look forward to with Visual FoxPro:

- **An easier time designing database, tables, forms, and queries.** Visual FoxPro has a complete set of design tools that enable you to build everything you need for a customized database program.

- **New and improved wizards.** A wizard is a program that asks a bunch of questions about a table, form, query, or whatever you're creating. Based upon your answers, the wizard goes ahead and builds the table, form, or query for you.

- **Improved search features.** You can join together tables into a View and then ask Visual FoxPro to look into all the tables to find the information that you need.

These features are just a few of the valuable enhancements over previous versions of Visual FoxPro. And, of course, all customized database programs that you build with Visual FoxPro are Windows-ready. You can create a complete Windows database application using Visual FoxPro.

About This Book

All the technical jargon is omitted from this book. (I leave the jargon for the documentation that comes with Visual FoxPro.) Instead, you find step-by-step instructions, detailed explanations, and illustrations for the stuff that can't easily be put into words. Pictures speak louder than words, so I keep the words to a minimum wherever an illustration can tell most of the story.

Visual FoxPro 5 For Dummies isn't a typical computer book that contains reams of information that makes nerds stay up all night reading. I am the friendly instructor who brings real world answers to real world questions in a way to assure that you get the job done — and have fun along the way.

How to Use This Book

You don't need to read this book from cover to cover. (Of course, I'm flattered if you do.) The book is designed for you to flip to the topic that is stopping you from getting your work done. Look up the topic in the index, turn to the page cited, and then read your confidential briefing that makes you an instant expert. (This technique is how those news reporters look so smart on camera during news conferences.) Then you can get back to work.

Throughout the book, I talk about many keyboard commands and menu shortcuts. These commands and shortcuts are really neat things to know. (They even make you a whiz kid in front of your colleagues.) Menu shortcuts look like this:

File⇨Exit

This lines means "hold down the Alt key, press *F* (for File), and then release both keys and press *x* (for Exit)." The *F* and *x* are underlined because that's how they appear on the menu.

Keyboard commands look slightly different:

Ctrl+F4

With this line, you need to hold down the Control (Ctrl) key, press F4, and then release both keys. You should have no problem with this stuff if you treat the Ctrl and Alt keys the same way as you treat the Shift key.

Visual FoxPro still uses a throwback to the olden days (when a pound cake was actually a pound of cake). Visual FoxPro has a Command Window where you can type instructions for Visual FoxPro. I show you these commands whenever they can help you do your job. Commands in the Command Window are formatted like this:

```
@ 3, 6 SAY  Hello world.
```

This line means that I want you to switch to the Command Window, type the entire line, including the quotes and the @ symbol, and then press the Enter key. (I talk more about entering a line in the Command Window in Chapter 8.)

What You're Not to Read

I throw in road signs called icons (see the section "Icons Used in This Book," later in the Introduction) to mark the text that has special interest or meaning. The technical garbage that I include is stuffed into sidebars. Read the sidebars if you're curious; otherwise, you can ignore them.

Foolish Assumptions

Books aren't a good medium to use to hold a conversation. And, as a writer, I need to know my audience. So because I can't know all of you personally, I assume several things about you. Chances are that you're by your computer, in transit, or someplace else where most people find reading a little therapeutic. Therefore, you don't have any chance to ask me those "How to" questions about Visual FoxPro that rattle your mind. Nevertheless, I've given many waking hours to thinking about you.

I also make the following assumptions about you. You work with a computer (maybe you own it) with Windows 95. You have a job to get done right away. Someone told you Visual FoxPro is the way to go (or your boss tells you that Visual FoxPro is what the company uses, so get cracking), and you're looking for help, tips, shortcuts, and maybe a big baseball bat to threaten your computer when it doesn't do what you want it to do. This book takes care of all but the baseball bat. (The marketing department couldn't figure out how to attach a good-sized baseball bat to this book.)

I can't cover everything in this book (no one can lift a telephone book-size *Visual FoxPro 5 For Dummies,* let alone read it), so I assume that you know the basics of Microsoft Windows. You know how to choose menu items, use the mouse, and know the mouse terms (click, double-click, click and drag, and right and left mouse buttons). You also know how to manipulate windows (moving, sizing, and closing). If you need help with Windows, pick up *Windows 95 For Dummies* (IDG Books Worldwide, Inc.), by Andy Rathbone.

How This Book Is Organized

This book is divided into parts, chapters, and smaller things. Parts are boundaries for broad topics that are covered by the book. Chapters concentrate on the major points of the topic. They contain the fascinating, the provocative, the sensational, and the good stuff that makes discovering Visual FoxPro a pleasurable experience. Within chapters are these itsy-bitsy, little things that contain nuggets of helpful information and answers your perplexing questions about Visual FoxPro.

The following sections give you a peek at what awaits you.

Part I: Databases and Tables

A prerequisite to creating databases and tables is to be able to identify data. After you know what data looks like, then you find out the techniques for storing, organizing, fixing, and erasing these little buggers. Part I is the meat of the book. After you've mastered Part I, you're all set to go.

Part II: Ways Programmers Manipulate Data

Some people may call asking for information a query. Others may call it an interrogation. But you're still asking Visual FoxPro to get you the data that you need. Visual FoxPro has a whole bunch of neat tools that make pulling information from a stubborn database a breeze. These tools help you ask your question the way Visual FoxPro can understand your request. This part helps you choose the proper tool for the job and gives you plenty of examples to successfully extract information from your databases.

Part III: Working with Forms

Part III is the time to create a game face for your database. You can take the drab look of the way you enter information into your database and later display the information on-screen by creating a fancy form. You have the chance to put all the bells and whistles on the form just like those you see in most Windows application. You can add command buttons, list boxes, radio buttons, combo boxes, or a spinner. Part III shows you how to build all these things into your form.

Part IV: Reports, Labels, and Graphs

Information that you place into a database and tables must debut publicly someday. (Is this like a coming-out party?) Visual FoxPro can ease your tensions about this public appearance, thanks to a bunch of presentation tools, such as report, label, and graph builders. These tools make dressing up the data fun and painless. Your data is bound to catch the eye of every-one in the public. The how-tos are in Part IV.

Part V: Things That Make a Big Difference

Try as I may, I couldn't find a home for a number of topics that make a big difference. So I stuffed this information all together in Part V. Here, you find the application builder, screen builder, and desk accessories. These items are too important to leave out of this book because they make a real differ-ence when their features are needed. You also find out how to create macros and organize a project. Read all about them in Part V.

Part VI: The Part of Tens

Finally, the part that makes a ...*For Dummies* book a unique experience: the Part of Tens. Read about problems, shortcuts, helpful commands, help instructions, and bold new frontiers in just one little part. This section is compact, helpful, and fun — you just can't beat that combination.

Icons Used in This Book

Road signs are helpful to point out important information whenever you travel through unfamiliar territory. You need the same kind of help when you venture out to master a new software tool such as Visual FoxPro. I include icons as road signs that point out the good stuff and make the book fun to read. Here's the graphical guide to my road signs:

Points out the easy way to do something. These icons mark tips that save you time, energy, and hair.

Marks useful reminders and buries them deep into your subconscious.

Offers friendly warnings about pitfalls, traps, and errors in the making. Don't overlook these warnings!

Identifies technical information that some people (you know — the geeky ones) like to know. If you want, you can skip these paragraphs, unless you're really up to reading it.

Where to Go from Here

Your briefing is concluded. You're qualified to begin using Visual FoxPro. Go anywhere you'd like. Start with the Table of Contents or jump right into creating a database. You may prefer to look at the report builder first. Whatever way you decide, *Visual FoxPro 5 For Dummies* is right there to help. So what are you waiting for?

Part I
Databases and Tables

The 5th Wave · By Rich Tennant

BOB WAS ONE OF THE MANY SUFFERERS OF MACINTOSH OBSOLESCENCE SYNDROME

OH GREAT! NOW THE "X3'S" BEEN UPGRADED!

In this part . . .

The whole idea of using Visual FoxPro is to help you manage your data. In Part I, you find out how to identify data and begin to do some work with Visual FoxPro.

You also see how to stuff data into tables and databases, and you see how data is sorted, searched, and displayed on-screen. By the end of Part I, you'll be barking commands and making all the data jump through hoops at the crack of your whip.

Chapter 1

Creating a Database

● ●

In This Chapter

▶ Installing Visual FoxPro

▶ Starting Visual FoxPro

▶ Building a database

● ●

Are you ready to build a database and a whole bunch of tables? Sure you are! Roll up your sleeves and prepare yourself for some interesting work.

Building a database — and everything else that goes along with the process — is much easier than trying to assemble those complicated toys your kids always want at holiday time. You're certain to find my directions much simpler to follow than those so-called instructions that the toy manufacturers write — and you don't need any tools, except Visual FoxPro.

Installing Visual FoxPro

You're probably as excited as I am about jumping into the world of Visual FoxPro, but hold on for a moment. You need to get the program installed onto your computer before you can start the engine.

If you already installed Visual FoxPro and know how to start the program, then skip to the section "Understanding Basic Database Terminology," later in this chapter.

However, if you haven't installed Visual FoxPro yet, read on.

Whether you have the disk or CD-ROM version of Visual FoxPro, the installation process is basically the same.

1. **Insert disk 1 or the CD-ROM into the appropriate computer drive.**

2. **Click the Start button and then choose** **R**un.

3. **Type** d:\setup.

   Be sure to replace the *d* with the appropriate letter for the drive that contains Visual FoxPro.

4. **Press Enter to begin the installation.**

The installation process is rather straightforward. You're asked a bunch of routine questions, and you choose the answer from a list of options. The first question — where you're asked whether you want the laptop, complete, or custom installation — is the most important one to answer correctly, so I offer a bit of advice.

The answer depends on how much space you have on your hard disk. If you have only 15MB free, then select Laptop installation — even if you're not installing Visual FoxPro on a laptop.

You need a little more than 100MB free for the complete installation, which is the typical installation. The difference between the Laptop and Complete installation is that Visual FoxPro is loaded with samples of databases and other things that you may find useful later.

If you really know what you're doing — you're not using Visual FoxPro for the first time, for example — and you want only certain features of Visual FoxPro, then select the Custom installation. The Custom installation lets you decide which Visual FoxPro files are loaded onto your hard disk. For this installation, you need anywhere from 15MB to 240MB free. As you make your selection, Visual FoxPro shows you the amount of free disk space and the amount of disk space that is required for the files you selected.

Stick with either the Laptop installation or the Complete installation. The Custom installation contains a lot of fancy stuff, most of which takes up valuable disk space — and chances are, you won't use these fancy features, anyway.

The rest of the installation process is so simple that I don't bother going into details. The questions are self-explanatory, and the answers are obvious. But if you need help, check out the appropriately titled sidebar "But if you need help . . . ," later in this chapter. However, an appendix at the back of the book does offer advice on how to customize installation.

But if you need help . . .

Well, you think you know what you're doing, but then you stumble across something during the installation of Visual FoxPro that you just aren't sure what to do. Don't panic.

You can find plenty of help in the Visual FoxPro Installation Guide and Master Index booklet that came with your copy of Visual FoxPro.

And don't worry about having to read thick, heavy manuals. The installation guide is very thin, and you need to scan through only about 30 pages before you find the answer to your question.

You'll also want to check out the Appendix at the back of this book for installation tips.

When the installation process is complete, you need to restart your computer.

Starting Visual FoxPro

After you install Visual FoxPro and restart your computer, a new program icon named Microsoft Visual FoxPro appears on your desktop. Double-click this icon to start the program.

Understanding Basic Database Terminology

To build a database in Visual FoxPro, you need to know some basic terminology. Think of your last trip to Europe — or your dream of traveling to Europe. Before you leave for uncharted waters, you usually brush up on the local customs and master a few key phrases. Traveling into Visual FoxPro land works in about the same way. You need to understand the words *database, table,* and *field* — the building blocks of Visual FoxPro — before you can truly master the program.

A *field* contains specific data. For example, fields can contain an address, and one data field contains the street address, another field the city name, and yet another field the zip code.

A *table* is a group of fields that are in some way related to one another. One table contains multiple fields, so you can have a table that contains an account identification number, an account name, a street address, a city name, a state name, a zip code, a telephone number, and all the other information that you expect to describe a particular account. These items are all contained in fields in that table.

A *database* is a group of related tables that you can refer to by a single name. You can, for example, say, "Let me see the accounting database." As part of the accounting database, therefore, you get to see the accounts payable table, the payroll table, the accounts receivable table, and all the rest of the tables that make up the accounting database.

A *relational database* is a collection of data that is stored into more than one table. These tables can be linked together by common values in fields found in both tables.

Creating the Database

To create a database, you need to use the Database Designer. The Database Designer is the place where you tell Visual FoxPro which tables you want to place into the database. After you create a database, you then create all the tables for it. (See Chapter 2.)

To create a database by using the Database Designer:

1. Choose File⇨New to open the New dialog box, shown in Figure 1-1.

Figure 1-1:
The New dialog box. Select the Database radio button to create a new database.

The New dialog box lists all the file types that you can create. Some file types are self-explanatory (the Query, Report, and Label file types, for example). Others, such as Program and Class, may be confusing, so I explain them throughout this book.

Picking the file type that you want to create is as easy as selecting the appropriate radio button. Of course, because you're creating a database, you need to select the Database file type.

2. **Select the Database radio button.**

3. **Click the New file button to display the Create dialog box, shown in Figure 1-2.**

The Wizard

Whenever you create a new table or another kind of file in Visual FoxPro, you usually have two choices in the New dialog box: the New file button or the Wizard button.

Although I usually tell you to click the New file button, you always have the option of using the Wizard button. The Wizard button runs a *wizard,* which is a program that asks you questions about the table or whatever file you're creating. The wizard then uses your answers to automatically create the table.

If the Wizard button is gray, then a wizard doesn't exist for the file type that you selected. For example, a wizard for creating a database doesn't exist, but you can use a wizard to create a table.

A wizard is so easy to use that you need no instruction to make any file using a wizard. If you really need to create a table, build a query, form, or a report fast, then use a wizard rather than do the work yourself. A wizard asks only for the minimal information that is necessary to do the job, and in a matter of minutes, you can have a working table, query, or report ready to use immediately.

Wizards are Microsoft's response to letters and calls saying that Visual FoxPro is a little too complex for the beginner to grasp. Some Visual FoxPro users want to be able to type in a few words and then click a few buttons to tap into the real power of Visual FoxPro. And, as a result, the wizard was born.

Although the wizard gets the job done fast, you only end up with the basic table, query, form or report, and you miss out on all the fancy stuff that I show you how to do in this book. To do the fancy stuff, you need to choose the New file button over the Wizard button.

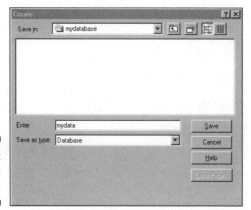

Figure 1-2:
The Create
dialog box.

**4. In the Save in drop-down list box of the Create dialog box, choose
which folder to store your database in.**

The Save in drop-down list box shows you in which folder on your hard
disk the program intends to place this database if you don't do anything to change the location.

You really don't want to put your database in just any old location.
Instead, you want to create a folder just for your databases. If you're
not sure how to do so, check out *Windows 95 For Dummies* by Andy
Rathbone (IDG Books Worldwide, Inc.).

5. Type the name of your new database in the Enter text box.

Visual FoxPro automatically names your first database DATA1.DBC.
This designation is obviously not a proper name for your database,
but it can serve as an acceptable temporary name until you devise a
better one.

To name your database, type up to eight characters and leave the file
extension blank. Visual FoxPro automatically adds the DBC extension
for you. Whatever you do, though, don't change the extension DBC
because Visual FoxPro uses this file extension for database files.

Be creative but practical when you name your database. Give the
database a name that describes its content.

6. Click the Save button.

Visual FoxPro displays the Database Designer, and you're ready to
create your first table. (See Chapter 2.)

Chapter 2

Adding Content to Your Database

· ·

In This Chapter

▶ Choosing the best data for your database

▶ Planning your table's format

▶ Creating a table

· ·

Roll up your sleeves and get ready for some tricky but fun work creating tables for your brand new database. Don't rush out for a hammer and saw. The table I'm talking about isn't for your kitchen. Instead, this table is where you stuff information that you later use in queries and reports.

In this chapter, you identify the kinds of information that you want to store in the table, such as a person's name, address, and telephone number. You also find out how to make the table just the right size for the information.

Choosing Your Data

To design the tables in your database, you need to make a list of all the data that you want to stuff into them.

When I say *data,* I'm referring to the information that you store in a file on the disk such as a floppy disk, your computer's hard disk, or a CD. A *file* is an electronic file folder, and stuffing data into a file is similar to storing important papers inside a manila file folder (except that the data inside my computer is better organized than in my file folders).

But just as you don't want to stuff travel information into a file folder containing your mortgage paperwork, you don't want to use any old data in a database. Selecting the kinds of data that you want to collect is critical to building a good database.

Because data is so critical to your database, you need to make sure that you're choosing the best data. Keep in mind that data out of context is not meaningful to anyone. For example, "555 Maple Street" is obviously a street address and data. Is it important data? Sure is! Without the street address, you don't know the house in which your special someone lives. But is the street address meaningful? Not unless you know the town and state where the house is located. Therefore, you need additional data — data that is related to the street address — to make 555 Maple Street mean something to you.

Following are points to consider when deciding what data to collect:

- ✔ **Select data that's important to you.** A person's name, address, telephone number and spouse's name are important when you create a database that is your personal telephone directory.

- ✔ **Select data that, when related to other data, has a special meaning.** A telephone number is a piece of data, but it doesn't have meaning until you relate the telephone number to a person's name.

- ✔ **Select data that is specific rather than too general to work with in your database.** Rather than a person's name, you'd really want a person's first name and a person's last name. (See the sidebar "Choosing specific data," later in this chapter, for more information.)

Say, for example, that you want to create an electronic address directory where you can store important information about your friends. From this database, you want to display the information and even print mailing labels. But before you can do these tasks, you need to list all the information that you'd like to store in the database.

Brainstorming

The first step to choosing your data is to brainstorm. When you brainstorm, you need to jot down anything that seems remotely appropriate for your database. Keep in mind that database designers don't reinvent the wheel; a database designer finds out what information is currently being used.

When you brainstorm, you also need to decide what other information can be helpful. For example, if you're creating an electronic address directory, you may want to include information that you'd find on business cards and in your personal telephone directory.

You also need to add to your list any other information that you may want to include in the database. If you're creating an electronic address directory, for example, you may want to include financial information from your checkbook or from a mailing list for your business or club.

Table 2-1 lists the information that I came up with during my brainstorming session. You can, of course, add more items to this list or even cut down this list to your liking.

Table 2-1	Potential Address Book Database Contents	
Name	Address	Telephone number
Place of business	Birthday	Wedding anniversary
Job title	Spouse name	Spouse's place of business
Spouse's job title	Spouse's birthday	

Refining your data list

After you brainstorm, you need to refine your list of information. For example, the address item on my list is too general for the database because the address actually consists of several pieces of data — the street, city, state, and zip code.

Following are tips to help you make your information more specific.

> ✔ **Check to see whether the item has components.** If so, you may want to include each component in the database. Say that you need to store addresses in the database. Components include the house number, street name, city, state, and zip code.

Choosing specific data

Data can be identified in a general way or a specific way. A general description of data is like an address. A specific description of data is a component of the address, such as the street or the city or the state. Collectively, these specific pieces of data form the general definition of the address.

Avoid general descriptions of data because they can be difficult to work with in your database. Say that you store an address as one long piece of data in the database (street, city, and state) and you want to print the address on a label. You'd end up with the street, city, and state stretched across one line on the label — not what you had in mind.

However, if the address is stored as three separate pieces of data, you can easily place each piece of data wherever you'd like it on the label. This flexibility is available only if you are specific when you identify data.

✔ **Determine how you plan to look up data in the database.** Whenever you ask the database software to find information in the database, you must specify the value that you are looking for and a specific field of the database where the value might be hiding. The value is called the *search criteria*. Each item that you use as search criteria should be a specific piece of data in the database. (For more information on searching, see Chapter 8.)

After I refined my data from the brainstorming session, I came up with the data names listed in Table 2-2. Of course, you may come up with a different kind of list, which is okay. Although most people develop a similar list of data, you can't expect any list to match 100 percent. As long as the final database works, then no one has made a mistake. You and I simply approached the problem differently.

Table 2-2	Refined Data Names
Item	*Components*
Name	First name, middle name, maiden name, last name
Address	P.O. box, street, apartment no., city, state, country, zip code
Phone number	Home phone
Employer	P.O. box, street, suite no., city, state, country, zip code, phone no., modem, fax no.

Planning Your Field Size

Before you create your database, you also need to decide the size of the *field*. A field is a place in the database where you store data. *Field size* determines the number of characters that can be stuffed into the field. Visual FoxPro automatically sets the size of some fields, such as numeric data types fields and date data type fields. The size chosen by Visual FoxPro is just fine because you can always change it.

You are on your own when it comes to setting the size of a character data type field. The best thing you can do is guess. In the address book example, you can try to guess the number of characters in a person's first name. For example, I'd probably allot ten characters, but someone's name could always be 11 characters long.

If you make the size too short, you'll cut off information. If the field is too long, you'll waste space. A good approach in determining the size of a field is to look at the data that you want to enter into the field.

For example, for the address book database, you may have data available on a printed form, such as a Rolodex. If not, you can probably arrive at a good estimate by looking at similar data (such as in a telephone book) to see the longest first name, middle name, and last name.

And what happens if you guess wrong? (And you will.) The answer depends on the nature of the data. If the information is critical, such as a person's name, street, town, or company name, then consider making the existing field bigger, which is also called *restructuring the database*. (See Chapter 6.) You can avoid restructuring, however, if you can abbreviate the information so that the data fits the size of the current field.

Table 2-3 lists my suggested sizes for various fields in my proposed address book database.

Table 2-3	Estimated Field Size	
Field Name	*Field Type*	*Field Size*
FName	Character	10
MidName	Character	10
MaidName	Character	25
LName	Character	25
PO_Box	Character	5
Apt_Num	Character	5
Street	Character	25
City	Character	25
State	Character	2
Country	Character	3
Zip	Character	10
HPhone	Character	16

Breaking Up the Data into Tables

After you identify and define the list of fields by name and size, you can break up the list into smaller lists. This concept is called *normalizing the data*.

You don't want to put all your data into one table because it slows down the process of finding information quickly. For example, if you place all your data into one table and you want to find an entry that matches your selection criteria, Visual FoxPro has to search through all the characters in the table.

You can reduce the search time by creating several smaller tables. Each table can hold a smaller number of fields that are logically related to each other. In Table 2-4, I show you how the address directory database can be grouped into three smaller tables: Address Table, Phone Table, and Employer Table.

The Address Table contains all the general information about the person. The Phone Table houses only the telephone numbers. The Employer Table holds only employer information.

You can be creative and come up with your own way to group these fields. How you group the fields doesn't matter as long as the groupings make sense and the information can be found quickly.

For example, if you need a telephone number, Visual FoxPro can search only the Phone Table to find the information that you seek; it doesn't need to plow through data stored in the other tables. Likewise, Visual FoxPro searches the Address Table if you ask for the person's address.

What if you need a person's address and telephone number? You can ask Visual FoxPro to use both the Address Table and the Phone Table. Whenever you need to find information in two or more tables, you must tell Visual FoxPro to *join,* or link, those tables, which means that records of the first table are matched with records of the second table. See Chapter 3 for more information.

I created an ID Number field for the tables in the address directory database (see Table 2-4). This field then becomes the common link to all the tables. (See Chapter 7 for information on linking.) So when you need a person's address and telephone number, you can ask Visual FoxPro to use the Address Table and the Phone Table and to join these tables using the ID Number field.

Table 2-4	Groupings for the Address Directory Database	
Address Table	*Phone Table*	*Employer Table*
ID_Number	ID_Number	ID_Number
FName	HPhone	Employer
MidName		Emp_PO_Box
MaidName		Emp_Suite
LName		Emp_Street
PO_Box		Emp_City
Apt_Num		Emp_State
Street		Emp_Country
City		Emp_Zip
State		Emp_Phone
Country		Emp_Modem
Zip		Emp_Fax

Building a Table

You can add tables to the database by using the Table Designer dialog box.

Visual FoxPro automatically sets the table name as TABLE1.DBF. The program names subsequent tables as TABLE2.DBF, TABLE3.DBF, and so on — you get the point. Follow the same steps in naming the table as I suggest in Chapter 1 for naming a database. Don't include a file extension because Visual FoxPro does that for you.

To create a table for your database:

1. **Open the database in the Database Designer.**

   The new table you create will become part of the database.

2. **Choose Database⇨New Table.**

   The New Table dialog box, shown in Figure 2-1, appears.

3. **Click the New Table button to display the Create Table dialog box, shown in Figure 2-2.**

   Type the name of the new table in the Enter table text box.

4. **Click the Save button.**

   The Table Designer, shown in Figure 2-3, appears.

Figure 2-1:
The New
Table dialog
box.

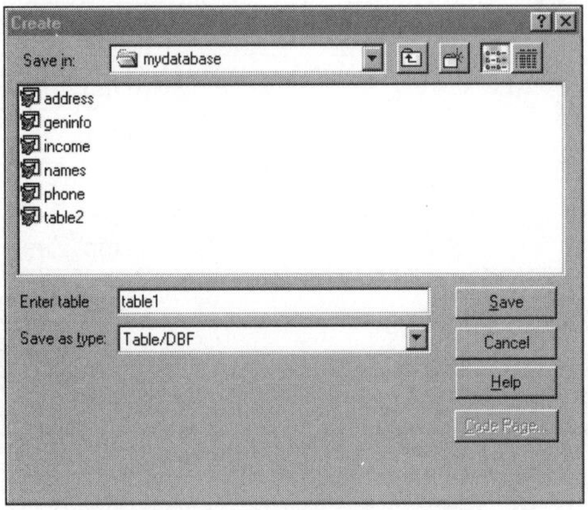

Figure 2-2:
The Create
Table dialog
box.

5. Enter information about fields.

See the following sections for information on how to add and define
fields for your table.

6. Click OK to create the table.

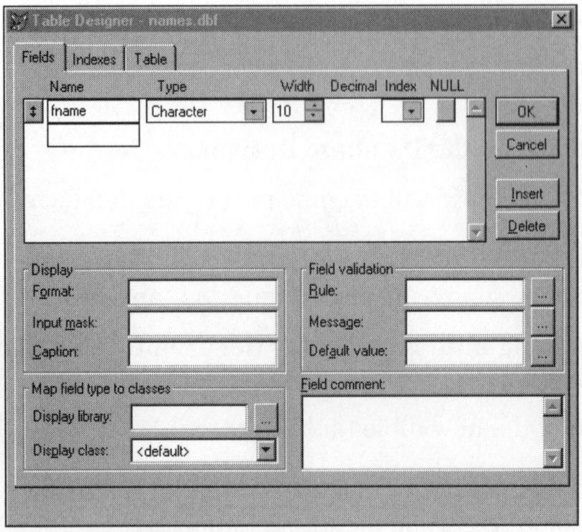

Figure 2-3:
The Table
Designer.

Setting special table properties

Sometimes you want Visual FoxPro to reject a record based on the value of more than one field. You can't give your database this kind of protection, however, by using field validation alone. (Field validation lets you specify conditions under which Visual FoxPro replaces a value placed in a field.) You can, however, provide such protection if you use *record* validation. *Record validation* enables you to specify conditions under which Visual FoxPro rejects the entire record. You can enter criteria for record validation by clicking the Table tab on the Table Designer dialog box, shown in Figure 2-4.

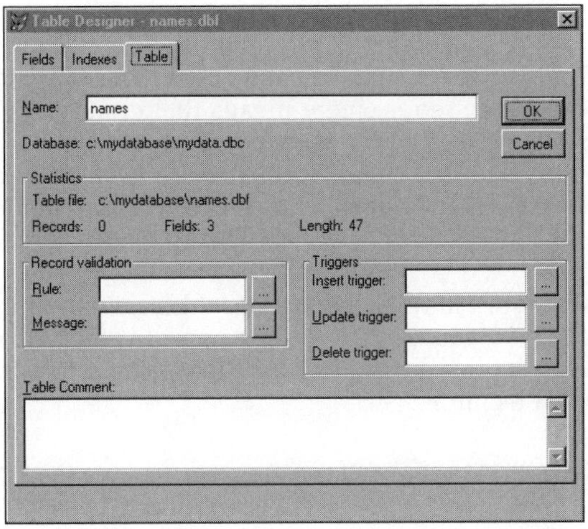

Figure 2-4:
Create a record validation whenever a validation rule involves more than one field in the table.

In the Table Designer dialog box, you can establish record validation rules by using the Record validation or Triggers areas.

You can, for example, have Visual FoxPro validate the record all the time by creating an expression in the Rule text box. (See Chapter 3.) Or you can have the validation occur right before someone inserts, updates, or deletes a record by writing the rule into the appropriate trigger text box.

A trigger is like a burglar alarm. The trigger sits quietly waiting for a particular event to occur. The events are inserting a record, updating a record, or deleting a record from the table. A burglar alarm waits until someone breaks into your house and then sounds the alarm. When an event sets off a trigger, Visual FoxPro checks the values entered into the record against the rules you created for the trigger.

The record validation area

In the section "Setting the field validation properties," later in this chapter, I discuss how you can develop validation rules for fields. You can also set the same kind of rules for each *record* in the table. This type of rule is called the *record validation rule*.

The record validation rule is an expression that Visual FoxPro uses to determine whether a record is valid based on rules that you set. Suppose that your database is recording grades of students. Two fields in particular are pertinent to this task. These fields are those for a percentage grade (0 – 100%) and for a grade point (1.0 – 4.0). The percentage grades consist of numbers in the 80s or 90s, for example, and the grade point of numbers such as 3.0 or 4.0.

The value of each field, however, must remain consistent with that of the other field. This consistency requirement means that grades of 90 and higher in the percentage grade field must accompany a 4.0 value in the grade point field; 80 to 89 must equate with 3.0; 70 to 79 must equal 2.0; and percentage grades of less than 70 must accompany a 1.0 value in the grade point field.

A field validation can't work in this case because the validation depends on the values in two fields. So you need to write a record validation rule that is an expression. The following expression is one that I came up with for the preceding grade report example:

```
(num_grade > 89 and grade_pt != 4) or (num_grade > 80 and
 num_grade < 90 and grade_pt != 3) or (num_grade > 70 and
 num_grade < 80 and grade_pt != 2) or (num_grade < 70 and
     grade_pt != 1)
```

This expression is actually four small expressions joined by the word *or* into one large expression. The large expression is true if any of the small expressions are true.

Each small expression is within a set of parentheses. The first small expression tells Visual FoxPro to examine the values of the num_grade (percentage grade) field and grade_pt (grade point) field. If the value in the num_grade field is greater than 89 and the value of the grade_pt field does not equal 4, then the expression is true. A true expression means that the validation rule is violated, which means that anyone who receives a percentage grade higher than 89 must have a grade point value of 4.0. (Don't be concerned if you're confused by expressions. I cover creating expressions in more detail in Chapter 3.)

If the record validation expression is true, Visual FoxPro displays an error message on-screen. The error message is the text that you enter into the <u>M</u>essage text box in the Record validation area of the Table Designer dialog box's Table tab. And if you're not familiar with creating expressions, you can always use the Expression Builder to help you create one. (See Chapter 3.)

You may be confused as to why a true expression displays an error message. You'd think the message appears when the expression is false. Well, true and false depends on your viewpoint.

A condition tells Visual FoxPro when to display the error message. You're saying to Visual FoxPro, "If this condition happens, then display the message." You identify the condition in the form of an expression. Therefore, for the condition to happen, the expression must be true. (See Table 2-5 to find out what each symbol means.)

Table 2-5	Common Symbols and Their Meanings
Symbol	*Meaning*
=	Equals
>	Greater than
<	Less than
>=	Greater than or equal to
<=	Less than or equal to
<>	Not equal
AND	Both expressions to the left and to the right of the AND operator must be true for the data to be valid.
NOT	The expression to the right must be false rather than true for the data to be valid.
	This explanation implies that you can write an expression such as salary<99000 NOT salary>100000. But this gives a syntax error and doesn't make sense. NOT salary>100000 means that only salaries under $100,000 are valid.
OR	Either expression expression to the left or to the right of the AND operator must be true for the data to be valid.

Triggers

A *trigger* fills a hole in your database security by forcing Visual FoxPro to examine conditions of a record before inserting that record into the database or whenever you update or delete an existing record. You create triggers in the Table tab of the Table Designer.

A trigger is actually an expression that Visual FoxPro evaluates whenever an event sets off the trigger. An *event* is the insertion, modification, or deletion of a record. A *procedure* is merely a set of instructions that tells Visual FoxPro to do something.

You can run a procedure by entering the name of the procedure in the appropriate trigger text box. You can find out more about procedures when you find out how to program in Visual FoxPro. For now, however, just use expressions as your triggers.

Keeping within Visual FoxPro boundaries

Here are the maximum limits of field, records, and tables. You'll probably never reach these limits, but they're always good to review when you design your database.

Fields	Maximum size of character fields is 254.
	Maximum number of characters in field names in a table not associated with a table is 10.
	Maximum number of characters in field names in a table associated with a database is 128.
Records	Maximum number of records per table file is 1 billion.
	Maximum number of characters per record is 65,500.
	Maximum number of fields per record is 255.
Tables	Maximum size of a table file is 2 gigabytes.
	Maximum number of tables open at one time is 2,551.
	Maximum number of characters per table field is 254.
	Maximum number of tables that can be related is unlimited.

Visual FoxPro uses three kinds of triggers:

- ✔ Insert trigger
- ✔ Update trigger
- ✔ Delete trigger

The following example is a typical expression for the Insert and Update triggers: `salary < 25000`. This expression tells Visual FoxPro to check to see whether the value of the salary field is less than 25,000. If so, Visual FoxPro sounds an error.

You can build an expression that checks values in various fields in the table before the program does anything with the record. If the program detects a violation, Visual FoxPro doesn't continue with the event. (That is, the program doesn't insert a record, update a record, or delete a record.) Instead, an error message appears. The information that caused the violation must be fixed before the event can continue.

Adding Fields to a Table

A field is the place where you put data after you build your table. You use the Table Designer to create fields.

1. **Open the table to which you want to add fields.**

   The Table Designer, shown in Figure 2-5, appears.

2. **Select the Table tab and then click OK.**

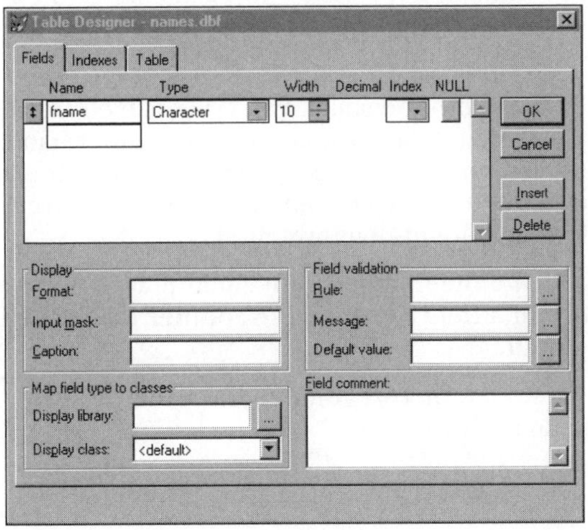

Figure 2-5:
The Table
Designer.

3. **Click the first box below the Name column head in the Table Designer dialog box and then type the name of your field.**

   The *field name* describes the kind of data you intend to store in the field (for example, fname for first name and lname for last name) and can be up to 128 characters in length, including letters, numbers, and symbols — but not spaces.

   Although you don't seem to have room enough for 128 characters in the Name column, you really do because Visual FoxPro scrolls the characters off the box as you type the name.

4. **Press the Tab key to move the cursor to the Type column and then choose a data type, if necessary.**

   The *data type* describes the kind of data you store in the field.

   Visual FoxPro sets the field type to Character by default, but you can easily change the data type by clicking the down arrow next to the type listing. This action opens a drop-down box that contains data types. Select the data type you want.

   Most of the time, you use the Character, Number, and Date fields. For information on the other field types, see the section "The 13 field types," later in this chapter.

5. **Press the Tab key to move the cursor to the Width column and tell Visual FoxPro the number of characters that you want to stuff into the field.**

   This field characteristic is called the *width* of the field or the field size.

    When you select the field type for the field, Visual FoxPro automatically establishes a default width for the field and displays that value under the Width column. You can change this established width for the field only if Visual FoxPro enables you to do so. If a spinner appears to the right of the width value in the column, you can change the Width value. If you don't see a spinner, you must accept the default width that Visual FoxPro determines.

   If you make the field width too small, you don't leave room in the field for all the data. Making the field too wide, on the other hand, increases the size of the table unnecessarily. So you must look at the information that you intend to put into the field and estimate the correct size for the field to hold that amount of information.

6. **If necessary, indicate the number of decimal places that Visual FoxPro can store in a field by using the spinner that appears beneath the Decimal column.**

   If you don't see a spinner in this column, however, you cannot set the number of decimal places.

Visual FoxPro doesn't enable you to set decimal values for field types that don't use decimals. You can't set a decimal value for an integer data type, for example, because an integer is a whole number and doesn't have a decimal value. The character field type obviously doesn't use a decimal value either.

7. **Skip the Index column and, if necessary, put a check mark in the NULL value check box to indicate that entering a blank value into the field is okay.**

   Click the NULL column if you want to permit a blank value in a field; a check mark then appears on the button. If you don't click the NULL button, you must always enter something into that field.

   Suppose, for example, that you want every record to include a Social Security number. The field that contains the Social Security number, therefore, can't be left blank. So you don't check the NULL value check box for this particular field.

   In contrast, you may find the fact that not every person has a middle name acceptable. The field that contains the middle name, therefore, can have an empty value. So you do check the NULL value check box for this field.

8. **If necessary, establish additional criteria.**

   You can set up additional criteria, such as a default value for the field. For information on doing so, see the section "Setting Special Field Properties," later in this chapter.

9. **Enter another field and repeat Steps 3 through 7 to define that field.**

   The chances are good that your table will include more than one field. To add another field, you simply give the cursor a push to the next field by pressing Tab. However, if you clicked the button in the NULL column, Visual FoxPro helps you with your next field: The cursor automatically returns to the first column and opens another field.

   If you don't define the field, Visual FoxPro discards the field from the table.

10. **Click OK; when the program asks whether you want to input data records into the table, click <u>N</u>o.**

    A box appears in the Database Designer. This box contains the name of the table that you just created and a listing of all the fields that the table contains (see Figure 2-6). I call this little box the *table box*.

    You double-click the table box whenever you want to select the table. You need to select the table if you want to see the data stored in the table or you want to add, delete, or modify records. I give you more information on this feature in Chapter 5.

    You can delete a table by clicking the table box and pressing the Delete key.

Setting Special Field Properties

When you enter data into a table, Visual FoxPro automatically takes the data and stuffs it into the appropriate field without making a fuss — unless, of course, the data you enter doesn't match the field's data type.

You may want to impose restrictions on how someone can input data into your table. You may want to separate the individual numeric components of Social Security numbers with hyphens, for example, or the area code from a telephone number with parentheses. And I suspect that you may want to use your own words as the label for the field whenever you use the field on a form or report.

Visual FoxPro can easily enforce these restrictions if you establish these requirements at the time you define the field. You can enter these restrictions by selecting a field in the Table Designer dialog box and then typing the appropriate value in the field property box.

Setting the Display properties

In the Display properties area of the Table Designer dialog box, you can set the Format, Input mask, and Caption. You don't need to set these values for most fields you create unless you decide to spruce up your table.

✓ **Format:** In the Format text box, specify the format, such as hyphens in a Social Security number or parentheses around the area code of the telephone number, that Visual FoxPro should use whenever the value of the field is displayed on-screen and in reports. Enter the necessary hyphens and parentheses for the format and substitute the 9 mark for the data characters. If you want to format a Social Security number, for example, you'd type 999-99-9999 into the format box.

✔ **Input mask:** In this text box, you indicate how you want data to look as someone enters information into a field. For example, to save time, you don't want someone to enter the hyphens every time a Social Security number is entered into the Social Security number field. By placing the hyphens in the input mask, the user doesn't need to enter the hyphens when they're entering data.

To do so, select the field that you want to preformat by placing the cursor on the name of the field and clicking. Type the characters that you want to use as the format for the field in the Input mask text box. You can substitute 9s for the actual data, as shown in Figure 2-7. Typing (999) 999-9999 in this text box is how you specify a telephone number, for example, and you type the data here as 999-99-9999 to define a Social Security number.

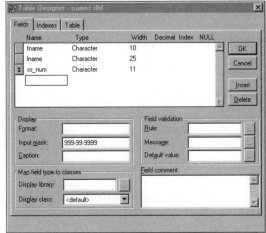

Figure 2-7:
The Table Designer, complete with an Input mask.

✔ **Caption:** A caption is used in place of the field name whenever the field is displayed on the screen or in a report. Type text for the field's caption in this text box.

Setting the field validation properties

You don't want erroneous information stuffed into a field. Sometimes, however, such an event is impossible to prevent. Anyone can enter any character into a Character data-type field. The field validation properties help you catch obvious errors.

You can, for example, specify that someone can enter only a specific range of numbers into a field, such as in the case of a person's salary. Most firms have minimum and maximum salary amounts. A salary outside this range is considered erroneous — especially if a validation rule determines the possible salary range. If you set such a validation rule for a field in your table, Visual FoxPro stops someone from entering a number that's outside the range you specify.

To set the field validation properties:

- **Rule:** In this text box, you specify validation rules by entering an expression that uses English words and math symbols. An expression is like those arithmetic problems you did back in grammar school. For example, say that you want only values greater than 50 to appear in the grade field of your table. The expression that tells Visual FoxPro to prevent a lower number from being entered into the table is `grade > 50`. Grade is the name of the field; the > symbol is the greater-than operator; and 50 tells Visual FoxPro not to allow any number into the field unless the number is higher than 50.

  If you don't want to type the expression into this text box — and most people don't — you can build the expression by using the program's Expression Builder (see Chapter 3).

- **Message:** Whenever someone attempts to violate your validation rule, Visual FoxPro displays a warning message on-screen and doesn't put the erroneous data into the field. You get the privilege of writing that message. Simply enter the text for the message into the Message text box.

  Make your message informative so that the person knows what mistake was made and how to correct it. A simple statement that displays the words `Error` or `You can t do that!` doesn't help the person who's entering incorrect data into the field. Instead, you may want to create a message that reads something like the following example:

  ```
  The number you entered exceeds the permissible range.
  Enter a number between 0 and 1001.
  ```

- **Default value:** In the Default value text box, you can set the *default value* for the field. This property is the value that appears on-screen whenever someone enters data into the field. The person entering the data can choose to accept the default value or overwrite the default value with another value. An order entry system, for example, usually includes a field containing the date of the order. You can set the default value of this field to today's date. Visual FoxPro automatically fills in the field with the system's current date.

Keep in mind that not all fields need a default value. A default value for a person's first and last name fields, for example, just doesn't make sense.

The 13 field types

In the Table Designer dialog box, you can set the appropriate field type. In all, Visual FoxPro offers 13 field types.

Why so many field types? The answer is rather technical, but I'll just say that certain field types take up more room in the database than other field types. Therefore, you help Visual FoxPro store your information the most efficient way by specifying the field type of a field. Following are descriptions of the field types:

- ✔ **Character:** A character field type is used to hold letters, numbers that will not be used in calculations (like house numbers), and punctuation. The most common data type, the character field can hold any characters.

- ✔ **Currency:** The currency field type holds currency values (dollars and cents). Visual FoxPro automatically takes care of the currency symbol whenever values in the field are used in calculations and in reports. And you can stick into this field numbers from –922337203685477.5808 to 922337203685477.5807.

- ✔ **Numeric:** The numeric field type holds whole numbers or fractions. These values can be used in calculations. You also can use a numeric field type for currency, although Visual FoxPro does not supply the currency symbol when the number is used in reports. And fields of this data type can hold numbers from $-.9999999999E+19$ to $.9999999999E+20$.

- ✔ **Float:** The float field type can hold the same types of values as the numeric type. So why have the same field type with two different names? The reason is that databases other than Visual FoxPro have a float field type. By having a float field type, Visual FoxPro can easily convert data from those databases.

- ✔ **Date:** The date field type is used for dates. Dates stuffed into these fields can be used in date calculations, such as the one that determines how many days before you get your birthday presents. Date values also can be used in fields that are character field types, but they cannot be used directly in date calculations. These values must first be converted to a date field type before they are calculated. Fields of the date field type can handle dates from 01/01/100 to 12/31/9999.

- ✔ **Datetime:** The datetime field type holds both the date and the time. (I see where they got that field type name from.) Visual FoxPro can use both date and time values placed into this kind of field in date and time calculations, which means you can subtract time values to find out how much time has past between values. These fields can hold dates from 01/01/100 to 12/31/9999 and time from 00:00:00 a.m. to 11:59:59 p.m.

✔ **Double:** The double field type holds precise numbers that are extremely large or small and that require accuracy out to the 16th decimal place. You rarely use this data type unless you deal with numbers from +/–4.94065645841247E-324 to +/–8.9884656743115E307.

✔ **Integer:** The integer field type contains whole numbers. You can't insert a decimal value in this field, but you can shove large or small whole numbers in these fields. These numbers can range from –2147483647 to 2147483646.

✔ **Logical:** Use this type when only two values, true or false, need to be placed into a field. Typically, you ask questions like, "Do you drive a BMW? Are your parents wealthy? Are you single? Are you free Friday night? Can you pick me up at 7?" All these questions can be answered either true or false (or if you're picky, yes or no). The answers to these questions can be stored in a logical field type field as True or False.

✔ **Memo:** Use this type when you want to save a lot of text into a field. Actually, the text is stored on your disk. The value in the field is only a reference to where the text resides on the disk. This field types allows you to easily add a notepad to your database.

✔ **General:** The general field type is reserved for fields that hold references to an OLE object (no bullfighting, please). *OLE* is the acronym for *object linking and embedding,* and an object can be an Excel spreadsheet, a Word document, or practically anything else that you create with another Windows program. You can link these objects directly into your Visual FoxPro database.

✔ **Character (Binary) and Memo (Binary) Field Type:** These field types contain the same kinds of data as the character and memo field types. However, the data is stored in the binary format, which prevents the data from being changed by programs written in Visual FoxPro programming language. Chances are that you'll never need to use these field types.

Chapter 3

Indexing Your Database

• •

In This Chapter

▶ Selecting the type of index to use

▶ Creating an index

▶ Turning on (and off) an index

▶ Inserting expressions and filters in your index

▶ Modifying an index

▶ Deleting an index

• •

*F*inding one record in a table containing a million records is like asking someone to find a needle in a haystack. You know that the information is in the table, somewhere, but you don't know whether the information is in the first record, the ten thousandth record, or the millionth record. Fortunately, you don't need to go through the painstaking procedure of looking through each field of each record to locate the information that you need. You can ask Visual FoxPro to do the work for you.

Even Visual FoxPro may move slowly in a search, however, unless you correctly build the database through which you're searching — and unless the table containing the information has a index. But create a good index to go along with your table and — wow! — just watch Visual FoxPro zip through millions of records at the speed of light. (Well, maybe that's a little exaggerated. . . .) Visual FoxPro can find data as fast as your disk drive can move — as long as you have those good indexes for your table.

This chapter takes you behind the scenes to see just how this indexing magic works — and how you can become an index magician.

Using an Index

Suppose that you remember something about a hot topic somewhere in this book, but you don't know which page discusses that topic. The book contains more than 300 pages and thousands of words, so how do you even begin to find the phrase that you need?

The answer to your quest lies in the back of the book: its index. An index contains important words, along with the numbers of the pages that contain those words. And to make your search even easier, these important words appear in alphabetical order. Look down the index, and you're bound to find the word that you need. Then you can turn to the corresponding page in the book and read all about the topic.

So I haven't told you anything that you didn't know, right? Ah, but I have. I've just described (in theory, at least) how Visual FoxPro can zip through millions of records to find the one you need. Like you, Visual FoxPro uses an index, as long as someone builds an index for the table. (And that someone is you.)

Keep in mind, though, that your database doesn't need to have an index. When your database does have an index, it's usually for one table. A table's index is similar to a book's index. Both indexes contain keywords to look up and numbers that refer you to the keyword's location in the book or in the database. You simply tell Visual FoxPro to copy into an index the values in the table for which you're likely to search.

You also can use these values to change the order of information in the table. These values are called the *key to the index.* Along with these values are the numbers of the records in the table that contain each value. In a database index, record numbers are like the page numbers of a book.

Time for an illustration before you become too confused. Table 3-1 shows a table that contains names and Social Security numbers. I include the record numbers in the table for your reference, but record numbers aren't really stored in the table.

Table 3-1 also shows the index for the table. Notice that the index file contains only two fields: the Social Security # and the Record # fields. The Record # field lists the number of the record in the table that contains the Social Security number. In this case, the index file stores the record numbers.

Table 3-1	**A Table and the Table's Corresponding Index File**					
Table				**Index**		
Record #	**Social Security #**	**FName**	**LName**	**Social Security #**	**Record #**	
1	444-44-4444	Bob	Smith	222-22-2222	2	
2	222-22-2222	Mary	Jones	444-44-4444	1	
3	888-88-8888	Sue	Adams	555-55-5555	4	
4	555-55-5555	Joe	Jobs	888-88-8888	3	

Pretend now that you're Visual FoxPro, and you're asked to find the name of the person who has the Social Security number 444-44-4444. You're told to use the index to conduct your search. So you open the index and read each Social Security number, looking for 444-44-4444. Bingo — you find the number.

Next, you look at the value in the index's Record # field. This field tells you the record number that you need to locate in the table — in this case, record #1. You open the table and go immediately to record #1, where you find the name that you seek: Bob Smith.

In essence, this process is how Visual FoxPro uses indexes to find the data that you need in the database.

Planning an Index

Before you create an index for your table, you need to decide which values to include in your index, as well as the type of index that you want to create.

Visual FoxPro offers four types of indexes:

- **Primary index.** A *primary index* is the main index for a table. The primary index determines the order in which Visual FoxPro processes records in the table if you specify no other index. A primary index also enables you to enter only unique values in the field(s) that you use as the key to the index. The index shown in Table 3-1 is a good choice as the primary index for that table because it contains Social Security numbers. Social Security numbers are unique, and that's why the index in Table 3-1 can be a primary index.

- **Candidate index.** A *candidate index* is similar to a primary index. The order of this index also can determine the order in which Visual FoxPro processes records in the table. A candidate index ensures that you enter only unique values in the *key field,* which is another term for the *key to the index.* Visual FoxPro enforces unique values. Each time you enter a new value in the key field, Visual FoxPro searches the key field to see whether the value is already there. If so, an error message appears.

Although you can have many candidate indexes, you can have only one primary index for each table. Also, the primary index is the only one you can use as a default index for the table. You need to tell Visual FoxPro that you want to use a specific candidate index for processing records in a table; otherwise, the program uses the primary index for this task by default.

✔ **Regular index.** A *regular index* also determines the order in which Visual FoxPro processes records in the table. This index type, however, differs from the other indexes in that a regular index can have duplicate values as its key to the index — that is, you can have the same value appear any number of times in the field that you use for the regular index.

To look up information in the table by last names, for example, you need to create a regular index rather than a primary or candidate index because a table can include several people who have the same last name.

✔ **Unique index.** Previous versions of FoxPro used a unique index. In the current version of the program, however, queries or views perform the functions that once were reserved for unique indexes — and queries and views are much easier to use. So forget about creating this type of index; I mention it only so that if you hear users of earlier versions talking about unique indexes, you know what they're talking about.

You can create several indexes for a table, so your decision as to which index type to create needn't be all that difficult. You can create one index of each type, if you want. But creating many indexes for each table really doesn't make much sense.

A primary index is ideal for most tables in which at least one field contains unique values, such as the Social Security number field or an identification number field. Visual FoxPro then can take advantage of the efficiency of an index that also serves as the default index for the table. In other words, you don't have to remember to turn on the default index. When you ask Visual FoxPro to find information, the program automatically searches the default index instead of looking at every field in the table.

Indexes also play an important role in the way that Visual FoxPro processes records in the table. Records go into a table sequentially. The first set of data entered into the table goes in the first record, the second set of data piles into the second record, and so on. This process is known as the *data-entry order*.

When you want to print records in the table, Visual FoxPro prints the first record and continues through to the last record. Sometimes, however, you may want the records printed in a different order — by last name, for example. To do so, you need to rearrange the records until the printing is complete.

You can have Visual FoxPro logically change the order of these records by creating one or more indexes. Suppose that you have a table containing a Social Security number field, a last name field, and a company name field (among others). You want to rearrange the records in three ways: by Social Security number, by last name, and by company name. The best way to accomplish this task is to create three indexes.

The first index uses the Social Security number as the key field. Because this field contains unique values, you can create from this field either a primary index (if none exists) or a candidate index (if a primary index exists). Visual FoxPro automatically arranges the index in order by Social Security number.

The next two indexes that you create need to be regular indexes: one for the last name field and the other for the company name field. The key fields to these indexes most likely contain duplicate values — two people who have the same last name or who work for the same company. Therefore, you can't use these fields for either a primary index or candidate index.

Each index stores the key value in alphabetical order. So if you want to see records in last name order, you tell Visual FoxPro to use the last name index. Then, if you want to see records displayed by company, you tell Visual FoxPro to switch to the company name index.

Don't go crazy creating millions of indexes, though — too many indexes can confuse you and slow data entry, data retrieval, sorts, and searches. The delay arises each time you add a new record, delete an existing record, or modify values in a record that contain the key to these indexes. Visual FoxPro has to update all the indexes. The more indexes you have and the more records each index covers, the more time Visual FoxPro takes to update the indexes. Checking scores of indexes can really bring down the performance of your database, so you're better off keeping the number of indexes to a reasonable number. I rarely go beyond three indexes.

Creating an Index on One Field

You create indexes by using the Table Designer. At the top of the Table Designer are three tabs, one of which is Indexes. Click the Indexes tab to put the index form on-screen.

Here's how you create an index for a table. (I assume, of course, that you have already created a database and at least one table for the database. I show you how to create a database and tables in Chapter 1 and Chapter 2.) Follow these steps:

1. **Open the database that you want to create an index for.**

   Visual FoxPro displays the Database Designer for the database.

2. **Double-click the table box to display the records in the table.**

3. **Choose Table⇨Properties.**

   Visual FoxPro displays the Work Area Properties dialog box.

4. Click <u>M</u>odify.

The Table Designer shown in Figure 3-1 appears.

5. Click the Indexes tab.

6. Click the Name box and type the name of the index.

The Name column contains the name of the index. Click the Name box and then begin typing the name. Each index must have a unique name that conforms to the Visual FoxPro naming restrictions. (The name has to be no more than ten characters long, must have no spaces, and must start with a letter.)

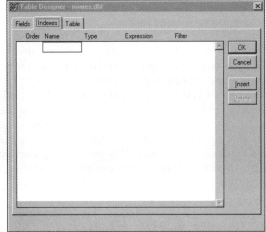

Figure 3-1:
The Indexes
tab of the
Table
Designer.

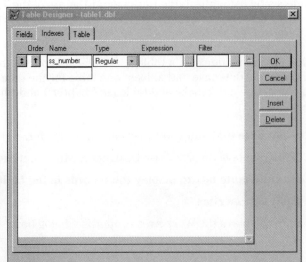

Figure 3-2:
Enter
the name
of the index
in the Name
column.

7. **Click the button to the right of the Expression column.**

   The Expression dialog box appears.

8. **Double-click the field name that is the key field for the index.**

9. **Click OK.**

   You return to the Indexes tab of the Table Designer.

10. **Click the Type combo box to select the type of index that you want to create (see Figure 3-3).**

    The Type column contains a combo box of valid index types. When you select an index type from this box, your selection appears in the Type column. The regular index type is the default value and suits most of your indexing needs.

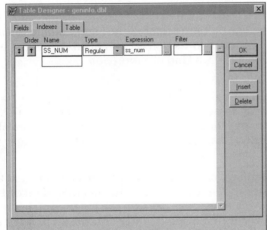

Figure 3-3: Select the type of index from the Type combo box.

11. **Click the button to the right of the Filter column.**

    The Expression box appears. The Expression column is where you identify the name of the field that you intend to use as the key to the index. Most of the time, you use one field as the expression, in which case you type that field name in the Expression column.

    You can, however, become fancy with the key value. You can use only part of the value of a field as the key, such as when create an index on just the month of a date that has 01/01/98. You also can use more than one field as the key. You can create an index on a salary field, for example, and then have an expression that includes key field values greater than $20,000. These expressions are unusual because you probably won't need to create similar expressions for indexes you use with your table.

I talk more about building unusual expressions in the section "Creating Multiple Field Indexes," later in this chapter. Don't skip that section, thinking that building expressions is out of your league, because you can use the Expression Builder to have Visual FoxPro do most of the complicated stuff for you. (You click the button next to the Expression box to access the Expression Builder.)

12. **Double-click the field name that is the key field for the index.**

13. **Click the equal sign in the Logical combo box.**

14. **Type the value of the field that you want to use as the filter for the index in the Expression box.**

    You use the Filter column to tell Visual FoxPro that you want to include only some of the table's records in the index. If you type Smith, for example, only records that have the value *Smith* as the key field are included in the index. If you don't specify a filter, Visual FoxPro indexes all the records in the table.

    You can click the button to the right of the Filter column to enter a condition for selecting records. This action opens the Expression Builder because a filter is a kind of expression.

    You may, for example, want the index to include only the last names of people who work for company XYZ. If so, the filter that you type in the Filter column looks something like mytable.company = "XYZ". The table name is mytable, and the field name is company. I talk more about filters in the section "Inserting Expressions and Filters," later in this chapter.

A filter is not required for an index; in fact, you typically don't use one. So why use a filter? A *filtered index* cuts the number of records that Visual FoxPro needs to process because the index contains references to only those records that meet the filter criteria. If you want to see only the records of people who work in company XYZ, you don't need to see all the other records, so set a filter on the index. Visual FoxPro ignores those records and responds to your request faster than if you didn't use a filter on the index.

15. **Click OK to close the Expression Builder.**

    You return to the Indexes tab of the Table Designer.

16. **Click the arrow button in the Order column to change the order of the index from ascending to descending.**

    You use the Order column to indicate whether the program places the values of the key field in ascending or descending order. *Ascending* means A–Z and 0–9, and descending means Z–A and 9–0. By default, all indexes are in ascending order, as indicated by the up arrow. Click the up arrow to change to descending order. A down arrow then appears.

17. Click OK to close the Table Designer.

You return to the Work Area Properties dialog box.

18. Click OK to close the Work Area Properties dialog box.

Visual FoxPro creates the index for you and returns you to the Database Designer.

Creating Multiple Field Indexes

You can use more than one field as the key value of an index. You're likely to use this technique more than you imagine. The following example describes a typical situation in which a multiple field index comes in handy.

Suppose that you want to look up information about a certain person, but you know only the person's first and last name. You already know that you can create an index based on last names. But what about first names?

Because your database could contain several people who have the same last name, you really need to create an index that uses both first name and last name fields. And you can do that. All you need to do is type both field names in the Expression column of the index. This process, however, can prove to be a little tricky.

Here's how you create an index on more than one field in your table:

1. Open the database that you want to create an index for.

Visual FoxPro displays the Database Designer for the database.

2. Double-click the table box to display the records in the table.

3. Choose Table⇨Properties.

Visual FoxPro displays the Work Area Properties dialog box.

4. Click Modify.

The Table Designer appears.

5. Click the Indexes tab.

6. In the Name column, enter the name of the index.

7. Click the Expression button to display the Expression Builder.

8. Double-click the first field that you want to use for the index.

The name of the field appears in the Expression box.

You must be careful of the order in which you place the field names. Visual FoxPro treats the values of these fields as one field, reading left to right.

9. Choose the plus sign from the String combo box.

You must separate the field names that you type in the Expression column with plus signs (+) — for example, lname + fname. You can include as many names as you need in a single field, but make sure that a plus sign connects each name with the next name. Don't worry about placing spaces between the field names and the plus sign; Visual FoxPro inserts the spaces automatically.

10. Double-click the next field that you want to use for the index.

Visual FoxPro displays the field name to the right of the plus sign in the Expression box.

11. Click OK to close the Expression Builder.

You return to the Table Designer.

12. Click OK to close the Table Designer.

You return to the Database Designer.

The multiple field index shown in Table 3-2 uses the last name and first name fields as the key to the index. Visual FoxPro combines these values and then stuffs the combined value into the index as the key value. The result is that the letters of the last name run directly into the letters of the first name.

Table 3-2		A Multiple Field Index				
Table				**Index**		
Record #	**Social Security #**	**FName**	**LName**	**Lname+FName**	**Record #**	
1	777-77-7777	Victor	Adams	AdamsSue	3	
2	222-22-2222	Mary	Jones	AdamsVictor	1	
3	888-88-8888	Sue	Adams	JobsJoe	4	
4	555-55-5555	Joe	Jobs	JonesMary	2	

If you tell Visual FoxPro to find *Sue Adams,* the program looks for *Sue Adams* in the index. Oops! You need to ask Visual FoxPro to find *Adams Sue* because the program creates the index on the basis of last name + first name — that is, last name followed by first name, not vice versa.

I set up this particular order for a logical reason, by the way: You want the names to appear in the index in alphabetical order by last name and then by first name because it's easier to find a person by his or her last name than by the person's first name. The moral of this story is that you need to carefully plan the way that you organize your fields in a multiple field index.

Inserting Expressions and Filters

An *expression* determines the values that the program uses for the index. All records are included in an expression. By contrast, a *filter* determines values for the index but uses only a subset of the records — records that meet the filter's criteria — in the index.

Inserting an expression or a filter into an index is not difficult, thanks to the nearly foolproof Expression Builder. The *Expression Builder* is a tool that lets you form complex expressions by selecting values, operators and other neat things from drop-down list boxes. You can define both an expression and a filter by making selections in the Expression Builder.

After you assemble your expression, the Expression Builder lets you verify that the expression does what you expect it to do. When you're satisfied, click OK, and the expression automatically appears in the field property. The Expression Builder includes a box in which you can type the expression for your index. If you fear making a typo, however, you can select components of the expression from the boxes that dot the Expression Builder.

Suppose that you want to create a filter that uses records in which the last name field has a certain value. Here's how you do it:

1. **Open the database that you want to create a filter for.**

   Visual FoxPro displays the Database Designer for the database.

2. **Double-click the table box to display the records in the table.**

3. **Choose Table⇨Properties.**

   Visual FoxPro displays the Work Area Properties dialog box.

4. **Click Modify.**

   The Table Designer appears.

5. **Click the Indexes tab.**

6. **In the Name column, enter the index name.**

Using the Expression Builder

The Expression Builder has three categories of list boxes:

- **Functions.** *Functions* are complex tasks that Visual FoxPro performs automatically. Functions are grouped into string functions, math functions, logical functions, and date functions.

- **Fields.** The Fields list displays all the fields that are available in the current table (the table that you are using when you display the Expression Builder dialog box). You'll use this list frequently as you create your own indexes.

- **Variables.** The Variables list displays information that Visual FoxPro stores. You won't need this information until you become an experienced Visual FoxPro user.

You can mix items in all three list boxes to form complex, powerful expressions that enhance the indexes you create for your tables.

7. **Click the button to the right of the Expression column or the button to the right of the Filter column.**

   Visual FoxPro displays the Expression Builder, shown in Figure 3-4.

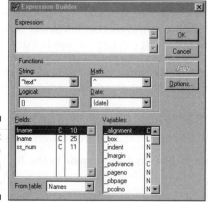

Figure 3-4:
The Expression Builder.

8. **Double-click the fname field in the Fields list to display the field name in the Expression text box.**

9. **Double-click the equal sign in the Logical combo box to display the equal sign to the right of the field name in the Expression text box.**

10. **Type the value that you want to the right of the equal sign in the Expression text box — including the quotation marks.**

Writing an expression

Writing a validation expression is a little tricky, but something that you can master with practice. The method I use works well if you're not comfortable writing math expressions. Here's how I do it:

1. **Write down the validation rule in English.**

2. **Substitute mathematical words (called *operators*) for your English words.**

Say that you want data to be greater than 5000 and less than 99000. (These numbers could be the valid salary ranges for your company.)

Follow the first step in my procedure and write this expression in English:

```
less than 99000 and greater than
5000
```

Now for the mathematical expression. Look up the less than operator and the greater than operator and then substitute the English words with the appropriate operator:

< 99000 AND > 5000

This process becomes even easier when you use Visual FoxPro's Expression Builder.

For example, if I want to create a filter that uses records in which the last name field has the value Smith, I type "Smith" to the right of the equal sign.

11. **Click OK to close the Expression Builder.**

You return to the Indexes tab of the Table Designer.

12. **Click OK to save the filtered index.**

You've built an index.

Turning an Index On and Off

Although you create an index (or several indexes), the mere fact of creation doesn't mean that Visual FoxPro is actually going to use the index. You must order the program to do so. To order Visual FoxPro to use an index:

1. **Open the table you want to create an index for.**

2. **Create two indexes.**

If you don't know how to do this, refer to the section "Creating an Index on One Field" and "Creating Multiple Field Indexes," earlier in this chapter. For this example, I call one index Names, with a key of lname + fname. I make this first index a regular index. I call the other index ss_num, with a key of Social Security number. I make this index a primary index.

When you finish, you again have the Database Designer with a table box on-screen.

3. **Right-click the name of the table in the Table box to open a shortcut menu.**

4. **Click Browse to display the contents of the table.**

   You see columns showing the field names and empty rows (unless you entered information in the table).

   As soon as the table is displayed on-screen, the Database menu changes to the Table menu.

5. **Choose Table⇨Properties.**

   The Work Area Properties dialog box, shown in Figure 3-5, appears. Near the lower-right corner of the dialog box, you find the Index order combo box. By default, <no order> initially appears in this combo box.

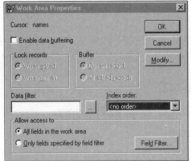

Figure 3-5:
The Work Area Properties dialog box.

6. **From the Index order combo box, select the index that you want to turn on.**

7. **Click OK to close the Work Area Properties dialog box.**

   Now the index is turned on. Records appear in the table in sort order of the key fields of the index in the Browse view of the table.

Modifying an Index

What happens if you make a mistake as you create an index? Golly gee, the whole world will collapse, your computer will go up in smoke, and your car won't start tomorrow! Right? Well, get those ideas out of your mind.

What *really* happens? You fix the problem. And you can do so by following these steps:

1. **Open the database that contains the index you want to change.**

   Visual FoxPro displays the Database Designer for the database.

2. **Click the name of the table box in the Database Designer.**

3. **Choose Database⇨Modify.**

   The Table Designer appears.

4. **Click the Indexes tab.**

5. **Modify the index attributes the same way that you created the index.**

   If you don't know how to do this, refer to the sections "Creating an Index on One Field" and "Creating Multiple Field Indexes," earlier in this chapter.

6. **Click OK.**

   You return to the Work Area Properties dialog box.

7. **Click OK.**

   You return to the Database Designer. You've fixed the index.

To make sure that you've fixed the index, try the index again with your table, using the same method that you used to discover the problem in the first place.

Deleting an Index

If you become frustrated while attempting to fix an existing index, stop. Walk away from the computer. Get a cool one from the refrigerator. And try again in an hour or so. Instead of repairing the index, you may want to start fresh by deleting the old index so that you can create a new one.

To delete an index:

1. **Open the database that contains the index you want to delete.**

   Visual FoxPro displays the Database Designer for the database.

2. **Click the name of the table box in the Database Designer.**

3. **Choose Database⇨Modify to display the Table Designer.**

4. **Click the Indexes tab.**

5. Click <u>D</u>elete.

6. Click OK.

The index is gone.

Refer to the section "Creating an Index on One Field" or the section "Creating Multiple Field Indexes," earlier in this chapter, when you're ready to build a new index for your table.

Chapter 4

Working with Data

In This Chapter

▶ Entering information into the database

▶ Viewing data

▶ Changing information that's already in the database

▶ Getting rid of data you don't want

*A*fter all the work of planning and creating your database, tables, and indexes, you finally begin to put stuff — *data* — into the database. Data can be your special someone's telephone number, your bank account, your boss's birthday, sales for your company's latest product line, and so on. Your database can consist of just about any information that you may want to retrieve later, whether you want to search for a specific value, display the information on a form, or print 2out the information in a report. (See Chapter 14.)

This chapter shows you how to enter each piece of data into an appropriate field of a table, display the data on-screen, change and save the data, and remove the data from the table. Make sure that you've properly defined the fields, or Visual FoxPro won't let you enter the data. (See Chapter 2 for more information about defining fields.)

Accessing Data Without Using a Form

You've probably heard about some whiz kid being able to break into a program by using the back door to the system. Sounds mysterious and dangerous, doesn't it?

Actually, *back door* simply refers to viewing tables from the Database Designer, which I describe in Chapter 1. Any database that is part of a *computer application* — a database, forms, and reports joined together to allow easy access to the information stored in the database — has a back door.

Most people, however, don't use the back door for entering your database; most use what I call the *front door:* forms. Forms are like credit card applications or bank deposit forms except that they appear on the computer screen. In a computer application, you use forms to manage data entry and data display. A form contains a title, directions on how to complete the form, labels for places where the user enters data, and the actual places where the user enters data. The person filling out the form doesn't see the database name, tables, indexes, and fields. In fact, someone new to using a computer may not realize that such things even exist. But they do exist, and you can see them by viewing tables from the Database Designer. You need to go through this back door of the database to:

- ✔ Enter data
- ✔ View data
- ✔ Modify data
- ✔ Delete data

You find out how to perform all these tasks in this chapter.

Inserting Records into a Table

When you want to insert more data into a table, you append a new record and enter the data in the blank fields of the new record.

Here's how to add a record to a table:

1. **Choose File➪Open.**

   The Open dialog box appears.

2. **Select the database that you want to add a record to and click OK.**

   The Database Designer appears.

3. **Double-click the name of the table in the Database Designer.**

   The table appears, as shown in Figure 4-1.

4. **Choose Table➪Append New Record or press Ctrl+Y.**

   Visual FoxPro inserts a blank record into the table and places the cursor in the first field.

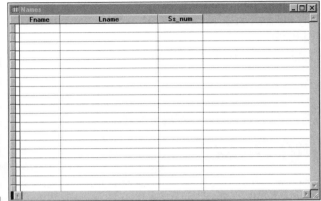

Figure 4-1:
After you get your table on-screen, you can append a new record.

When you have a fresh new record on-screen, simply start typing the fields. The new record remains on-screen when you finish typing data in the fields. Press Ctrl+F4 to close the table and return to the Database Designer dialog box.

Here are things to note:

✓ If you define a field to appear with certain characters to separate pieces of the field's data — for example, Figure 4-2 shows the Ss_num field with dashes for separating the Social Security number — those characters appear in the fields as *input masks*. As you type, the cursor automatically skips the input mask character. (I show you how to create an input mask in Chapter 2.)

Figure 4-2:
You can see an input mask in the Ss_num field in this table.

> ✔ If you type more characters than the field can hold, the cursor automatically moves to the next field and overwrites data that's already in the next field.

> ✔ Press Tab to move from field to field.

Paying Attention to Indexes When Adding Data

As you enter data into a table, you need to remember all the rules that you established for the table when you created it, especially if you created a primary index for the table. Both indexes permit only unique values as the key to the index. The primary index is the default index for the table. Suppose that your table consists of a first name, a last name, and a Social Security number and uses the Social Security number field as the key value for the primary index. Visual FoxPro doesn't like it if you try to enter a Social Security number that's already being used by another record. (I show you how to create indexes in Chapter 3.)

But the program just watches you silently as you make your invalid index values and doesn't pounce until you try to leave the record, at which time Visual FoxPro displays a warning message. You can't continue until you remove the invalid index value. You have three choices:

> ✔ **OK:** Returns you to the record without changing any data. You need to make all the changes to the record yourself to make the data acceptable to the indexes for the table.

> ✔ **Revert:** Erases all the data you entered into the record and returns you to the record so that you can re-enter the record.

> ✔ **Help:** Provides online assistance just when you're about to panic.

When Visual FoxPro is satisfied that the data in your record is acceptable for your indexes, it updates all the indexes that are associated with the table.

Displaying the Data: The Browsing Method

You have many choices for displaying the information that you stuffed into a table: You can display the data in reports or on forms, you can display all the data or just some of it, and so on. You can check out Part III for the fancy methods, but for now, focus on the simplest way: *browsing the table.*

Browsing allows you to display — and edit — all the table's data in a spreadsheetlike form, just like the kind of display that you use when you enter the data. (See Figure 4-3.)

Figure 4-3:
When you
browse a
table, you
can view
and change
all the
records in
the table.

Ss_num	Fname	Lname	Title
111-11-1111	Tom	Smith	Manager
222-22-2222	Mary	Jones	Manager
333-33-3333	Joan	Gates	Manager
444-44-4444	Mike	Smith	Clerk
555-55-5555	Mark	Russell	Supervisor
666-66-6666	Joanne	Collage	Manager
777-77-7777	Sandra	Jones	Manager
888-88-8888	Anne	Gates	Manager
2	3	4	3

Here's how to browse:

1. **Choose File⇨Open.**

   The Open dialog box appears.

2. **Choose the name of your database and click OK.**

   The Database Designer dialog box appears.

3. **Double-click the name of the table in the Database Designer.**

   Alternatively, you can right-click the table name and choose Browse from the shortcut menu, or click the table name in the Database Designer and then choose Database⇨Browse.

   Your data appears in a window. Notice that the column headings are the field names and that each row is a record of information.

The window that appears doesn't show all the data. Use the horizontal scroll bar (at the bottom of the screen) to display fields that can't fit in the window; use the vertical scroll bar (on the right side of the screen) to bring additional records into the window.

Editing the Data in Fields

To make changes to information in a record, first browse the table (refer to "Displaying the Data: The Browsing Method," earlier in this chapter) to find the data that you want to modify. Then click the field that holds the offending data and use one of these methods:

> ✔ To erase the character to the left of the cursor, press the Backspace key.
>
> ✔ Press the Delete key to erase the character to the right of the cursor.
>
> ✔ To erase all the data in the field, select the data and press the Delete key.
>
> ✔ To insert text into the field, place the cursor where you want the text to appear and then start typing.
>
> ✔ To replace all the text in the field, select the data and then begin typing the new text.

Although you're modifying data in the table, you don't use the Modify command that appears on the Database menu and on the context menu. That command is for changing the definition of fields in the table, not for modifying the data in the table.

Deleting Data

Now's the time for some magic — you know, the now-you-see-it-now-you-don't kind. You can delete a record from the table and then make the record reappear again.

The magic is that when you ask for a record to be deleted, Visual FoxPro marks the record for deletion at a later time but doesn't actually get rid of it. The record is still around and available until then, even though Visual FoxPro treats marked records as though they don't exist if you enter SET DELETED ON in the Command Window. I show you how to hide deleted records in the section "Hiding (and unhiding) records that are marked to be deleted," later in this chapter.

You can unmark the marked records and bring them back into the fold, if you like. You also can make Visual FoxPro hide marked records from view. And you can control when Visual FoxPro does the final deed and deletes marked records for good.

Deleting and undeleting records

To mark a record (or range of records) for deletion later or to unmark a record (or range of records) that you previously marked for deletion, follow these steps:

1. **Display records by following the steps in the section "Displaying the Data: The Browsing Method," earlier in this chapter.**

   A record that's marked for deletion has a black arrowhead in the column next to the first field in the record, as shown in Figure 4-4.

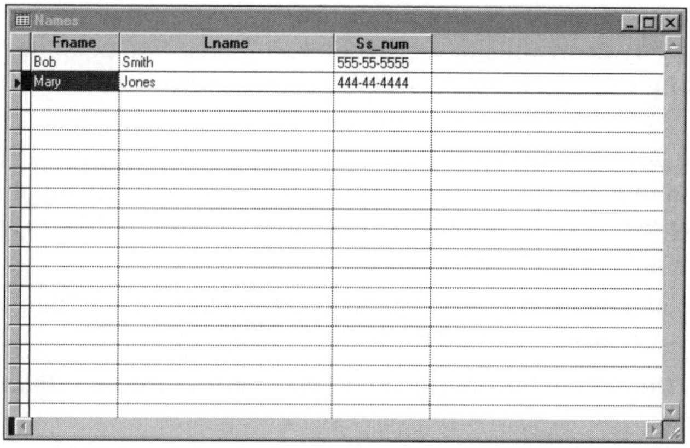

Figure 4-4:
The black
arrowhead
in the far-
left column
indicates a
record
that's
marked for
deletion.

2. **Click the record that you want to mark or unmark for deletion.**

3. **Click the column to the left of the record's first field or choose Table⊏>Delete Records to delete the record; to undelete the record, choose Table⊏>Recall Records.**

   Notice that the black arrowhead in the far-left column is a *toggle,* which means that you click to make the arrowhead appear and then you click again to make it disappear.

   If you're deleting, the Delete dialog box, shown in Figure 4-5, appears. If you're undeleting, a similar dialog box appears. (The following steps apply to both dialog boxes.)

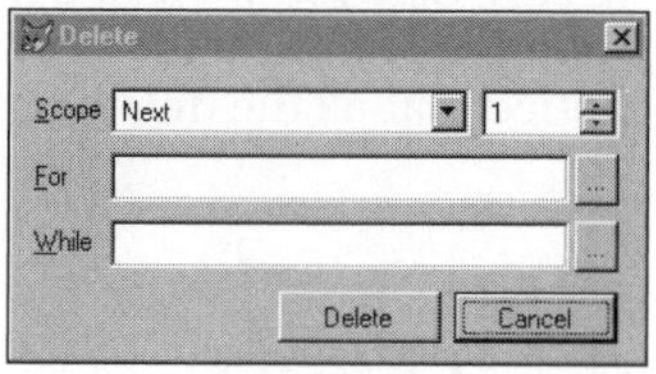

Figure 4-5:
The Delete
dialog box.

4. **In the dialog box, specify the records to be deleted or undeleted.**

   In the Scope combo box, select Next if you want to act on just the next record, All for all the records in the table, Record for the currently selected record, or Rest for the current record plus all subsequent records.

   Or use the box next to the Scope box to specify the number of records to delete or undelete. The default is one record.

You can enter an expression to define the criteria for the records to be deleted by using the <u>F</u>or and <u>W</u>hile text boxes. For example, you can enter fname = "Bob" in the For box and salary = < 25000 in the While box.

And if writing expressions isn't your thing, you can always click the button that appears to the right of these text boxes to display the Expression Builder. In Chapter 3, I show you how to build expressions by using the Expression Builder.

Note: Don't expect these expressions to delete all matching records unless you also select All from the combo box.

5. **Click the <u>D</u>elete button (or the Recall button, for undeleting) to finish the job.**

You return to browsing the table. Notice that the arrowhead appears next to the current record, which is the record you can change. You can make another record the current record by moving the cursor to that record and clicking the left mouse button.

Deleting records for good

Here's how you can get rid of the marked records for good:

1. **Display the records by following the steps in the section "Displaying the Data: The Browsing Method," earlier in this chapter.**

2. **Choose Table⇨Remove Deleted Records.**

Visual FoxPro asks whether you're sure that you want to delete the records; if you answer Yes, those records are lost forever. You return to browsing the table, where you'll notice that all the deleted records have been removed from the table.

Hiding (and unhiding) records that are marked to be deleted

If you don't want to see records that are marked for deletion in the list of records, you can make Visual FoxPro hide those records. Follow these steps:

1. **If the Database Designer isn't on-screen, open it.**

See Chapter 2 if you need to brush up on how to open the Database Designer.

2. **Choose <u>W</u>indow⇨<u>C</u>ommand Window or press Ctrl+F2.**

The Command Window appears. You can display the Command Window at any time while you're in Visual FoxPro.

3. **To hide records that are marked to be deleted, type the following command, as shown in Figure 4-6:**

```
SET DELETED ON
```

4. **Press Enter (see Figure 4-6).**

Figure 4-6:
The
Command
Window.

5. **Click the table box in the Database Designer that contains the records that are marked for deletion.**

Records that aren't marked for deletion appear on-screen.

6. **Choose Window⇨Command Window or press Ctrl+F2.**

The Command Window appears again.

To make those records visible again, follow the same steps, typing the following command in Step 2:

```
SET DELETED OFF
```

Saving Data

You won't find any Save Data button on-screen when you enter or modify data. When you close the window that contains the table, Visual FoxPro assumes that you want to save the data and saves it automatically.

You put a lot of work into building your database and entering data. You don't want to lose all the work due to a power outage or a computer crash, so make sure that you copy the database and tables to a floppy disk before you shut off your computer. Don't worry about which files to copy. Simply copy everything from the folder that you created for the database. You'll be sure that you haven't overlooked a file by mistake.

The Command Window

The Command Window is where you give Visual FoxPro written directions to follow, such as to hide records that are marked for deletion. You use the Visual FoxPro Language Commands, rather than a menu or a dialog box, to give these directions. Many instructions (such as hiding and unhiding records that are to be deleted) can be given only by using Visual FoxPro Language Commands.

Each time you use a menu or dialog box (to create a new table, for example), Visual FoxPro automatically displays the corresponding Visual FoxPro Language Command in the Command Window.

The Visual FoxPro language is beyond the scope of this book, but you can find a complete discussion of the language in the documentation that came with your copy of Visual FoxPro.

Chapter 5

Rearranging the Data

● ●

In This Chapter

▶ Displaying certain fields

▶ Moving fields in a table

▶ Simple sorting of records

▶ Sorting records into another table

● ●

*Y*ou can feel proud of yourself when you find out how to build a database and some tables and then stuff them with information. Something is still missing, though. Sometimes, the information in your table is orga-nized just the way you expect, but at other times, you'd like to switch things around a little.

Fields appear in the order in which you entered them when you built the table, for example, but you may want to rearrange the fields to appear in a different order from the way that Visual FoxPro displays them when you browse the table. Maybe the records are just not the way you need to see them. Or maybe too many records may be on-screen, and you may want Visual FoxPro to chop them down to a more manageable number. Or you may simply want to get more creative and change the way Visual FoxPro displays the data in the table. Well, get as fancy as you'd like: Visual FoxPro can fulfill any request that you can imagine. I show you all these techniques in this chapter.

Displaying a Selection of Fields

Whenever you browse a table, Visual FoxPro displays every field that you create in the table. Actually, you see only those fields that can fit into the window. You need to use the horizontal scroll bar, shown in Figure 5-1, to see those fields that are just out of sight.

	Lname	Fname	Salary	Ss_numb
▶	Smith	Bob	30000.0	111-11-11
	Jones	Mary	35000.0	222-22-22

Figure 5-1:
You can't see all the fields at the same time.

Horizontal scroll bar

Sometimes, however, seeing all the fields doesn't make sense. Suppose that you have a table that contains a person's first name, last name, address, Social Security number, and salary. And suppose that you are interested in viewing only the person's name and salary. But the name fields are the first two fields in the table, and the salary field is the last field in the table (and probably not visible in the window). The solution to this problem is to ask Visual FoxPro to display *only* the name fields and the salary field.

To select the fields that you want to display:

1. **Open your database.**

   The Database Designer appears.

2. **In the Database Designer, double-click the table box of the table that you want to browse.**

   The table's records appear.

3. **Choose Table⇨Properties.**

   Visual FoxPro displays the Work Area Properties dialog box, shown in Figure 5-2.

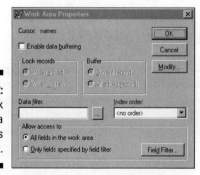

Figure 5-2:
The Work Area Properties dialog box.

4. Click the Fiel**d Filter button.**

The Field Picker dialog box, shown in Figure 5-3, appears.

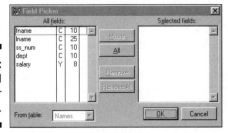

Figure 5-3:
The Field
Picker
dialog box.

5. In the All fields area of the dialog box, double-click the names of the fields that you want to display.

The fields that you want to display move from the All fields list box to the Selected fields list box.

6. Click OK.

You return to the Work Area Properties dialog box.

7. Click OK.

The Work Area Properties dialog box closes, and only the selected fields appear in the table, as shown in Figure 5-4.

Displaying just the fields that you need to see becomes helpful whenever you have many fields in a table. The fields that you don't need to see simply clutter the screen and can make reading information difficult. The Field filter is the perfect tool to break through the information logjam.

Figure 5-4:
After you
select the
fields to
display, you
see only
those
fields.

Fname	Lname	Salary	
Bob	Smith	30000.0	
Mary	Jones	35000.0	

Moving Fields in a Table

If you're like me, you sometimes want to move the fields around when you browse the data in a table — but you don't want the change to be permanent. (Refer to Chapter 6 if you want to permanently change the table's structure.) Moving fields is a little different from selecting fields. In this case, you still want to see all the fields contained in a record, but in a different sequence. When you select fields, you see only the fields that you choose; the other fields do not appear on-screen. I suggest that you move fields whenever you need to reference all the fields but find that some fields that you need to see don't fit on-screen.

Suppose that you stuffed a person's name, address, telephone number, Social Security number, salary, and other important information into a database. Now you want to see the person's Social Security number, name, and salary. However, other fields are between the fields that you want to look at.

You'd have to flip-flop the horizontal scroll box back and forth to see both the name and the salary — that is, unless you move the fields around. You can point to the field name of the salary field and then drag the salary field next to the last name field. When you release the mouse button, Visual FoxPro quickly reshuffles the fields, shoving the other fields out of the way so that you can insert the salary field just where you want it.

Follow these steps to move a field:

1. **Open your database.**

   The Database Designer appears.

2. **Double-click the table box of the table that you want to browse.**

   Records of the table appear.

3. **Point to the field name that you want to move and hold down the left mouse button.**

   The mouse pointer changes to a down arrow.

4. **Drag the mouse pointer to the position where you want to insert the field.**

   The field name moves as you move the mouse pointer.

5. **Release the mouse button.**

   Visual FoxPro relocates the field name and the data in the field.

Now you've organized the fields that way you want to see them without having to scroll across the records to see the fields that are out of sight.

Squeezing Fields onto the Screen

In a table that has many fields (or in a table where the width of a few fields are wide) viewing all the data in the record at one time may be difficult. (See Figure 5-5.)

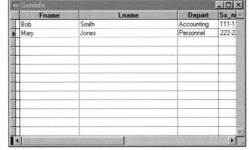

Figure 5-5:
Fields before you change the default field width.

Of course, you can choose those fields that you want to see, or you can rearrange the fields, which may just do the trick. (Refer to the sections "Displaying a Selection of Fields" and "Moving Fields in a Table," earlier in this chapter.)

Sometimes, however, you don't have to go to all that fuss. Instead, you can use some of that extra space in the fields that already appear in the window. After you reclaim this valuable window territory, fields to the right of the window pop into sight.

Here's the trick to getting rid of extra space when you're browsing a table: With the mouse, grab and drag a *column line,* which is a line that separates the gray field names in the top row in the table. You know you're on the column line when you see a two-headed arrow. Visual FoxPro temporarily shrinks the field width and covers empty spaces and characters that are part of the data, as shown in Figure 5-6.

Figure 5-6:
Fields after you change the default field width.

As the width of the field shrinks on-screen, fields to the right move to the left to make room for fields that can't fit in the window.

To change the width of the table in the browse window:

1. **Open your database.**

   The Database Designer appears.

2. **Double-click the table box of the table that you want to browse.**

   Records of the table appear.

3. **Point to a column line (vertical line in the table) in the gray field names and hold down the left mouse button.**

   The mouse pointer changes to a double arrow.

4. **Drag the line right or left to adjust the field width on-screen.**

   The column line moves to the new location in the table.

The new column width appears only when you browse the table and has no effect on the size of the field in the table. The field size determines the field's permanent width. I show you how to change the size, name, type, and other attributes of a field in Chapter 6.

5. **Release the mouse button.**

   Visual FoxPro adjusts all the fields accordingly.

Grabbing a column line and repositioning the column width on-screen is handy when all the fields don't fit on-screen at the same time and some fields contain blank spaces. I find plenty of blank spaces in fields that contain names and cities because I always leave enough room for the largest name that I can think of. I temporarily remove the spaces by changing the field width when I browse the table. The spaces are still in the field, but you don't see them on-screen. You can always widen the column width. The data isn't lost, though. You can reverse the process and stretch the field back to its original width.

Sorting Records

You may need to change the order of the records, which is called *sorting* the records. You're probably familiar with the idea of sorting — *A* comes before *B*, for example, and 1 comes before 2, which is *ascending order*. When *B* comes before *A* and 2 comes before 1, that's *descending order*.

Sorting records is handy when you want to browse records in the order of the values in one or more fields, as is the case when you sort records by last name. Your job is to tell Visual FoxPro how to sort the information that you stuffed into a table. Probably the easiest way to sort information is to create an index. You can find out how to create an index in Chapter 3.

You can create a different index for each way that you want to sort information in the table. Each time you want see the information sorted in a different way, you turn on the appropriate index.

To turn on an index:

1. **Open your database.**

   The Database Designer appears.

2. **Double-click the name of the table in the Database Designer.**

3. **Choose Table⇨Properties.**

   The Work Area Properties dialog box appears.

4. **Select the name of the index from the Index order combo box in the Work Area Properties dialog box, shown in Figure 5-7.**

   You must create an index before you can select the index. I show you how to create an index in Chapter 3.

5. **Click OK.**

   Records in the table appear in sort order.

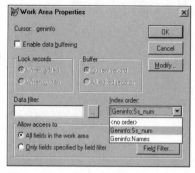

Figure 5-7: You select an index from the Index order combo box.

Making the Sort Permanent

Indexes are a great way to shift records around the table without having to change the data-entry order of the records. *Data-entry order* is the sequence in which Visual FoxPro stores information in the table — the first record entered in the table is the first record in the table, and the last table that you see in the table is the last record that someone entered in the table.

You need to maintain data-entry order if you want to trace the flow of information into the table. Suppose that you have a table that stores information about each customer who calls your place of business. Each time you receive a call, you enter information in the table. You can see the order in which customers called by browsing the table. The first record in the table contains information about the first caller, the second record contains information about the second caller, and so on.

Visual FoxPro always maintains data-entry order whenever you use an index to sort records. You need only turn off the index; Visual FoxPro shows you the records in data-entry order.

Sometimes, you may want to permanently rearrange all the records in the table, such as when you want to send, or *export,* the data to another application, such as a spreadsheet program. One way that you can permanently rearrange all records is to use the SORT command.

Using the SORT command

You won't find the SORT command in any menu. Instead, you have to type several commands in the Command Window (including the SORT command) to have Visual FoxPro perform the sort.

You use the Command Window to give written commands to Visual FoxPro by using the Visual FoxPro language. In fact, each time you use menus to tell Visual FoxPro to do something (such as create a table), the Visual FoxPro Language Command for the task appears in the Command Window automatically. As you become comfortable with Visual

FoxPro, you'll find that entering Visual FoxPro language commands in the Command Window is faster than choosing items from menus.

Visual FoxPro was one of the first PC databases — before Windows and Macintosh databases. Visual FoxPro (or FoxPro, as it was known) also was (and is) a programming language. Therefore, the program has a command language, a Command Window, and a program editor. The *Visual* features make building objects such as databases, tables, forms, and reports easier, but they do not write commands; you still have to do that the old-fashioned way.

Sorting is more complicated than simply choosing items from a menu or clicking buttons in a dialog box; you need to enter commands from the keyboard in the Command Window. Just be careful when you type commands; otherwise, Visual FoxPro complains by displaying Unrecognized command verb in a message box. When you see this message, you probably misspelled the command. Don't worry; Visual FoxPro gives you an endless number of chances to correct your spelling. If you don't enter the command correctly, Visual FoxPro won't know what you want it to do (and, in this case, won't sort your table correctly).

To sort

1. **Display the Command Window by pressing Ctrl+F2.**

2. **Type the following commands in the Command Window, pressing Enter after you type each command line:**

```
CLOSE DATABASES
OPEN DATABASE ('\vfp\mydata\mydatabase')
USE names
SORT TO newfile ON ss_num
```

Visual FoxPro recognizes commands entered in uppercase or lowercase letters, so type them however you want. Remember to replace (\mydatabase') with the name of the database that contains the table you want to sort. In line 3, you also need to replace names with the name of the table you want to sort. In line 4, replace newfile with the name of the new table and replace ss-num with the record you want to sort by.

Your screen should look like Figure 5-8.

If you made a typo, Visual FoxPro displays a message box telling you that it didn't understand your command. If you get such a message, click OK and re-enter the command in the Command Window.

Figure 5-8:
The
Command
Window.

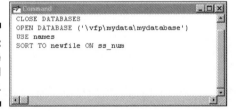

```
CLOSE DATABASES
OPEN DATABASE ('\vfp\mydata\mydatabase')
USE names
SORT TO newfile ON ss_num
```

3. Click the Close button to close the window.

The Command Window disappears, and you return to a blank screen.

If you made an error, however, a message box appears. Close the message box and repeat the procedure, starting with Step 2. Alternatively, close the message box and then close the Command Window; Visual FoxPro ignores the errors that you typed in the Command Window.

The commands in Figure 5-8 look like they're written in some archaic language, but they're really English with a Visual FoxPro accent. You recognize some of the words as English, but the sentence structure is a little peculiar.

Here's what each command line says, in plain English. Whenever you see `mydatabase`, replace it with the name of your database.

- ✔ `CLOSE DATABASES` This code closes any open databases so that Visual FoxPro doesn't get confused about which database you want to sort.

- ✔ `OPEN DATABASE ( \mydatabase )` This code opens the specified database.

- ✔ Be sure to replace the name of the directory, database, and table with the name of your directory that contains the data and with your database and table names. If you use long Windows 95 names that contain spaces, you must place the name in parentheses and inside single quotation marks — for example, `USE ( long table name )`.

- ✔ `USE names` This code tells Visual FoxPro to use the `names` table that you built in the database. This table contains the data that you want Visual FoxPro to sort.

- ✔ `SORT TO newfile ON ss_num` Copy all the values from the `names` table to a new table called `newfile`; then sort the records in the new table by `ss_num` (Social Security number).

To display the sorted data, type the following code in the Command Window, replacing `newfile` with the name of the new table:

```
USE newfile
BROWSE
```

The preceding code displays the contents of the new file, sorted by Social Security number.

Sorting selected fields with the SORT command

The SORT command gives you flexibility in how you display the data in the new table. You can do any of the following:

- ✔ Copy only certain fields to the new table.
- ✔ Sort the data in descending order (ascending order is the default).
- ✔ Select only the records that you need for the new table.

The commands that you use to select fields to sort and to specify the direction of the sort are basically the same bunch of commands that you use to sort. (See the section "Sorting Records," earlier in this chapter.) Two things are different from those steps, however. First, you use the argument to change from the default sort order (which is ascending) to descending sort order. (An *argument* is a word that tells Visual FoxPro to perform the task in a way other than the default way.)

Next, you use the FIELDS argument to list the field names that you want to copy to the new table, as follows:

```
CLOSE DATABASES
OPEN DATABASE ( \vfp\mydata\mydatabase )
USE names
SORT TO newfile ON lname DESCENDING FIELDS fname, lname,
salary, dept
```

Here's what the code says, in English:

- ✔ CLOSE DATABASES This code closes any open databases, so that Visual FoxPro doesn't get confused about which database you want to sort.
- ✔ OPEN DATABASE (\mydatabase) This code opens the specified database.

   Be sure to replace the name of the directory, database, and table with the name of your directory that contains the data and with your database and table names. If you use long Windows 95 names that contain spaces, you must place the name in parentheses and inside single quotation marks — for example, USE (long table name).

- ✔ USE names This code tells Visual FoxPro to use the names table that you built in the database. This table contains the data that you want Visual FoxPro to sort.
- ✔ SORT TO newfile ON lname DESCENDING FIELDS fname, lname, salary, dept This code creates a new table called newfile; copies the first name, last name, salary, and dept fields to the new table; and sorts the data by last name in descending order.

Sorting selected records

You can tell Visual FoxPro to pick just the records that you need for the new table. The following code is almost the same as the code in the previous section. In this example, however, I want only the records of people who are assigned to the accounting department. Be sure to replace \vfp\mydata\ mydatabase with the path and name of your own database file. Replace newfile with the name of your file and replace the field names lname, fname, salary, and dept with the names of the fields in your table. And change accounting in the value in your field.

```
CLOSE DATABASES
OPEN DATABASE ( \vfp\mydata\mydatabase )
USE names
SORT TO newfile ON lname DESCENDING FOR dept =  accounting
           FIELDS fname, lname, salary, dept
```

You specify as an expression for the FOR argument the field name dept; for the value of the field in the records that you want to sort, you specify accounting . For more information about arguments, refer to the section "Sorting selected fields with the SORT command," earlier in this chapter.

You can use the FOR argument (see the section "Sorting selected fields with the SORT command," earlier in this chapter) with an expression. I talk about expressions in Chapter 4 (and show you how to use the Expression Builder to create an expression the easy way). You can use the Expression Builder to create your expression when you enter commands in the Command Window, but you have to type the expression in the Command Window yourself.

Only those records that meet the criteria defined by the expression are copied to the new table. Visual FoxPro brings into the new table only those records that have the value accounting in the dept field.

Here, in English, is how you tell Visual FoxPro to sort selected records:

- ✔ CLOSE DATABASES This code closes any open databases so that Visual FoxPro doesn't get confused about which database you want to sort.

- ✔ OPEN DATABASE (\mydatabase) This code opens the specified database. Make sure you replace mydatabase with the name of your database.

- ✔ USE names This code tells Visual FoxPro to use the names table that you built in the database. This table contains the data that you want Visual FoxPro to sort. Replace names with the name of your own table.

✔ SORT TO newfile ON lname+fname DESCENDING FOR dept = accounting FIELDS fname, lname, salary, dept **This code creates a new table called** newfile; **copies just the first-name, last-name, salary, and dept fields to the new table (if the dept field has the value** accounting **); and sorts the data by last name in descending order. Make sure you replace these field names with names of fields in your table. You also need to replace** newfile **with the name of your own file and** accounting **with the name of the value of your field.**

You can do other things with the SORT command, such as include records that have a salary value greater than $30,000, but those things are beyond the scope of this book. This chapter gives you enough of a head start that you can perform the most common sort operations.

Whenever you use the SORT command to sort a table, Visual FoxPro duplicates all or some of the records in the table. Therefore, you must be sure that your hard disk has sufficient room to store duplicate records. Check out the upcoming sidebar "Do you have enough room on your disk?" to make sure that you have enough room.

Do you have enough room on your disk?

Visual FoxPro copies records from the current table to a new table whenever you use the SORT command, which means that you must have enough room on your hard disk to store all the new data. If you don't have enough room on your hard disk, you can't use the SORT command to sort the table. Visual FoxPro displays an error message when your disk has no more room for the new table — but don't worry about your data. Your original data remains untouched in the old table.

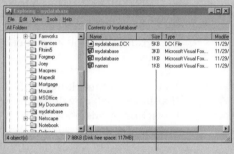

Table size

You should have three times the size of the table that you want to sort available on your hard disk. The following steps show you how to check the size of a table:

1. **Click Windows Explorer.**

   The Windows Explorer dialog box appears.

2. **Click the folder that contains the table.**

   The number that appears to the right of the table name shows the number of kilobytes that the table takes up on your hard disk. (See the figure.)

   If you see only the name of the table, choose View⇨Details.

To determine the available disk space, open Windows Explorer. The available disk space appears at the bottom of the Explorer window.

The number that appears on-screen is the number of bytes that are free on your hard disk. This number must be equal to three times the size of the table that you want to copy. But there's one trick: Because Windows Explorer shows the size of the table in kilobytes, you have to multiply that number by 1,000 to compare it with this available space number, which is the number that appears at the bottom of the Explorer window.

If the number displayed on-screen is less than three times the size of the table, you must free disk space by deleting files on the disk before trying to sort the table.

Chapter 6

Changing the Structure of a Table

. . . .

In This Chapter

▶ Changing a field's definition

▶ Adding a field to a table

▶ Deleting a field from a table

. . . .

*T*hat saying about the best-laid plans of mice and men sometimes going astray often applies when you create a table in Visual FoxPro. Perhaps you thought you did your best to plan all the fields that you want in your table. But instead, you left out some things, and then the table didn't have enough room to store all the data. In addition, everyone who looks at the table wonders what the field named nfame means.

Okay, you made a few mistakes. No one's perfect. You're forgiven. And correcting the mistakes doesn't take very long.

If you haven't guessed by now, making changes in your table is what I talk about in this chapter. In this chapter, I show you all the tricks to get your table back into shape.

Modifying the Table Structure

When you tell Visual FoxPro the field names, the field widths, and the other attributes of a field definition when you create a table (refer to Chapter 2), you are creating the *structure of the table*.

You can compare creating the structure of a table to building a house. A builder designs a house based on the number of people who will be living in it. Likewise, when you create a table, you design it based on the amount of data you want to enter. If the number of residents of the house increases, the builder considers modifying the structure to make more room. Similarly, if you need to add more data to your table, you must revise the table to accommodate the additional data.

Fortunately, making changes to your table is not as difficult or as expensive as modifying the structure of your house.

You can make changes to your table by using the Table Designer. To display the Table Designer dialog box, try this shortcut:

1. **Open the table you want to change.**

   The table appears as a box in the Database Designer.

2. **Right-click the table box of the table that you want to modify.**

   A shortcut menu jumps onto the screen, as shown in Figure 6-1.

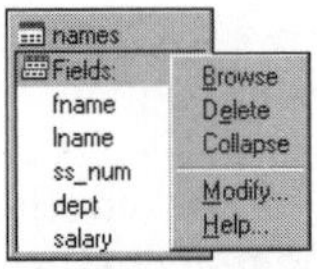

Figure 6-1:
Right-click
the table
box to see
this menu.

3. **Choose Modify from the shortcut menu.**

   The table appears in the Table Designer. The following sections give you information on changing items in this dialog box.

Be careful, however — modifying the structure of a table is different from creating the table. When you *create* a table, the table doesn't contain any data. When you *modify* a table, the table already contains data which can be seriously affected by the changes that you make.

Changing a field's definition

The field definition consists of the following attributes that tell Visual FoxPro how much space that you need to stuff data into the field:

- ✔ Field name
- ✔ Field data type
- ✔ Field width
- ✔ Decimal places
- ✔ NULL attribute

Simply make the changes to the fields the same way that you defined the field when you created the table (refer to Chapter 2). You can change the attribute of any field this way.

Changing a field name

To change any field name:

1. **Display the Table Designer, if it's not already displayed.**

2. **In the Table Designer, click the field name that you want to change.**

   Visual FoxPro highlights all the letters in the name.

3. **Enter the new name for the field.**

   Visual FoxPro replaces the old field name with the new field name. You must be sure that the new name falls within the naming rules (see the upcoming "Naming rules" sidebar); otherwise, Visual FoxPro becomes annoyed and rejects the new name.

4. **Click OK.**

   You return to the Database Designer.

The next time you browse the table, you see the new field name. Notice that the new field becomes the rightmost field of the table. You can always rearrange the order of the fields, as I show you in Chapter 5.

Naming rules

Here are the rules for naming a field:

✔ A field name can have up to 128 characters and can contain any characters (including numbers) except for spaces. Avoid using long field names because they can be difficult for humans to work with.

✔ Only one field in the table can have a specific name. Visual FoxPro does not allow duplicate field names in the same table.

✔ The field name should describe the kind of data that you store in the field. Although this rule is not mandatory, it makes sense.

Changing a field's data type

You may not think that you'll ever need to change the data type of a field because you've spent all that time planning the layout of your database and tables. But even I sometimes go back and modify the data type of a field. Here's how you modify a data type:

1. **Open the Table Designer, if it's not already open.**

2. **In the Table Designer, click the data-type combo box of the field that you want to change.**

   Visual FoxPro highlights the name of the current data type.

3. **Click the data-type combo box arrow.**

   Visual FoxPro displays a list of field types.

4. **In the <u>T</u>ype list, click the new field type.**

   The new field type replaces the old field type. The values for the Width and Decimal attributes of the field may change to the default values automatically. For example, changing from a Character field type that had a width of 25 to a Float causes the width to change to 20, which is the default width for the Float field type.

5. **Click OK.**

   You return to the Database Designer.

Visual FoxPro can modify or delete current data in the field type that you change, depending on the new field type. If you change the field type of the field that contains first names from Character to DateTime, for example, all the first names are replaced by the date type mask (/ / : : AM). See the upcoming "Pitfalls of changing field types" sidebar for more information about changing field types.

Changing a field width

You can increase or decrease the width of a field by following these steps:

1. **Open the Table Designer, if it's not already displayed.**

2. **In the Table Designer, click the width column of the field that you want to change.**

   Visual FoxPro highlights the current width of the field.

3. **Enter the new width value by using the width column spinner to increase or decrease the current value.**

   The value changes incrementally as you click the spinner.

Pitfalls of changing field types

You may need to change field types sometime. (If you need to brush up on your knowledge of field types, refer to Chapter 2.) Suppose that you have an integer field type, which accepts only whole numbers; Visual FoxPro doesn't make room for decimal numbers. Then, one day, you need to put a decimal number in the field. Visual FoxPro won't let you do that, however, because the field has no room for the decimal numbers. So you have to modify the structure of the table and change the integer field type to a numeric field type.

Changing a integer field type to a numeric field type works well because you've gone from an integer to a numeric field type. Because the numeric field type has more room for data than an integer field type does, you don't lose any data when Visual FoxPro makes the changes in the structure of the table.

You can lose data, however, if you change from a roomier field type to a smaller field type — when you change a numeric field type to an integer field type, for example. The decimal values stored in the numeric field type field get chopped off when you switch the field to an integer field type. You lose the decimal values in the field forever.

Always compare the values in the field with the values permitted by the new field type. The new field type must be compatible with the current values in the field; otherwise, you can permanently lose data from the field.

Whenever you change an integer field type to one that accepts decimal numbers, be sure to set the number of decimal places that you want to store in the field. Just because the field is now a numeric field type doesn't mean that you can start storing decimal numbers in the field; you still must tell Visual FoxPro the number of decimal places that you need. (See the section "Changing the number of decimal places," later in this chapter.)

4. Click OK.

You return to the Database Designer.

The change in the field width occurs the next time you browse the table.

You can easily lose data if you are not careful. Increasing the field width doesn't cause you any problem — nothing happens to the data that is currently in the field. Decreasing the field width, however, can be hazardous to the health of your data. if you decrease the field width, you can lose data and have no chance of recovering it.

For example, say that your first name field has a width of ten characters. You can enter the name *Jacqueline,* which is ten characters long, as shown in Figure 6-2.

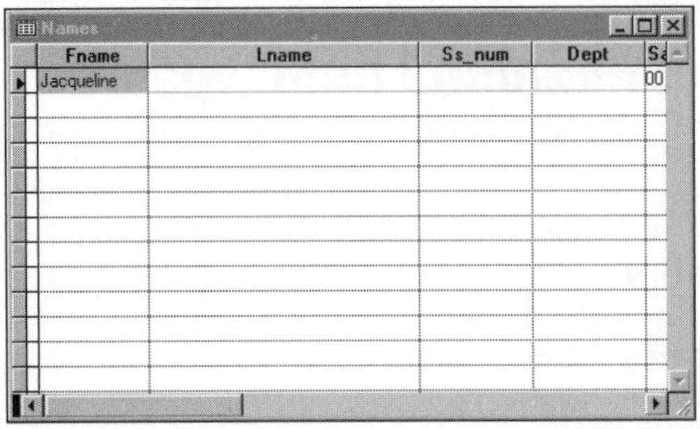

Figure 6-2:
Make the
field wider
to accept
the name
Jacqueline.

Now say that you decide to stretch the field width a little, modifying the field width to 15 characters. Perfect! You've given *Jacqueline* more breathing room.

Suppose, however, that you accidentally *decrease* the width of the field to five characters instead of *increasing* the width by five characters. You made a mistake, but didn't catch it in time to correct it. Visual FoxPro follows your directions and puts the squeeze on *Jacqueline.* Now *Jacqueline* is *Jacqu,* as shown in Figure 6-3, and all the other names that are more than five characters long also have been chopped off, or *truncated.*

Figure 6-3:
Oops! You
accidently
truncated
Jacqueline.

Jacqueline and all the other long names in the field will never be the same again. The letters chopped off the name are missing forever.

Changing the number of decimal places

Changing the number of decimal places in a field is a straightforward process. Follow these steps:

1. Open the Table Designer, if it's not already open.

What to do if you lose data

Changing a field's width may seem simple, but you're still subject to data loss. Suppose that you have the number 5.545 stored in a numeric-type field. Think of this number as representing the 5-million-plus shares of Billy's Company that you own. (Don't you wish?) The number is really 5,545,000, but you abbreviated the number to save space.

Now you want to increase the number of decimal places, but instead, you accidentally reduce the number of decimal places by two.

The current decimal value is 3, and with your change, the value is now 1. Visual FoxPro follows your orders and adjusts the table accordingly. As a result, the number of your shares in Billy's company is now 5.5 million, or 5,500,000. You lost 45,000 shares. (Wow!)

As you can see, Visual FoxPro truncates decimal numbers that can't fit into the new width of the field. And you can't bring back the lost numbers.

2. **In the Table Designer, click the Decimal column of the field that you want to change.**

   Visual FoxPro highlights the current decimal value of the field.

3. **Enter the new value for the decimal by using the decimal column spinner to increase or decrease the current value.**

   The value changes incrementally as you click the spinner.

4. **Click OK.**

   You return to the Database Designer.

The next time you enter a decimal number in the field, the change in the decimal size of the field occurs.

Changing the NULL attribute

Null is the term for nothing, empty, blank. You use the NULL attribute to tell Visual FoxPro whether you're going to allow the field to remain empty when you enter a new record in the table.

By default, each field must have a value. Here's how you change the NULL attribute:

1. **Open the Table Designer, if it's not already open.**

2. **In the Table Designer, click the NULL column of the field that you want to change.**

   NULL appears in the column.

3. Click the NULL button.

A check mark appears on the button to indicate that the field can have a NULL value. Click the NULL button again to remove the check mark if you want to make sure that a value is always entered in the field.

4. Click OK.

You return to the Database Designer.

When you enter a new record, Visual FoxPro enforces the selection that you made for the NULL attribute of the field.

 Determine whether the field is part of an index before you allow NULL values to be entered in a field that previously prohibited NULL values. Primary, candidate, and unique indexes require unique values in the key value of the index. You can brush up on indexes by reading Chapter 3.

Adding a New Field to a Table

Suppose that you review your table and notice that you don't have a place to enter middle names. You can solve this problem by adding another field.

You can add a new field to a table in three places:

- At the top of the list of fields
- At the bottom of the list of fields
- In the middle of the list of fields

Here's how to enter a new field at the bottom of the list of fields.

1. Open the table that you want to change.

The table appears as a box in the Database Designer.

2. Right-click the table box of the table that you want to modify.

A shortcut menu appears.

3. Choose <u>M</u>odify from the shortcut menu.

The table appears in the Table Designer.

4. Type the name of the field in the empty box that appears at the bottom of the Name column, just after the last field in the table.

Make sure that you enter the other attributes of the field.

5. **Click OK.**

Your change is made.

You also can insert the new field into the middle of the field list, as shown in Figure 6-4.

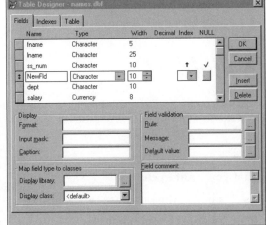

Figure 6-4: You can insert a field into the middle of a table.

You can use the same technique to insert a field at the top of the table. Follow these steps:

1. **Open the table that you want to change.**

The table appears as a box in the Database Designer.

2. **Right-click the table box of the table that you want to modify.**

A shortcut menu jumps onto the screen.

3. **Choose Modify from the shortcut menu.**

The table appears in the Table Designer.

4. **In the Table Designer, click the button to the left of the field where you want to insert the new field.**

A double-headed arrow appears on the button.

5. **Click Insert.**

A new field replaces the selected field. The selected field and the fields below it move down in the Table Designer.

6. **Enter the name of the new field in the Name column of the Table Designer.**

The default NewFld name is replaced by the new field name.

7. Set the other attributes the same way that you set the attributes of the other fields in the table (refer to Chapter 2).

8. When you finish, click OK.

The field is added to the table.

The new field becomes the rightmost field of the table the next time you browse the table. You can always rearrange the order of the fields, as I show you in Chapter 5.

Deleting a Table Field

You can delete any field in a table. You lose all data in that field, however, and you cannot recover the lost data.

To delete a field:

1. Open the table that you want to change.

The table appears as a box in the Database Designer.

2. Right-click the table box of the table that you want to modify.

A shortcut menu jumps onto the screen.

3. Choose Modify from the shortcut menu.

The table appears in the Table Designer.

4. In the Table Designer, click the button to the left of the field that you want to delete.

A double-headed arrow appears on the button.

5. Click Delete.

The selected field is deleted from the field list. All the other fields below the deleted field move up in the field list.

6. Click OK.

The field is removed from the table, and all the data in the field is gone forever.

Checking Indexes and Common Fields

Changes that you make in the structure of your table can affect other parts of your database, such as indexes and common fields. A *common field* is a field whose value also appears in other tables in the database. You use common fields when you join two tables; you can see how joining works in Chapter 7.

For now, you don't want the changes that you make in the table structures to have a negative impact on indexes and other tables.

Before you begin to modify your table, follow this simple checklist:

✔ **Determine whether the field joins another table.** If so, changes that you make in the field must also be made in the common fields of the other tables.

✔ **Determine whether the field is a key to an index.** If so, you must determine whether the changes will have a negative effect on the index. If the changes will have a negative effect, rethink the changes. If not, make sure that you change the index by using the Indexes tab of the Table Designer, which I show you how to do in Chapter 3.

Chapter 7

Tricks with Views

*I*n Chapter 2, you use data in one table at a time. In reality, you may want to use data in more than one table. To do so, you need to create a view, which links tables together by a common field. When you click the view in the Database Designer, records in the fields of the linked table look like one big table. In this chapter, you find out how to create a view from tables.

Creating a View

Suppose that you want a database to contain the complete background of every employee in your company. You probably can imagine the kinds of data that you'd need from each person: Social Security number; first, middle, and last name; address; telephone number; work assignment; and much more.

You could stuff all this information into a single table in the database, but this method is likely to slow the response time of your queries. So you follow the tips in Chapter 1 and divide all the data into multiple tables. Now, though, you don't know which table to use when you're looking for specific data.

Fortunately, Visual FoxPro lets you call up the data the way you need to see the information and still maintain the efficiency of a relational database.

The compromise is called a view. A *view* is a description of how you want Visual FoxPro to display the information in your database. You simply tell Visual FoxPro how you want to see the data in a view and then save the view with a new filename.

Each time you want to see, as a group, the data contained in more than one table, you use the name of the view to tell Visual FoxPro to show you the view. Visual FoxPro goes through all the hassles of matching records in each table to show you those records as a single record, while you sit back and wait. Best of all, you can create any number of views.

Before you can create a view, you must create the database and the tables. (See Chapters 1 and 2.) Figure 7-1 shows the tables that I use in this chapter; you can use your own tables.

Figure 7-1:
In this chapter, I use these tables to create a view.

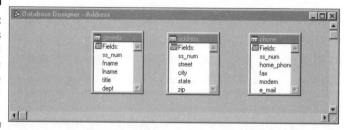

To select tables for a view, follow these steps:

1. **Open the database of your choice.**

   If you haven't created a database, refer to Chapter 1.

2. **Choose Database➪New Local View.**

   The New Local View dialog box appears.

Linking tables

Tables can be linked together only if the same value is in both tables. In other words, a field in each table must have the same value. Visual FoxPro uses this value, known as the *common field,* to match records.

You need to follow certain rules before a field can be used as a common field to join two tables.

✔ **Values must be unique.** That is, a duplicate value cannot be in the common field.

Otherwise, Visual FoxPro becomes confused as to which records belong to each other.

✔ **The common fields must be the same data type.**

✔ **The same value must appear in both common fields.**

Note: You can choose either Database⇨New Local View or Database⇨ New Remote View to create a view. New Local View (which you'll use most of the time) allows you to create a view for a database on your hard drive. New Remote View allows you to create a view for a database that resides on a network drive.

3. Choose New View.

The Add Table or View dialog box, shown in Figure 7-2, appears.

Figure 7-2:
The Add
Table
or View
dialog box.

4. Select the Tables radio button in the bottom-right corner of the dialog box to display a list of table names.

Note: You can choose which table to include in your view. If you select the Views radio button rather than the Tables button, a list of existing views appears. You can create your new view from existing views, but you rarely have to do so.

5. In the Tables in database area, double-click the name of the first table that you want to include in the view.

Visual FoxPro displays the table box in the View Designer.

6. Repeat Step 5 until all the tables you need for the view appear in the View Designer.

Visual FoxPro links the first table that you selected with the second table that you selected, using a field that is common to both tables. Visual FoxPro displays the Join Condition dialog box, shown in Figure 7-3, in which you pick the fields that will be used to link, or *join*, the tables. If you add a third table to the view, you need to repeat Step 5.

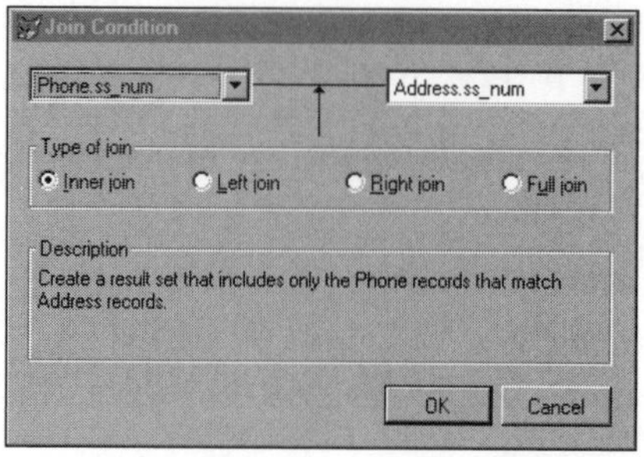

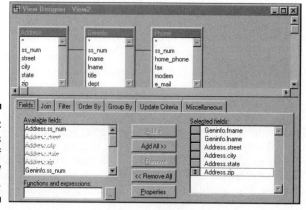

Figure 7-3:
The Join
Condition
dialog box.

7. **Select the Inner Join radio button, which is the default setting.**

8. **If you need to join other tables to the view, then continue selecting tables by repeating Steps 5 through 7; then click OK.**

   The Join Condition dialog box closes, and you return to the View Designer dialog box. Visual FoxPro displays the tables in the View Designer and draws a line between the fields that are common to each table.

9. **Click the Fields tab of the View Designer, shown in Figure 7-4.**

   After you join the tables for your view, you need to select the fields that you want to see whenever you call the view. When you select the fields, you can forget that you create the view from several tables. Simply pretend that you are dealing with one big table containing all the fields.

Figure 7-4:
The Fields
tab of
the View
Designer.

Choosing a condition that defines a join

Most of the time, you'll want to accept the default when you define a join, which is typically the first fields in both tables that have the same field name. However, you may occasionally want to use two other fields to join together two tables.

Any fields that contain the same unique values can be used as the condition for the join, even if the values are stored in two fields that have different names. For example, the Social Security number is a unique value that is typically used to join two tables. In one table, the Social Security number could be in a field called ss_num. In the other table, the same value could be stored in a field called tax_id. Yet you can use both fields to join the tables because they contain the same unique values.

Following are descriptions of the joins and suggestions as to when to select them.

✔ **Inner join:** Shows only records that match the join condition, such as the Social Security-number field in both tables. This join (the default) is the one that you'll be using most of the time. This kind of join is handy to use when you need to see records from both tables that have the same join condition value.

✔ **Left join:** Shows all records in the second table and only the records in the first table that match records in the second table. Say you have two tables. The first table contains names and Social Security numbers of employees in the accounting department. The second table contains salary information and Social Security numbers of all the employees in the company. You can use the Social Security numbers in both tables to join the tables.

You want to compare the salary of each employee in the accounting department to salaries of employees in the company. However, you want to keep the names of employees in confidence, except for those of the accounting department. The Left join shows you just the records you need. You have the names contained in first table (employees of the accounting department) joined with their corresponding record in the second table (salaries). In addition, you see all the records in the second table (all the salaries).

Table 1

Social Security Number	First Name	Last Name
111-11-1111	Bob	Smith
222-22-2222	Mary	Jones

Table 2

Social Security Number	Salary
333-33-3333	25000
222-22-2222	50000
555-55-5555	35000

✔ **Right join:** Shows all records in the first table and only records in the second table that match records in the first table. If you use a right join to join the preceding tables, you see all the records in Table 1 and you see the record with 222-22-2222 50000 in Table 2.

✔ **Full join:** Shows all records in the first table and second table, whether or not any records match.

10. In the Available fields list box, select the name of the field that you want to include in the view; then click the Add button.

Visual FoxPro displays the field names that are contained in every table that you selected for the view and moves the fields that you selected to the Selected fields list box. These fields now appear whenever you choose your view.

You don't have to click the Add button each time you want to move a field from the Available fields list to the Selected fields list. Instead, you can drag the field from the Available fields list to the Selected fields list.

11. Click the Order By tab of the View Designer, shown in Figure 7-5.

When you tell Visual FoxPro to show you the view, you see records in data-entry order. *Data-entry order* is the sequence in which the data was entered in the tables. Chances are that you want to see the data in a more orderly way, such as alphabetical order, which is called *ordering the data.* You can order the data by using one or more fields that you selected for the view. The list box shown in Figure 7-5 contains all the fields that you selected for the view.

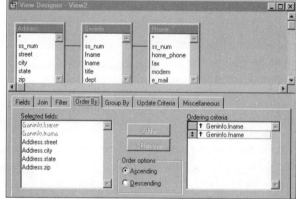

Figure 7-5:
The Order
By tab of
the View
Designer.

12. In the Selected fields list box, select the first field that you want to use for the order; then click the Add button.

The field moves from the Selected fields list to the Ordering criteria box. All the fields that you selected to be part of the view appear in the Selected fields list box. Suppose that you want the records to appear in alphabetical order, by last name. To do so, simply select the last-name field and then the first-name field. Visual FoxPro does all the ordering for you when you display the view.

Whatever fields you select for the view appears in the Ordering criteria box. In my example, I selected fname and lname, so they both appear in the Ordering criteria box.

13. **In the Order options area, select the Ascending or Descending radio button to specify the direction of the sort.**

    Ascending is A–Z or 1–10 and is the default sort order, which you'll use most of the time. Descending is Z–A or 10–1.

14. **Repeat Steps 12 and 13 until you select all the ordering criteria.**

    If last name is the only ordering criteria for the view, records appear in alphabetical order by last name. For example:

Social Security Number	First Name	Last Name
222-22-2222	Mary	Jones
666-66-6666	Mary	Smith
777-77-7777	Jane	Smith
111-11-1111	Bob	Smith

If you select a second field, such as first name, in the ordering criteria, records appear in alphabetical order first by last name and then by first name. For example:

Social Security Number	First Name	Last Name
222-22-2222	Mary	Jones
111-11-1111	Bob	Smith
777-77-7777	Jane	Smith
666-66-6666	Mary	Smith

15. **Click the Group By tab of the View Designer, shown in Figure 7-6.**

    Group By lets you place similar records near each other on-screen or summarize groups of records into in a single record, such as when you want to know how many employees are in each department or the sum of the salaries of employees by department.

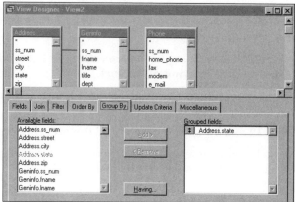

Figure 7-6:
You can summarize like records in a single record by using the Group By tab.

16. In the Available fields list box, select the fields that you want to group by.

Note: The fields that you did and did not select for the view in the Fields tab are also listed. This way, you can group records together or summarize records, even if you decide not to display the field used in the summary expression.

17. Click the Add button to add the selected fields to the Grouped fields list box.

Visual FoxPro takes care of grouping the records for you whenever you display the view.

18. Click the Having button.

The Having dialog box, shown in Figure 7-7, appears. You use this dialog box to specify an expression for summarizing records in a view.

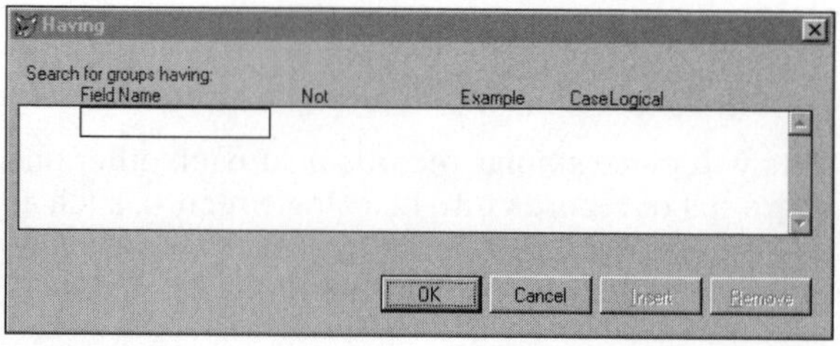

Figure 7-7:
The Having dialog box.

19. Select Expression from the Field Name column combo box.

The Expression Builder dialog box appears. You use this dialog box to create an expression to summarize records in the view. (See Chapter 3 to brush up on using the Expression Builder.)

20. Click OK to close the Expression Builder

You return to the Having dialog box.

21. Click OK to close the Having dialog box.

You return to the View Designer.

> If you want to test your view, click the Run button, which resembles an exclamation mark, to test your view. When you click the Run button, Visual FoxPro joins the necessary tables and displays in the view only the information that you asked for. If what appears isn't what you had in mind, close the browse window and modify your view criteria. Continue running and modifying the view until you get the results that you require.

You also need to save your view, just as you would save a database. After you save the view, it appears as part of your database and in the Database Designer, shown in Figure 7-8.

Figure 7-8:
Your view
in the
Database
Designer.

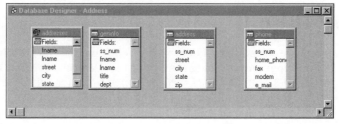

To close the View Designer, click the Close button, and you return to the Database Designer.

Displaying the View

You can display data in a view by double-clicking the view in the Database Designer. Displaying a view displays all the selected fields in what appears to be one table, but in reality are parts of more than one table joined together by Visual FoxPro.

Visual FoxPro shows you the data in the same column-and-row format in which you normally see data in a table. Unlike a table, however, data changed in a view is not saved in the related tables. In other words, you can change the data on-screen, but the data doesn't change in the table. The only way to make those changes permanent is to change the data in the table.

To display a view, follow these steps:

1. **Open the Database Designer.**

2. **Double-click the view.**

   The View appears in the Database Designer just like a table, except that the icon in the View box is a pencil. You probably won't notice the difference between a table and a view in the Database Designer if you don't see the icon in the View box.

Removing a View

You can remove a view from a database by clicking the View box in the Database Designer and pressing the Delete key. Deleting a view is handy when you no longer need to see records joined together using the criteria for the view. Including unnecessary views clutters the Database Designer.

Visual FoxPro asks you whether you're sure that you want to remove the view from the database. Click Yes, and the view is gone forever. Click No, and Visual FoxPro pretends that you never asked to remove the view.

If you mistakenly delete a view, you can't recover your loss.

Part II
Ways Programmers Manipulate Data

By Rich Tennant

"I ALWAYS BACK UP EVERYTHING."

In this part . . .

*W*ho is the most eligible person you know? The person must be warm and tender, have a good job, and come from a wealthy family. You can publish your request in the singles section of the newspaper or ask Visual FoxPro — if you entered information about eligible people in your database.

The reason to put information in a database is to be able to find the information that you need in a matter of seconds. Visual FoxPro can zip through millions of records in the blink of an eye and zero in on the information that matches your specifications.

Before Visual FoxPro can begin the hunt for your data, however, you must say the magic words — and I don't mean *please*. I show you those words and the proper way to phrase your request in Part II.

In this part, you find out how to search for information in a database and write complex queries to find the information you need.

Chapter 8
Searching Databases

• •

• •

*B*efore you realize it, the amount of information that you shove into your database can grow beyond your wildest dreams. Your database may contain so much data that you have a difficult time locating information in it.

As a result, finding information by browsing tables of the database doesn't work well any more. You can scroll down into the list of records but still not find the information that you need; the number of records is too great for anyone except a nerd to search the table by scrolling through records. There must be a better way to find information — and there is! You can simply tell Visual FoxPro what data you need and then sit back while the program searches for it. In this chapter, I show you how to find data in a database.

Using Edit⇨Find (A Simple Search)

The simplest way to find information in a table is to use the Edit⇨Find command. Suppose that you want to see the name of the person who makes a million dollars in salary. You can scroll through the table that contains salary information, or you can ask Visual FoxPro to do the searching for you. To do the latter, follow these steps:

1. **Open the database that you want to search.**

2. **Double-click the table that you want to search.**

3. Choose Edit⇨Find.

Visual FoxPro displays the Find dialog box shown in Figure 8-1, in which you enter search criteria.

Figure 8-1:
The Find
dialog box.

4. In the Look for text box, type the characters that you want to find.

5. In the Options area, select the options that you'd like Visual FoxPro to follow during the search.

You can make your Visual FoxPro searches more specific by choosing various options in the Find dialog box. The four search options that you'll use the most are Match case, Match whole word, Search backward, and Wrap around. Match whole word is the option that you'll use most of the time.

- **Match case:** When you select this check box, you're telling Visual FoxPro to search for characters that are the same as the characters that you entered in the Look for text box — characters that have the same pattern of uppercase and lowercase letters. If you type **MA** in the Look for text box and select the Match case option, Visual FoxPro skips *Mary* because you typed uppercase letters. *Mary* is not a match for *MA*.

- **Match whole word:** This option tells Visual FoxPro to find the characters that you typed in the Look for text box. If you type a space, followed by **MA**, in the Look for text box and then select Match whole word, Visual FoxPro skips *Mary* because you told it to find *MA* preceded and followed by spaces. *Mary* is not a match.

- **Search backward:** Visual FoxPro normally starts searching from the record that is currently selected (which is the first record when you start to search the table) and continues until a match is found or the last record is read. When you click the Find Next button, the search continues with the next record. Visual FoxPro does not return to records that it has already read. But if you want Visual FoxPro to search from the current record back to the beginning of the table, you need to select the Search backward option.

- **Wrap around:** Chances are that if you searched the table a few times, the current record won't be the first record in the table. Instead, the current record is likely to be somewhere else in the table — a situation that can cause a problem when you conduct the next search. You won't know whether to tell Visual FoxPro to search the current record and the remainder of the records or to search the current record and the preceding records. Simply put, you don't know where records that match the search criteria are located. When you select Wrap around, Visual FoxPro searches all the records in the table.

You can select a combination of options, such as both Match case and Match whole word. When you select both these options, you're telling Visual FoxPro to match exactly the characters that you typed in the Look for text box.

6. **Click the Find Next button.**

   Visual FoxPro cranks away until the data is found or all the records in the table are searched. The field that contains the data is highlighted. If no field is highlighted, Visual FoxPro cannot find the information that you need. You'll hear a beep, and the message Not found appears in the message bar at the bottom of the window.

   Note: Just because Visual FoxPro highlights a field doesn't mean that the table doesn't contain other fields that contain your search data. Visual FoxPro stops searching whenever a match occurs or when no more records are available to search. Even though Visual FoxPro stops searching when it finds a match, the records that it has not yet searched still may contain a match.

7. **To tell Visual FoxPro to continue the search, click the Find Next button.**

   Visual FoxPro stops at the next occurrence. Keep clicking the Find Next button until you locate the record that you want.

Although the Edit⇨Find command tracks down the data that you need, this method has a down side: Visual FoxPro takes a long time to locate information in a table that contains a great deal of information.

Visual FoxPro begins the search by comparing the search criteria with the first letter in the first field of the first record of the table. Then Visual FoxPro moves to the next letter, and so on. Going through every letter of each piece of data in the table is time-consuming, even for a computer.

The search is not isolated to a particular group of records or to a particular field of the table; all the data in the table is fair game. Another drawback is that Visual FoxPro can search only one table at a time unless you join tables in a view. (Chapter 7 covers views.)

How searching works

After you specify the search criteria and give the go ahead to start the search, the database software proceeds to the field and compares all the values stuffed in the field against the value that you are seeking.

If the value matches the search criteria, then the database software displays the record that contains the value.

If the search criteria is not found, then a message appears.

You must include a field in the database for each kind of data that you plan to use as search criteria. Plan ahead for all possible searches, and your database won't let you down.

Use Edit⇨Find to locate information in a table that contains only a few records or when you're unsure which field to search. But don't use Edit⇨Find to search for data in a table that contains many records. You'll be waiting forever, and you can perform the same kind of search in other ways with much faster results, as you see in the remaining sections of this chapter.

Using Table⇨Go to Record

I prefer to find information in a table on the fly by opening the table that I want to search and then choosing the Table⇨Go to Record command. This command enables you to poke around records in the table without having to scroll through the records by using the vertical or horizontal scroll bar.

The Go to Record submenu gives you six choices: Top (move to the first record of the table), Bottom (move to the last record of the table), Next (move to the next record), Previous (move to the previous record), Record # (go to a particular record number), and Locate (locate the record that has the search criteria you specify). The following sections describe these options.

Top, Bottom, Next, and Previous

The Top, Bottom, Next, and Previous options instruct Visual FoxPro to move the record pointer, which shows you which record is the current record. The next time you browse a table, look at the left side of the window. The arrow that points to the current record is the record pointer. (See Figure 8-2.)

Record pointer

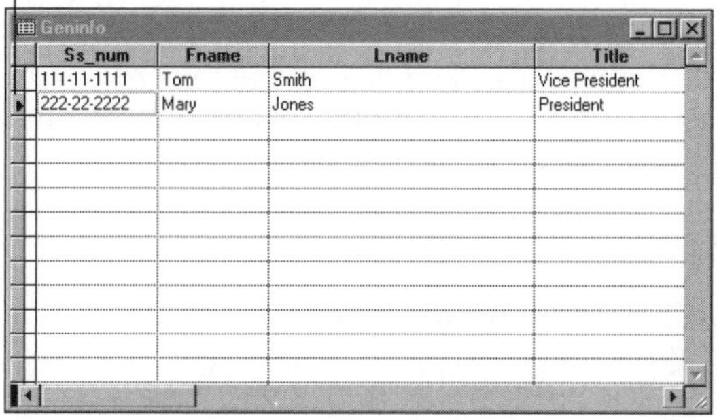

Figure 8-2:
The record
pointer
identifies
the current
record.

Ss_num	Fname	Lname	Title
111-11-1111	Tom	Smith	Vice President
222-22-2222	Mary	Jones	President

Here's how you use these options:

1. **Open the database that you want to search.**

2. **Double-click the table that you want to search.**

3. **Choose Table➪Go to Record.**

    A submenu appears.

4. **From the submenu, choose Top, Bottom, Next, or Previous.**

    Top makes the first record in the table the current record. Bottom
    makes the last record in the table the current record. Next makes the
    following record the current record. Previous makes the preceding
    record the current record.

Although these options don't find data in the table, they do help you move
about the table, and using them sometimes is faster than using the vertical
scroll bar.

Record

Use Record # when you're searching for a particular record number rather
than a value that is stored in a field of the record.

Suppose that you have a stack of 25 index cards containing names and
addresses that you're entering into a table. Two people have the same first
and last names, and you entered the wrong zip code for one of those people.
Which record contains the mistake? A fast way to answer this question is to
find out where the corresponding index card falls in the stack of index cards.

Now suppose that the mistake occurred with the 13th card. The 13th index card probably has the same information as the 13th record in the table because records in the table are in data-entry order (as long as you haven't changed the order of the records). So you can use Record # to move the record pointer to the 13th record of the table, where you can make the necessary corrections.

Here's how you use the Record # option:

1. **Open the database that you want to search.**

2. **Double-click the table that you want to search.**

3. **Choose Table⇨Go to Record.**

   A submenu appears.

4. **Choose Record #.**

   The Go to Record dialog box, shown in Figure 8-3, appears.

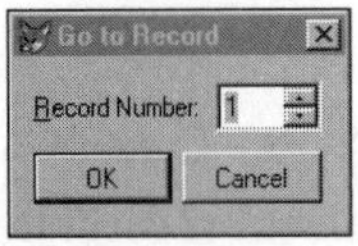

Figure 8-3:
The Go to
Record
dialog box.

5. **Enter the record number.**

   The record number that you enter is the number of the record in the table. The first record you enter into the table is record 1, the second record entered is record 2, and so on. If you want the fifth record you entered into the table to become the current record, then you enter the number 5 in the Go to Record dialog box.

6. **Click OK.**

   The record pointer moves to the record number that you entered.

Locate

Locate is my choice for finding data in a table. Locate allows you to specify the field that you want Visual FoxPro to search, as well as an expression to be used as a search criterion. (I talk about expressions and how to use the Expression Builder in Chapter 3, when I show you how to build an index for your table.)

When you choose Locate, Visual FoxPro displays the Locate Record dialog box, which is where you specify the criteria for the search. The dialog box gives you room to specify the scope of the search and to enter a For expression and/or a While expression. I discuss those options later in this section. You can brush up on expressions in Chapter 3.

To use Locate, follow these steps:

1. Open the database that you want to search.

2. Double-click the table that you want to search.

3. Choose Table⇨Go to Record.

A menu appears.

4. Choose Locate.

The Locate Record dialog box, shown in Figure 8-4, appears.

Figure 8-4:
The Locate
Record
dialog box.

5. From the Scope drop-down list, select a search option.

The Scope drop-down list contains four options. Stick with the default All option because you probably want Visual FoxPro to search all the records in the table. If you're interested in the other options, check out the upcoming sidebar "Other search options."

6. In either the For or While text box, type the name of the record that you're looking for.

Although the For and While text boxes both allow you to enter expressions as search criteria, they instruct Visual FoxPro to conduct the search in different ways. You'll probably use For all the time, though, because you normally want to find a specific value in a field.

Here's how to choose between these text boxes:

- **For.** The entry in the For text box tells Visual FoxPro (in English), "Search for these characters in this field."

- **While.** The entry in the While text box tells Visual FoxPro to continue searching while the expression is true. If the expression is true, then Visual FoxPro goes to the next record and continues the search. If the expression is false, then Visual FoxPro stops the search.

Other search options

Although you'll usually want to search all the records in a table, other search options do exist in the Scope drop-down list:

✔ **Next:** This option tells Visual FoxPro to use the next record for the search. When you select the Next option, a spinner appears, allowing you to specify the number of records that should be included in the search. You can select Next and then specify the number by using the spin

wheel or typing the number in the text box. When you click the Locate button, Visual FoxPro searches that number of records.

✔ **Record:** This option tells Visual FoxPro to search a particular record. You can use the spinner to select the record number or type the number in the text box.

✔ **Rest:** This option tells Visual FoxPro to start at the record pointer and search the rest of the records in the table.

---

7. Click the Locate button.

Visual FoxPro highlights the record that contains the value you're looking for. If it doesn't find the value in any field, Visual FoxPro highlights the last record of the table.

Locate is a great tool to use whenever you need Visual FoxPro to point to the record that contains the search criteria. A major drawback, however, is that you see all the fields in the record that contain the matching information. You don't have the opportunity to choose the fields that you want to see. You may have to click the horizontal scroll bar to see fields that are just out of sight.

Another drawback of Locate is that you see all the records in the table, including those that don't match the selection criteria. You can easily become confused because you have to keep one eye on the record pointer. If you accidentally move the record pointer, you may end up reading information from the wrong record. I show you how to work around this problem in the next few chapters.

Searching by Using the Command Window

If you really want a challenge, try searching a table by using commands that you enter in the Command Window. Although this search method involves a great deal of work, you have greater control. This manner of searching also starts you on your way to developing a Visual FoxPro program. A Visual FoxPro program is written commands entered in the Command Window and saved in a file. You can tell Visual FoxPro to read the file and follow your written instructions, so you don't need to choose menus and enter information into dialog boxes to search your table.

If you find that you like giving commands, don't hesitate to explore the world of programming. You don't need a degree from MIT to program, and you may make some money in programming.

Using the Command Window

Normally, the Command Window is open when you start Visual FoxPro. As you open databases, dialog boxes, and designers, however, the Command Window becomes hidden. You can make the Command Window active by pressing Ctrl+F2. (See Figure 8-5.)

The Command Window is empty when Visual FoxPro starts. As you create or open databases, tables, forms, and other objects, Visual FoxPro automatically enters commands in the Command Window. These commands are the same ones that you can enter instead of using menus and dialog boxes.

Figure 8-5:
Press
Ctrl+F2 to
make the
Command
Window
active.

Setting the stage for the search

When you choose items from a menu or use a dialog box to specify your search criteria, you're really giving commands to Visual FoxPro. Instead of going through all the gyrations of clicking and pointing, you can enter a one- or two-word command in the Command Window.

The first thing that you normally do before you begin a search is make sure that all databases are closed. Also, make sure that you've already created an index for the table (refer to Chapter 3) because the index is needed to conduct the search.

To set up a search in the Command Window, complete the following steps. When you're finished, your screen looks like Figure 8-6. Remember, you should always enter all the commands and not assume databases are open or closed. First, you close any databases that are opened and then open the database you need. These methods are good programming style.

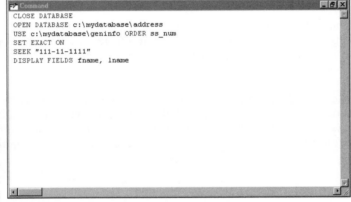

Figure 8-6:
To set up
a search
in the
Command
Window,
you type
these
commands.

Keep in mind that you need to substitute your own database, table, index, search criteria, and field names if you try this method on your computer.

1. Press Ctrl+F2.

The Command Window appears.

2. Type CLOSE DATABASE **and press Enter.**

You can type either uppercase or lowercase letters.

3. Type OPEN DATABASE c:\mydatabase\address **and press Enter.**

Substitute the name of your database for c:\mydatabase\address, of course.

4. Type USE c:\mydatabase\geninfo ORDER ss_num **and press Enter.**

(Remember to substitute your information.) The table is opened but remains hidden. The ORDER command tells Visual FoxPro to use the index for the search.

The SEEK command, which I describe in the following step, works only on an indexed table.

5. Type SEEK "111-11-1111" **and press Enter.**

Be sure to include the quotations and to replace 111-11-1111 with your search criterion. Visual FoxPro tries to compare the search criterion with the key value of the index that you specified in Step 4 using the ORDER command. When it finds the data in the index, Visual FoxPro reads the number of the record in the table that contains the value; then it finds that record in the table.

If Visual FoxPro finds a match, it displays, at the bottom of the screen, the number of the record that contains the value. The display record 2/2, for example, means that the record that contains the matching value is record 2 and that the table contains 2 records. If Visual FoxPro doesn't find a match, it displays the message No Find in the bottom-left corner of the screen.

6. Type DISPLAY FIELDS fname, lname **and press Enter.**

Visual FoxPro displays the values of the fname and lname fields of the record that matches the search criterion. You can specify any number of field names that you want to display.

Finding an exact match or partial match

As you do in the other methods of searching, you can use the Command Window to tell Visual FoxPro to look for a complete match or a partial match of the search criterion. The command that you use to search for an exact match is

SET EXACT ON

The command that you use to search for a partial match is

SET EXACT OFF

When you conduct a partial search, Visual FoxPro begins by comparing the leftmost character of the search criterion with the key value of the index.

Suppose that you're looking for information about a person, but you're not sure whether that person's last name is Johnson or Johnston. Enter the SET EXACT OFF command in the Command Window and press Enter; then type the SEEK command as shown in the steps in the section "Setting the stage for the search," except use *Johns* as the search criterion. Visual FoxPro reports that a match is found as soon as it finds a match of *Johns* in the last name field in the index.

Chapter 9

Filtering Data

- -

In This Chapter

▶ Creating a data filter for a table

▶ Filtering records that match part of a value

▶ Filtering records in multiple tables

- -

*W*hen you have records upon records, you can go crazy every time you need to look up information in the database. Where is all this efficiency that you've been hearing about in these confounded devices that are going to save the world?

Keep your shirt on — I'm coming to the fun stuff. Before you start clicking buttons and making Visual FoxPro your slave, you have to pay your dues and plow through rudimentary steps.

In this chapter, I show you how to cut down your table so that only the records that you want to see appear in the table. Don't be alarmed — you won't lose the rest of the records. You just use a filter that leaves those unwanted records out of sight.

Understanding Filters

A *filter* is a gizmo that lets some data through to the screen and forces other data to wait. Think of a filter as the admissions office of a college. The office accepts some applicants, but other applicants must keep trying. Likewise, a *data filter* is a filter that keeps out some data and lets other data through.

You can use a filter to see just some of the records that meet your needs. Suppose that you create a table that contains information about all the employees of your company, but you want to see only information about employees who work in the accounting department. Rather than scroll through all the employees to find just those who are assigned to accounting, you can create a filter. The filter displays only the records of employees of the accounting department.

Every filter uses criteria to determine what is allowed to pass through the filter. A college admissions office uses a set of guidelines set up by the people who run the college. The guidelines are the filter criteria.

You determine the filter criteria for a data filter on your tables by establishing an expression. I cover expressions in Chapter 3.

Figure 9-1 displays all the records in the geninfo table, which I created to show you how a filter works.

Ss_num	Fname	Lname	Title	Dept
111-11-1111	Tom	Smith	Manager	52-133
222-22-2222	Mary	Jones	Manager	52-134
333-33-3333	Joan	Gates	Manager	54-120
444-44-4444	Mike	Smith	Clerk	55-454
555-55-5555	Mark	Russell	Supervisor	54-876
666-66-6666	Joanne	Collage	Manager	52-342
777-77-7777	Sandra	Jones	Manager	52-344
888-88-8888	Anne	Gates	Manager	55-222

Figure 9-1:
The geninfo
table.

Creating a Filter

A *filter expression* tells Visual FoxPro which records you want to see. To enter filter expressions, follow these steps:

1. **Open the database file that contains the table for which you want to create a filter.**

   The Database Designer appears.

2. **In the Database Designer, double-click the table box of the table that you want to filter.**

   Records appear in the browse window of the table.

3. **Choose Table⇨Properties.**

   The Work Area Properties dialog box, shown in Figure 9-2, appears.

4. **Click the button that appears to the right of the Data filter text box.**

   Visual FoxPro displays the Expression Builder dialog box, shown in Figure 9-3, in the center of your screen.

5. **In the Fields list, double-click the field name you want to use in the expression.**

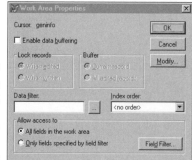

Figure 9-2:
The Work
Area
Properties
dialog box.

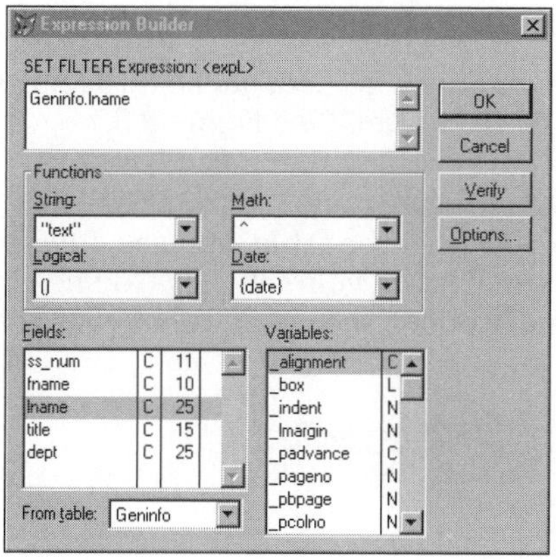

Figure 9-3:
The
Expression
Builder.

6. **In the Logical combo box, select the equal sign.**

7. **In the Set Filter Expression box, type the value of the field that you want to use for the filter to the right of the equal sign to complete the expression.**

   If the value is a numeric value, such as a person's salary, you don't include the number in quotations. If the value isn't a numeric value, such as a person's name, then you place quotations around the value.

8. **Click OK to close the Expression Builder.**

   You return to the Work Area Properties dialog box.

   Notice that the expression is squeezed into the Data filter text box, as shown in Figure 9-4. Sometimes, you can't see the complete expression in the text box because the expression is wider than the box, but don't worry. Visual FoxPro uses the complete expression, including parts that won't fit in the Data filter text box.

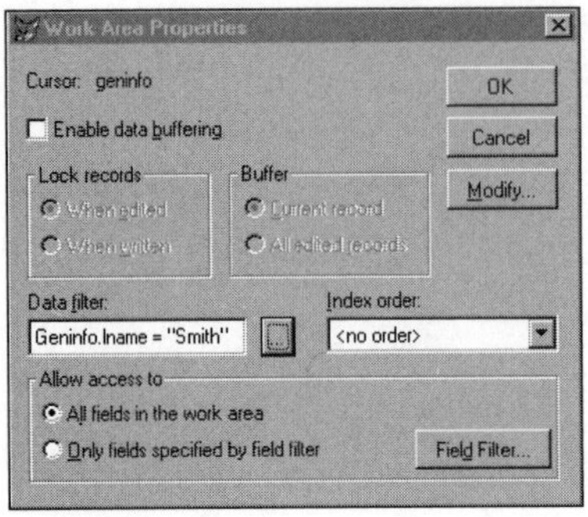

Figure 9-4: The expression appears in the Data filter text box.

9. **Click OK to close the Work Area Properties dialog box.**

You return to the browse window where Visual FoxPro shows you just those records that pass the data filter. (See Figure 9-5.)

Note: The data filter is not automatically removed from the table when you close the table. The next time you open the table, you see only records that meet the filter criteria — and you'll scare yourself silly. You need to remove the data filter (see the following section) so that all the records appear again.

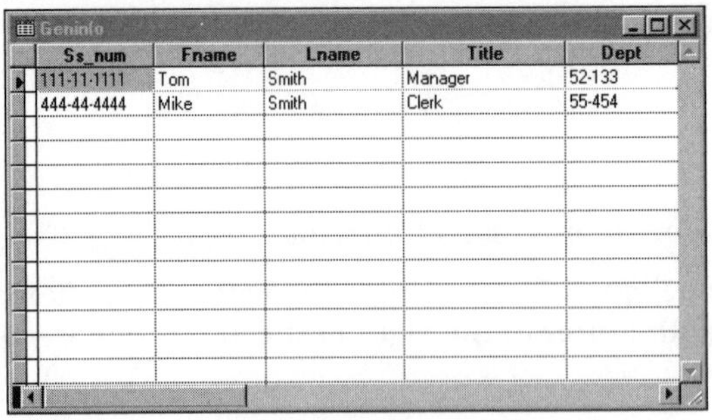

Figure 9-5: Only records that meet the filter criteria appear on-screen.

Removing a Data Filter

You'll probably want to get rid of a data filter after you use it so that you can see all the records again. The first time I used a data filter, I thought I'd lost the rest of the records in the table. I just wanted to get back to where I started and make sure that all the other records still existed. Yes, the other records existed.

Delete the data filter expression in the Work Area Properties box, and you'll see all your records reappear. To delete a data filter:

1. **Open the database file that contains the table for which you want to create a filter.**

   The Database Designer appears.

2. **In the Database Designer, double-click the table box of the table that you want to filter.**

   Records appear in the browse window of the table.

3. **Choose Table➪Properties.**

   The Work Area Properties dialog box appears.

4. **Select the expression in the Data filter text box.**

   Note: Sometimes, the expression is wider than the text box, so you have to drag across and let the expression scroll.

5. **Press the Delete key on your keyboard.**

   Visual FoxPro deletes the expression from the Data filter text box.

6. **Click OK to close the Work Area Properties dialog box.**

   Visual FoxPro displays all the records in the table in the browse window.

Filtering on More Than One Field

You can create a data filter on more than one field by building the proper expression. To do so:

1. **Create your first data filter.**

   (See the section "Creating a Filter," earlier in this chapter, if you're not sure how.)

   In the expression field name, you should have an equal sign and a value (for example, fname = Bob).

2. **Select the AND operator from the Logical combo box list in the Expression Builder.**

   AND is placed at the end of the expression. AND is the operator that tells Visual FoxPro to join together the expression you already created with another expression that you still need to create.

3. **Repeat Steps 6, 7, and 8 in the section "Creating a Filter," earlier in this chapter, to create the second expression.**

   In the expression field name, you should have an equal sign and a value from the first expression followed by AND field name equal sign and value for the second expression (for example, fname = Bob AND lname = Smith).

4. **Click OK to close the Expression Builder and return to the Work Area Properties dialog box.**

5. **Click OK to close the Work Area Properties dialog box and return to the browse window.**

   Visual FoxPro shows you only those records in the browse window that pass the data filter. (See Figure 9-6.)

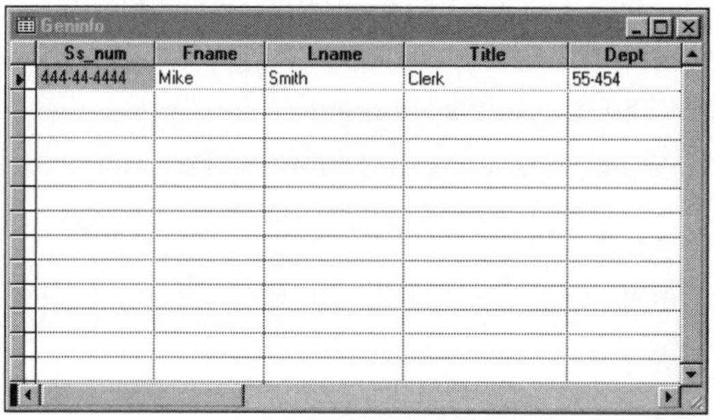

Figure 9-6:
Visual
FoxPro
displays the
records that
meet the
filter
criteria.

Filtering on a Partial Value of a Field

If you're like most people, you're probably impressed with the magic that Visual FoxPro can perform. Click a few buttons, and puff! Records disappear. What more can you ask for? Well, how about making records appear based on some of the values that are stuffed into a field?

Suppose that you own a medium-size company. You divide the company into departments, such as sales, accounting, and personnel. To keep track of these departments, you give each department a number — say, 52 for the accounting department.

The departments are large, so you decide to create subdepartments in each department. The accounting department, for example, has accounts receivable, accounts payable, and payroll subdepartments. You assign a number to each subdepartment — 52-133, for example — so that you can track information associated with the subdepartment.

Make the department number (52) part of the subdepartment number (52-133). Why? When you look at the subdepartment, you can immediately tell the department to which the subdepartment belongs.

Now suppose that you want to see all the subdepartments that are part of the accounting department. The accounting department is 52, and the first two digits of subdepartments that are members of the accounting department are also 52. You need to create an expression that tells Visual FoxPro to show you all the records in which the first two digits in the department field are 52.

Using substrings in a filter expression

Most fields that you use in a table are Character field type, which allows you to enter any character on your keyboard in the field. The letters and other characters in a Character field are called a *string,* and part of a string is called a *substring.* So when you want to use some of the characters in a field as a filter for the table, you need to use a substring of the string. Suppose that the department number 52-133 is a string of characters in a field. The characters 52 are a substring of 52-133.

A substring can be one or more characters that are part of the string. This example uses two characters — 52 — because you want to see only records in which the value of the department field starts with 52. Visual FoxPro can take part of the string — a substring — from a string if you give it enough information and use the substring to filter records in a table.

To do so, you first need to call the function SUBSTR( ). (A *function* is a complex task that Visual FoxPro already knows how to perform.) All you need do to is call the function by the function name.

The information that you must provide before running the SUBSTR( ) function is called an argument. *Arguments* are pieces of information needed for the function to work.

You need three pieces of information for the SUBSTR( ) function:

- ✔ **Field name.** The field name is, obviously, the name of the field. For this example, use dept, which is the name of the department field.

- ✔ **Starting position.** Starting position is the number of the first character that you want to use as part of the substring. For this example, you want Visual FoxPro to begin the substring with the first character of the string. If the string is 52-133, the first character of the substring is 5.

> ✔ **Number of characters in the substring.** The number of characters in the substring is the total number of characters that you want Visual FoxPro to use for the substring. For this example, the number of characters is 2. You want Visual FoxPro to begin the substring with the first character and to use the first character and the next character in the string as the substring (52).

Here's how you enter arguments. The arguments tells Visual FoxPro to go to the dept field (SUBSTR(dept, 1,2)). Start with the first character in the field (SUBSTR(dept, 1,2)) and read the first and second character (SUBSTR(dept, 1,2)) to create the substring.

Using a substring in an expression

You can use the SUBSTR() function as part of the expression for a filter. Follow these steps:

1. **Open the database file that contains the table for which you want to create a filter.**

   The Database Designer appears.

2. **Double-click the table box of the table that you want to filter.**

   Records appear in the browse window of the table.

3. **Choose Table⇨Properties.**

   The Work Area Properties dialog box appears.

4. **Click the button that appears to the right of the Data filter text box.**

   Visual FoxPro displays the Expression Builder in the center of your screen.

5. **Select** SUBSTR(, ,) **from the String combo box.**

   Visual FoxPro drops the function into the Set Filter Expression box.

6. **Enter the arguments inside the parentheses, making sure that the arguments are separated by the commas that already appear inside the parentheses.**

7. **Click the equal sign (=) in the Logical drop-down list.**

8. **Type** value to match **in the Set Filter Expression box.**

   You need to include all characters within quotes.

9. **Click OK to close the Expression Builder.**

   You return to the Work Area Properties dialog box.

10. Click OK to close the Work Area Properties dialog box.

Visual FoxPro shows you all the records in the browse window that belong to the accounting department. (See Figure 9-7.)

Ss_num	Fname	Lname	Title	Dept
111-11-1111	Tom	Smith	Manager	52-133
222-22-2222	Mary	Jones	Manager	52-134
666-66-6666	Joanne	Collage	Manager	52-342
777-77-7777	Sandra	Jones	Manager	52-344

Figure 9-7: All records that have the substring appear on-screen.

Make sure that the record pointer is pointing to the first record of the filtered records; otherwise, you see fewer records than actually meet the filter requirements. Always move the vertical scroll box to the top position to see the first record in the list of filtered records.

Filtering Data Across Multiple Tables

You may wonder how you filter records in more than one table. (At least that question came across my mind when I started building filters.) Typically, you group data into more than one table to make tables small and fast to search. You can join tables you need into a view (see Chapter 7), which makes multiple tables appear as one table. You can treat a view as a single table when you want to filter data. Here's what you do, but you need to join tables for the filter into a view (see Chapter 7) before beginning these steps:

1. Open the database file that contains the table for which you want to create a filter.

The Database Designer appears.

2. Double-click the view box of the view that you want to filter.

Records appear in the browse window of the table.

3. Create a filter. (If you're not sure how, see the section "Creating a Filter," earlier in this chapter.)

Chapter 10

The Fancy Way to Query Data

- -

In This Chapter

▶ Creating your query

▶ Running your query

▶ Saving your query

▶ Modifying your query

- -

Mirror, mirror on the wall, who's the richest one of all? If only a mirror could answer your questions. Don't fret if your mirror clams up; you can ask Visual FoxPro any question. As long as you ask the question in the proper form, and as long as the answer is in the database, Visual FoxPro gives you the answer within seconds of your request — a much better response than the mirror's.

Nothing can be that easy, you say. Well, you have a point. You must phrase your question in a way that Visual FoxPro understands: in the form of a query. A *query* is a formal way of asking for information from a database.

In this chapter, I show you how to create a query. And I assure you that creating a query is not difficult. So sit back, relax, and get started doing some fun stuff.

Creating a Query

You create a query by making choices in the Query Designer. A *query* is a formal way of asking for information from a database. The Query Designer resembles the View Designer. (Refer to Chapter 7.) This chapter shows you all the fancy stuff that you can do with the Query Designer.

To use the Query Designer:

1. **Open the database that you want to query.**

2. **Start a new query by choosing File⇨New.**

   The rather long New dialog box, shown in Figure 10-1, appears.

Figure 10-1:
The New
dialog box.

3. **Select the Query radio button.**

4. **Click the New file button to open the Query Designer.**

   The Add Table or View dialog box, shown in Figure 10-2, also appears, displaying the table names from which you select the tables that are to be used in the query.

Figure 10-2:
The
Add Table
or View
dialog box.

5. **Double-click the table names that contain the information you need for the query.**

You need to choose at least one table for the query. However, you can select more than one table if the information you're looking for is contained in multiple tables. The first table that you select pops into the Query Designer as a table box.

6. **If you select more than one table in Step 5, Visual FoxPro asks how you want to join the table with the first table that you selected by displaying the Join Condition dialog box.**

   A *join* is how Visual FoxPro links two tables by a common field.

   If you planned your database correctly (refer to Chapter 1), all the tables should have a common field. Chances are that you gave the common fields the same name. Visual FoxPro suggests these fields as the join in the Join Condition dialog box, shown in Figure 10-3.

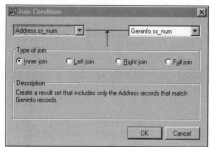

Figure 10-3:
The Join
Condition
dialog box.

   If Visual FoxPro isn't sure which fields to use as the join, you see two blank text boxes at the top of the Join Condition dialog box. These text boxes contain a drop-down list of field names. Select the field in each table that you want to use to join the tables. The same value must appear in both fields; otherwise, the tables cannot be joined.

   You can use several types of joins for the query. I explain the types of joins in Chapter 7 when I show you how to create a view.

   Speaking of views, you can select a view rather than a table for the query by selecting the Views radio button in the Add Table or View dialog box. Visual FoxPro displays all the views that are available in the database. Double-click the name of the view that you want to use; the view pops into the Query Designer. You can switch back and forth between tables and views to add a combination of tables and views to the query.

7. **Click OK to add the second table to the Query Designer.**

   You return to the Add Table or View dialog box, where you repeat Step 5 if you want to add another table to your query.

Using the query wizards

You may notice that whenever you create a new table, view, and query, I always tell you to click the New file button rather than the Wizard button. The Wizard button starts the wizard for whatever you are creating. A wizard is a great way to have Visual FoxPro do most of the work for you.

Click the Wizard button the next time you create a table, view, query, or any of the other things that I show you how to build in other chapters of this book. The wizard (figuratively) holds your hand throughout the process.

The wizard asks you questions in order. When you respond and click the Next button, the wizard asks you the next question. When you reach the last question, click the Finish button; Visual FoxPro does the rest.

Wizards are fast and easy to use, but I find that you don't really master the fun features of Visual FoxPro when you use wizards. That's my reason for having you explore wizards on your own.

8. **Click the Close button after you add all the tables and views that you require for the query.**

   The Add Table or View dialog box disappears.

9. **In the Available fields list in the Fields tab of the Query Designer (see Figure 10-4), click the name of the first field that you want to display in your query.**

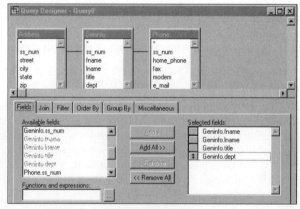

Figure 10-4: The Fields tab of the Query Designer.

10. **Hold down the mouse button and drag the field to the Selected fields list; release the mouse button.**

   The field name drops into the list.

As an alternative to Steps 9 and 10, you can double-click the field name in the Available fields list. Visual FoxPro displays the field in the Selected fields list automatically.

11. **Repeat the drag-and-drop process until all the fields that you want to see in the query appear in the Selected fields list.**

12. **(Optional) Click the Filter tab.**

The Filter tab tells Visual FoxPro what records you want to see on-screen. If you want to see all the records, skip this step. This tab consists of columns, below which you place the criteria for the filter. The tab looks confusing, but you'll breeze through the process of entering the information.

- Click the box below the Field Name column.

  A combo box lists available fields (see Figure 10-5). All the fields in the tables that you selected for the query appear in the list — not just the fields that you want to see in the query.

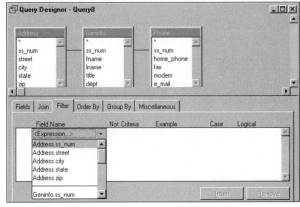

Figure 10-5:
All the available fields for the filter appear in the Field Name combo box.

Suppose that you're looking for the name of the person who is associated with the Social Security number 222-22-2222. You don't want to see the Social Security number; you want the Social Security number to be used as the criterion for the query. Click the Field Name box and select the field that you use for Social Security numbers.

- Click the Not column button to tell Visual FoxPro to do the opposite of what the expression says to do.

Say the expression tells Visual FoxPro to display all the records in which the last name is *Smith*. (See Chapter 3 to brush up on creating expressions with the Expression Builder.) The expression that conveys your wish is `lname = Smith` (which should look familiar, because I use the same expression throughout this book). The Not button does not contain a check mark.

Now you want to tell Visual FoxPro to display all the records in which the last name isn't *Smith*. Simply click the Not button and the check mark appears telling Visual FoxPro to reverse the logic of the expression.

- Click the down arrow to the right of the Criteria box to display a list of symbols that you use to set the criteria for the query.

Table 10-1 contains all the symbols in the Criteria drop-down list and typical values that you may enter in the Example column.

Table 10-1	Criteria Symbols	
Symbol	*Meaning*	*Example*
=	The value of the field is exactly the same as the Example column.	**Smith** The value in the field must equal *Smith.*
Like	The value in the field is like the Example column. You can use a question mark (?) to replace an unknown character in the Example column or an asterisk (*) to replace several unknown characters in the Example column.	**S?i*** The value in the field must have the first letter *S* and the third letter *i.* The second letter can be any character, and any number of characters can be the letter *l.*
==	The value in the field must match the text in the Example column character for character.	**le Smith** Each character in the field must match all the letters, including the space between *le* and *Smith.*
>	The value in the field must be greater than the value of the Example column.	**15** The value in the field must be greater than 15.
<	The value in the field must be less than the value of the Example column.	**15** The value in the field must be less than 15.
<=	The value in the field must be less than or equal to the value of the Example column.	**15** The value in the field must be less than or equal to 15.

Symbol	Meaning	Example
>=	The value in the field must be greater than or equal to the value of the Example column.	**15** The value in the field must be greater than or equal to 15.
Is Null	The value in the field must be null — in other words, the field must be empty.	No example
Between	The value in the field must be between the first value in the Example column and the second value in the Example column. Values must be separated by commas.	**15, 20** The value in the field must be between 15 and 20.
In	The value in the field must be one of the values in the Example column. Values must be separated by commas.	**Smith, Jones, Adams** The value in the field must be *Smith, Jones,* or *Adams.*

The Example column is where you enter the value that is used as part of the criteria for the query. If you want to use Social Security number 222-22-2222, you enter 222-22-2222 in the Example column (see Figure 10-6).

• Click the Case column button to require the filter criteria to match the uppercase and lowercase pattern in the Example column.

A check mark appears on the Case column button to indicate that the filter is case-sensitive. Click the Case column button a second time to remove the check mark and make the filter case-insensitive, which means that uppercase and lowercase characters

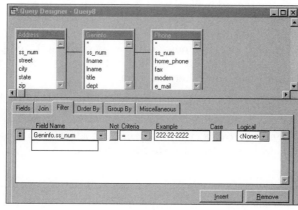

Figure 10-6:
In the Example column, enter the value that you want to find.

are treated the same. Suppose that you enter Smith in the Example column and then click the Case column button. Visual FoxPro passes up records that have *smith* in the last-name field because the name is not capitalized in that field.

- Click the combo box in the Logical column to display ways to link two filter criteria.

You can use more than one criterion for the filter. When you finish entering the first criterion, Visual FoxPro opens another line in the Filter tab, allowing you to enter another criterion. You must indicate in the Logical column whether both criteria or either criterion must be met for a record to pass through the filter.

You link the criteria by using the Logical column. The Logical column drop-down list contains three choices: <none>, AND, and OR. If you use a single line, you set the value of the Logical column to <none>, which tells Visual FoxPro that no more criteria are coming.

If you use more than one line, you must tell Visual FoxPro whether the record must meet the criteria in both lines or the criterion in just one of those lines. If both criteria must be met, set the Logical column value to AND. Set the Logical column value to OR if either criterion must be met.

Confused? An example may clear up the confusion. Suppose that the first line says that the value of the last name must be *Jones*, and the second line says that the value of the first name must be *Mark*. You're sure that the person you're looking for is Mark Jones, so you tell Visual FoxPro that the record must have the last name *Jones* AND the first name *Mark* before the record is displayed.

Here's another example. Suppose that you know the person's first name or his last name, but you aren't sure about both names. To continue the preceding example, you tell Visual FoxPro that the record must have the last name *Jones* OR the first name *Mark* before the record is displayed (see Figure 10-7).

- Click the Insert button to insert a new criterion for the filter.

You can also insert an new criterion by clicking the empty box that always appears after the last criterion in the Filter tab. Follow Step 12 to create another criterion.

- Click the criterion that you want to delete and then click the Remove button to remove the criterion from the filter.

When you remove a criterion, you can't recover it unless you use the Insert button to re-create the criterion.

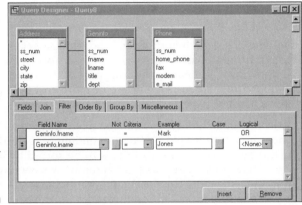

Figure 10-7:
Only records that have the last name *Jones* or the first name *Mark* will be displayed.

13. (Optional) Click the Order By tab of the Query Designer.

You see two lists: Selected fields and Ordering Criteria. The Selected fields list contains all the fields that you chose to see in the query. The Ordering Criteria list is where you place the field names in the order in which you want the records to be organized.

• In the Selected fields list, double-click the name of the field that you want to use to order the query.

Visual FoxPro automatically places the field name in the Ordering Criteria list box.

Suppose that you want records to be ordered by last name and then by first name. Double-click the last-name field in the Selected fields list; then repeat the step for the first-name field (see Figure 10-8).

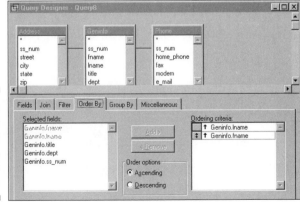

Figure 10-8:
Records appear in last name, first name order.

- Select one of the radio buttons in the Order Options section to specify sort order.

  Ascending is the default sort order. When you select the Descending radio button, the arrow next to the currently selected sort field points down, indicating that this part of the sort will sort in descending order. If you're using two or more sort fields, the other sort fields don't change.

  This feature can be handy; you can have one field sort in ascending order and another field sort in descending order, for example. But if you want two or more sort fields to be sorted in descending order, you have to set each sort individually by selecting each field and then selecting the Descending radio button. Alternatively, you can select the Descending radio button before you start moving fields; then the default order is descending.

14. **(Optional) Click the Group By tab of the Query Designer.**

    You see an Available fields list box and a blank Grouped Fields list box.

    - In the Available fields list, double-click the field names that you want to group records by. Visual FoxPro automatically displays the fields in the Grouped Fields list. For a complete discussion of grouping records, refer to Chapter 8.

    - Click the Having button in the Group By tab to specify a criterion for grouping records.

      Visual FoxPro displays the Having dialog box, shown in Figure 10-9, which resembles the Filter tab. You create a criterion in the Having dialog box the same way that you create a criterion in the Filter tab. The major difference is that the criterion in the Having dialog box affects only the way that records are grouped on-screen, whereas the criterion in the Filter tab determines which records you see on-screen.

15. **Close the Query Designer by choosing File⇨Close.**

    If you want to run or save the query, see the following two sections.

Figure 10-9:
The Having dialog box affects the way that records are grouped on-screen.

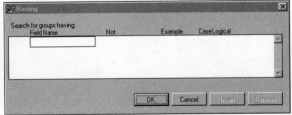

Running the Query

After you create a query, you get to run the query. You can run a query in the following ways:

- ✔ Click the Run button in the toolbar.
- ✔ Press Ctrl+Q.
- ✔ Choose Query➪Run Query.

No matter how you run the query, Visual FoxPro displays the records that you requested. When you finish viewing the records, click the window's Close button (the one with the X). The record's window closes, and you see the Query Designer again.

Saving the Query

The benefit of creating a query is that you can use the query any time without having to making all those decisions again. To save a query, choose File➪Save As; enter a name for the query in the Save dialog box; select the directory in which you want to save the query; and click OK.

Make sure that you save the query in the same directory as your database, so that everything you need is in the same place on your disk. I show you how to move the directories on your disk in Chapter 1, when you build your first database.

After you save the query, close the Query Designer by choosing File➪Close.

The next time you run the query, it applies the same questions to whatever the data is at that time. Suppose that you have a sales database, and you set up a query to show total sales by product. You can run the query in September to see the sales through that time. You can run the query again after December without changing it one bit and see your total sales through Christmas.

Running an Existing Query

To run a query from your disk, choose Program➪Do. The Do dialog box, shown in Figure 10-10, appears, displaying the query. Double-click the query name to run the query.

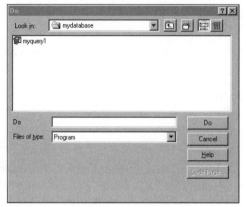

If you don't see the query name in the Do Program File list box, you probably are in the wrong directory on your disk. Change directories until you find the directory that contains your query.

Notice that the Query Designer does not appear on-screen when you run the query; only the data that you requested appears. After all, you don't need to see the query — you want to see only the records.

Modifying an Existing Query

You can always change the criteria for a query by changing your choices in the Query Designer. Follow these steps:

1. Choose File⇨Open to display the Open dialog box (see Figure 10-11).

Figure 10-11:
The Open
dialog box.

Notice the Files of type drop-down list near the bottom of the dialog box. Values in this list act like filters, displaying the names of the files in the current directory that are of the type specified in the Files of type list.

2. **From the Files of type drop-down list, select Query.**

   All the query filters in the current directory appear on-screen.

3. **Double-click the name of the query that you want to change.**

   Visual FoxPro displays the query in the Query Designer.

4. **Make your changes.**

5. **Save the query.**

   See the section "Saving the Query," earlier in this chapter, if you're not sure how.

6. **Close the Query Designer by choosing File⇨Close.**

Specifying a Destination for Your Query

You can use the information that a query retrieves for a variety of purposes. So far, you've seen the information displayed in Browse mode, in which the data is slapped together quickly. You also can use the information gathered from the query in a table, graph, screen, report or labels. No matter which one you choose, each item is called a destination.

How to avoid work

If you're like me (and like most computer programmers), you try to borrow from your previous work whenever you create a new database or program. The same holds true for creating a query.

Suppose that you built a query that displays records by people's names. Now you want to see the records by each person's department and name.

You could start fresh and create a new query, but why? You did most of the work when you set up the query for the person's name. Why not recall that query, modify the selection criteria to include the department, and save the query under a different name?

Computer professionals perform this little trick (sometimes called cut and paste) every day. You simply take an existing query and modify its criteria to form a new query. To find out how, see the section "Modifying an Existing Query," earlier in this chapter.

To see the complete list of destinations for a query, choose Query⇨Query Destination; the Query Destination dialog box appears (see Figure 10-12). Simply select a destination, answer a few questions (more questions!), and click OK. Visual FoxPro uses the result of the query as data for the destination that you selected.

Figure 10-12:
Click the
appropriate
button
to set the
query's
destination.

If you click the Table destination, for example, you can automatically enter into a table records that meet the criteria of your query. Visual FoxPro prompts you for the name of the table and then stuffs the records into the table every time you run the query.

To keep things simple, use the Browse destination, which is the default setting. You use the more common destinations later in the book, when I show you how to create screens, graphs, reports, and labels.

Part III
Working with Forms

The 5th Wave · By Rich Tennant

Re·al Pro·gram·mers

Real Programmers curse a lot, but only at inanimate objects.

In this part . . .

You can customize the way that you interact with data in your database by creating a form. A form is the face of your database; you use it to display the information that is in the database, enter new information, or change the existing data. In a sense, you're building your own Windows program on top of the database. You can place buttons, list boxes, text boxes, and practically everything else that you find in a typical Windows program in your forms.

Best of all, Visual FoxPro provides a host of tools called builders, which make creating a form as easy as snapping together toy building blocks.

You find out how to produce professional-looking forms for your database in this part of the book.

Chapter 11
Creating Forms

*O*n those rainy days when you were a tot, Mom probably let you loose in an old trunk filled with retired clothes. (Saying "retired clothes" has a little more class than saying "old clothes.") Dress-up day was here! You put on old hats, jackets, and oversize shoes and then pretended to be the people in your neighborhood.

Well, today is dress-up day for your database. In this chapter, you're let loose in a box — really, a toolbox on your screen — filled with buttons, combo boxes, text boxes, and all the other things that you find in a typical Windows program. You use these tools to paint a screen for your database.

Get ready for some real fun. Creating forms is the best part of Visual FoxPro.

Understanding Forms

You must be able to access information from a database in an easier way than opening a database, selecting tables, and so on. There *is* an easier way. You can simplify using your database by creating a screen.

A screen is called a *form,* which is something that's familiar to you. A form (see Figure 11-1) has the following elements:

✔ Text that gives instructions for completing the form

✔ Text that describes information you enter in the form

✔ Places to enter information

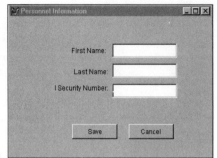

Figure 11-1:
Use this simple form to collect a person's name and Social Security number.

A Visual FoxPro form is similar to a credit-card application or any other form that you use. The form has places for text in the form and places for data. The only difference between a Visual FoxPro form and a credit-card application is that you create the Visual FoxPro form to appear any way you want it to. In this chapter, I show you how to create a form.

Creating a Form

To create a form, you use the Form Designer. Follow these steps:

1. **Open the database that you want to use with the form.**

2. **Choose File➪New or press Ctrl+N to display the New dialog box.**

3. **Select the Form radio button and then click the New file button to display the Form Designer, shown in Figure 11-2.**

   Visual FoxPro automatically displays a blank form. The form doesn't appear to be a blank form, however, because it contains dotted lines. These lines, which are called *grid lines,* help you align pieces of the form. Grid lines are not part of the form because the lines disappear when you use the form with your database.

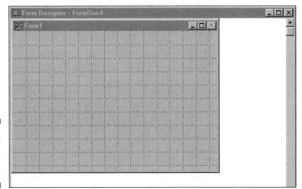

Figure 11-2:
The Form
Designer.

You can turn off the grid lines by choosing View➪Grid Lines, but
creating a form is easier if you display the grid lines. Repeat this
command to turn on the grid lines again.

 4. Click the Data Environment button in the Form Designer toolbar to associate tables with the form.

Visual FoxPro displays the Add Table or View dialog box, shown in
Figure 11-3, and also the Data Environment dialog box (behind the Add
Table or View dialog box).

Figure 11-3:
The
Add Table
or View
dialog box.

5. Double-click the names of the tables that you want to use with the form.

Each table that you double-click pops into the Data Environment
dialog box.

6. Click Close after you select all the tables that you require.

The Add Table or View dialog box disappears.

7. **Click the form to display the form's Properties window.**

   If the Properties window is not visible, click the Properties button in the Forms Control toolbar.

8. **Click the All tab or the Other tab, click the Name property, and then highlight the current name of the form in the text box just below the tabs (see Figure 11-4).**

Figure 11-4:
Enter the
form's
name in the
text box
just below
the tabs.

9. **Type the new name of the form; press Enter.**

10. **Click the form to make the form's Properties window active.**

    If the Properties window is not visible, click the Properties button in the toolbar.

11. **Click either the All tab or the Layout tab and then click the Caption property.**

    Visual FoxPro identifies a form by name. Anyone who uses a form, however, recognizes it by its caption. The form's *caption* is the word or words that appear at the top of the form, serving as a title. You can see the caption in the top-left corner of the form (see Figure 11-5).

    By default, Visual FoxPro uses form1 as the caption of the first form; it captions subsequent forms as form2, form3, and so on. Just as you can change the name of a form to something more meaningful, you can change the caption.

12. **Highlight the current caption in the text box below the tabs at the top of the dialog box and then type the new caption for the form; press Enter.**

    The new caption appears in the form. Keep in mind that captions can include spaces and can be up to 256 characters long.

Caption

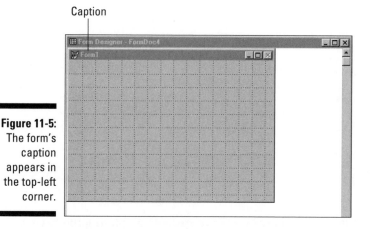

Figure 11-5:
The form's
caption
appears in
the top-left
corner.

13. Click the form to make the form's Properties window active.

If the Properties window is not visible, click the Properties button in
the toolbar.

**14. Click either the All tab or the Layout tab; scroll down to the
BackColor or ForeColor property, depending on which one you're
changing.**

Battleship gray probably isn't the color that you had in mind when you
decided to build a form for your database, so change the color of
the form.

A form's color properties are broken into background color and foreground color. By default, the form's background color is gray; the
foreground color, which is used for the text, is black by default.

Three numbers specify the colors: 0,0,0 for the foreground color
(black) and 192,192,192 for the background color (gray). You don't
enter numbers to choose colors; you choose colors from a color chart.

15. Double-click either the ForeColor or BackColor property.

Visual FoxPro displays the Color dialog box, shown in Figure 11-6.

16. Click a color and then click OK.

If you changed the background color, Visual FoxPro changes the gray
form to whatever color you chose in Step 14. If you changed the
foreground color, you won't see any change in the form until you insert
controls into the form. I show you how to make this change in the
section "Using Controls," later in the chapter.

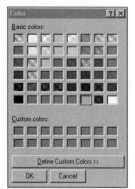

Figure 11-6:
The Color
dialog box.

---

17. Save the file by choosing File⇨Save As and completing the Save As dialog box.

Make sure that you enter the form's name in the Save Form text box, shown in Figure 11-7.

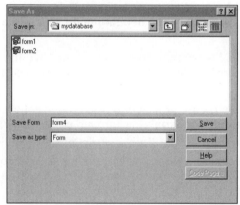

Figure 11-7:
Enter the
form's
name in the
Save Form
text box.

If you've already named the form, choose File⇨Save.

Save the form frequently as you create it so that you don't lose changes if someone or something cuts the electricity to your computer.

Using the Form Designer Toolbar

The Form Designer toolbar is below the standard toolbar, located at the top of the screen. The Form Designer toolbar contains buttons that display the following:

- The Properties window
- The Forms Control toolbar
- Other elements that you use to design a form

Table 11-1 lists the buttons on the Form Designer Control toolbar.

Table 11-1	**Form Designer Control Toolbar Buttons**	
Button	*Name*	*Description*
	Set Tab Order	Determines the order in which controls in the form are selected when you press the Tab key
	Data Environment	Associates a database and tables with the form, if you need to link the form to a table
	Properties window	Displays the Properties window, where you set values for properties of the form and for controls in the form
	Code window	Displays the Code window, where you enter commands that Visual FoxPro follows when specific events occur in the form
	Color Palette	Displays a palette of colors that you can use to color the form
	Layout toolbar	Displays the Layout toolbar, which you use to align controls in the form

(continued)

Table 11-1 *(continued)*

Button	Name	Description
	Form Builder	Displays the Form Builder, which helps you build a simple form
	AutoFormat	Displays the AutoFormat Builder, which enables you to apply standard styles (color, font, and so on) to the form

Buttons, list boxes, combo boxes, and other objects in a Windows program are called *controls*. Each control has a unique function and solves a particular problem in working with information.

A list box, for example, is a control that you're familiar with because a list box contains the names of files in a folder that you see whenever you choose File➪Open. You use a List Box control whenever you need to list items in a form. A list box does more than just display a list of names; the List Box control also enables the user to scroll the list and to select an item by double-clicking it.

Other controls have functions that are similar to and different from the functions in the List Box control; I cover the controls in detail in Chapter 12. I talk about the List Box control in this chapter just to familiarize you with the concept of a control.

Each control has features that you can modify: color, screen location, source of the data displayed in the control, and other features that I discuss later in Chapter 12. These features, called *properties,* are displayed in the Properties window.

You build your form by using controls and by modifying the properties of those controls.

Understanding the Form Properties

Every control that is used in a form has properties that you can change to meet the needs of your database. Likewise, a form has properties that you can modify. You can see a selection of properties by clicking the Properties button in the Form Designer toolbar. The properties appear in the Properties window, shown in Figure 11-8.

Figure 11-8:
The
Properties
window.

The Properties window contains five tabs:

- **All:** The All tab contains a list of the properties in the other tabs. I use the All tab often because I don't like wasting time clicking the other tabs. Sometimes, however, the other tabs are useful, such as when you want to find out whether a property exists for the form (or control) and you know only the category of the property, not the name of the property.

- **Data:** The Data tab, shown in Figure 11-9, contains only the properties that affect data used to display the form, such as where to place the form on-screen.

Figure 11-9:
The
Data tab.

- **Method:** The Method tab, shown in Figure 11-10, lists event properties for the form. An *event* is something that happens. Displaying, clicking, and closing forms are all considered to be separate events.

Figure 11-10:
The Method
tab.

✔ **Layout:** The Layout tab, shown in Figure 11-11, shows display properties for the form. These properties include color, the font used to
display information in the form, and other neat things that I discuss
later in this chapter.

Figure 11-11:
The Layout
tab.

✔ **Other:** The Other tab, shown in Figure 11-12, contains properties that
don't belong in any of the other tabs (except the All tab). This tab lists
the property used to name the form, as well as the type of window that
is used in the form.

Figure 11-12:
The Other
tab.

Assigning an Icon to the Form

 Whenever you minimize the form, Visual FoxPro displays the form as a icon at the bottom of the screen. The fox head is the default icon; you can change it to something more to your liking.

You have to get hold of your own icon from a third party. Visit your local computer store and ask for clip-art software that includes icons. Not all clip art can be used as icons, so be sure to ask the salesperson before you buy.

If you have an icon, here's how you assign it to a form:

1. **Click the form to make the form's Properties window active.**

   If the Properties window is not visible, click the Properties button in the toolbar.

2. **Click either the All tab or the Layout tab.**

3. **Double-click the name Icon.**

   Visual FoxPro displays the Open dialog box.

4. **Click the icon that you want to assign to the form.**

5. **Click OK to return to the Properties window.**

6. **Press Enter.**

   Visual FoxPro displays the name of the new icon in the properties list beside the Icon property name.

Note: Many other properties are used to describe the features of a form. You'll rarely change most of those properties, so I don't discuss them in this book. See the Visual FoxPro online help system for information on how to change a property that I do not discuss in this chapter.

Using Controls

After you're satisfied with the properties of the form, you can turn your attention to inserting controls into the form. You can always return to the form's Properties window and modify any of the properties at any time.

Controls are list boxes, combo boxes, buttons, and other objects that you use to navigate a Windows program. You can use these objects in your form by choosing them from the Form Controls toolbar.

Displaying the Form Controls toolbar

Click the wrench-and-hammer button in the Form Designer toolbar to display the Form Controls toolbar, shown in Figure 11-13. Notice that the Form Controls toolbar appears as a window alongside the form. This toolbar is called a *floating toolbar* because you can move the toolbar around the screen as you build your form. To move a floating toolbar, simply drag it to the desired position on-screen.

Figure 11-13:
The Form
Controls
toolbar.

The buttons in the Form Controls toolbar can be confusing. If you place the mouse pointer on a button and leave it there for a second, Visual FoxPro displays the name of the button.

Placing a control in the form

To grab a control and drop it into the form:

1. **Click the toolbar button that represents the control.**

   The mouse pointer changes to a cross when the cursor is positioned on the form.

2. **Move the cross to the spot in the form where you want to place the control.**

3. **Click the left mouse button.**

   Visual FoxPro displays the control in the form.

To find out how to place a control in a form, place a Label control in the form, following the preceding steps. A label is the simplest kind of control — it is just text, like the instruction text in a credit application. (The Label button is the *A* button in the Form Controls toolbar.) I describe the other controls in Chapter 12.

Notice that the word Label1 appears in the form, surrounded by eight tiny squares, as shown in Figure 11-14. The word Label1 is the caption for the label.

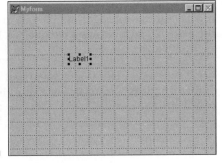

Figure 11-14:
Eight tiny squares surround the default name of the label.

You can change the caption of a Label control by changing the Caption property of the label, just as you changed the Caption property of the form, earlier in this chapter. (Refer to the section "Creating a Form," earlier in this chapter.)

The eight tiny squares are size boxes, which you use to change the size of the control in the form. To change the size of a control:

1. **Point to a size box and hold down the left mouse button.**

   The mouse pointer changes to directional arrows.

2. **Move the mouse pointer in the direction in which you want to resize the control and release the mouse button.**

   Visual FoxPro resizes the control in the form.

Repositioning a control in the form

If you don't like where you positioned the control in the form, move the control by dragging it to a new location. You can click anywhere but the size boxes when you drag a control. If you accidentally click the size boxes, you resize the control rather than move the control. What do you do? Don't worry: Simply choose Edit⇨Undo. Visual FoxPro returns the control to its former size.

Using the Layout Toolbar

Placing controls in the form isn't difficult; in fact, it's fun, and it gives you a way to release your creative talents.

The tricky part of placing controls in the form is getting the controls aligned with one another. You probably want to have certain controls, such as Label controls, lined up horizontally or vertically.

You can try to line up controls by sight, if you have a steady hand with the mouse. I find aligning controls by sight to be frustrating at times, however. Better ways of positioning controls on the form are to

- ✔ Use grid lines in the form
- ✔ Use the position marker
- ✔ Have Visual FoxPro handle the fine details of aligning controls by using the Layout window

Grid lines

You can use grid lines to help you through the process of aligning controls. I show you how to display grid lines in "Creating a Form," earlier in this chapter.

Grid lines can do more for you than simply provide a rule for your eye. You can have Visual FoxPro automatically align controls with:

- ✔ The vertical grid line
- ✔ The horizontal grid line
- ✔ Both grid lines

As soon as you place a control near a grid line, Visual FoxPro immediately snaps the edge of the control to align with the grid line. You can turn this snap-to-grid feature on and off by using the Options dialog box. Follow these steps:

1. **Choose Tools⇨Options to display the Options dialog box.**

2. **Click the Forms tab to display the options for the form (see Figure 11-15).**

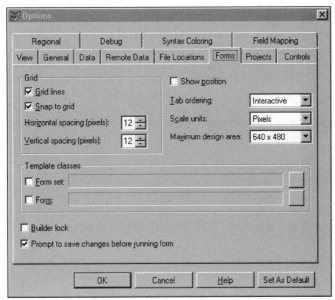

Figure 11-15: The Forms tab.

3. **Select the Snap to grid check box to turn this feature on or off.**

   If the check box is checked, the feature is turned on. If the check box is unchecked, the feature is turned off. You also can turn the Snap to grid feature on and off without leaving the Options dialog box by choosing Format⇨Snap to Grid.

4. **Click OK to close the Options dialog box.**

Position marker

The position marker consists of two sets of numbers located at the right end of the status bar (see Figure 11-16). If you don't see these numbers, chances are that the position marker isn't turned on.

Figure 11-16:
The position
marker is
located at
the right
end of the
status bar.

Position marker

Figure 11-16:
The position
marker is
located at
the right
end of the
status bar.

To turn on the position marker, choose <u>V</u>iew⇔Sho<u>w</u> Position.

The first set of numbers in the position marker identifies the horizontal and vertical position of the active control. You make a control active by clicking the control. Each time you reposition the control in the form, the numbers in the position marker change, reflecting the new position of the control.

The second set of numbers in the position marker tells you the size of the control. The first number is the control width; the second number is the control height.

You use these measurements to align controls in the form:

- ✔ If you're aligning one control with the top of another control, both controls need to have the same horizontal number.

- ✔ If you're aligning controls next to each other, both controls need to have the same vertical number.

Likewise, if you want to make the controls the same size (as typically is the case with command buttons), both controls should have the same second set of values in the position marker.

Layout window

A shortcut method of aligning controls in the form involves using the Layout toolbar. Display the Layout toolbar by clicking the Layout button in the Form Controls toolbar (the seventh button from the left in the toolbar).

The Layout toolbar, shown in Figure 11-17, is a little confusing. Rather than try to understand the buttons, simply place the mouse pointer on each button to read its caption.

Figure 11-17:
The Layout
toolbar.

You use the buttons to align controls in various ways, as shown in Table 11-2.

Button	Name	Description
	Align Left Sides	Aligns the left sides of the selected controls with each other
	Align Right Sides	Aligns the right sides of the selected controls with each other
	Align Top Edges	Aligns the tops of the selected controls with each other
	Align Bottom Edges	Aligns the bottoms of the selected controls with each other
	Align Vertical Center	Aligns the vertical centers of the selected controls with each other
	Align Horizontal Center	Aligns the horizontal centers of the selected controls with each other
	Same Width	Makes the selected controls the same width
	Same Height	Makes the selected controls the same height
	Same Size	Makes the selected controls the same width and height
	Center Horizontally	Centers selected controls horizontally
	Center Vertically	Centers selected controls vertically
	Bring to Front	Displays the selected controls on top of other controls on-screen
	Send to Back	Displays the selected controls behind other controls on-screen

Most alignment buttons are self-explanatory, but the Bring to Front and Send
to Back buttons need explanation. Controls can be positioned on top of each
other. You can place a Shape control in the form and then place a Label
control on top of the Shape control, for example. (A Shape control is used to
draw squares, rectangles, and circles in the form to enhance the appearance
of the form. Read more about the Shape control in Chapter 12.)

If you place the Label control in the form first, however, and then put the
Shape control in the same place, the Shape control covers the Label control.
You really want the Shape control to be behind the Label control. Follow
these steps:

1. **Click the control that you want to place behind the other control.**

   For this example, click the Shape control.

2. **Click the Layout Toolbar button in the Form Designer toolbar.**

   The Layout toolbar appears.

3. **Click the Send to Back button in the Layout toolbar.**

   Visual FoxPro does the rest.

Although Visual FoxPro aligns the controls in the form for you, you must tell
it two things: which controls are to be aligned and what kind of alignment
you require. You identify the group of controls that are to be aligned by
drawing a box around the controls. The box enables you to select more than
one control at the same time.

Here's how you select a group of controls in the form:

1. **Click the form alongside the controls that you want to select and
   hold down the left mouse button.**

2. **Drag the mouse to draw a box around the controls that you want to
   select (see Figure 11-18).**

Figure 11-18:
Tiny boxes
appear
around
all the
selected
controls.

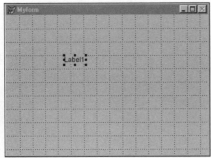

3. **Release the left mouse button.**

   Size boxes surround the controls, indicating that the controls are selected.

4. **Click the Layout Toolbar button in the Form Designer toolbar.**

   The Layout toolbar appears.

5. **In the Layout toolbar, click the button that you need to use.**

   Visual FoxPro aligns the selected controls.

Setting Tab Order

Although many people who use Windows programs favor using the mouse to select controls in a window, others prefer to use the Tab key. In nearly all Windows programs, including Visual FoxPro, you can move to the next control by pressing the Tab key.

Which control is the next control depends on the tab order of the controls. The *tab order* is the sequence in which each control is selected when the Tab key is pressed.

Visual FoxPro automatically assigns tab-order numbers to your controls. The first control that you place in the form is tab-order number 1, the second control is tab-order number 2, and so on. Visual FoxPro is being helpful, but sometimes that help gets in the way.

Suppose that the first control you place in the form is at the bottom of the form and the second control is at the top of the form. The control at the bottom of the form is the first tab position, and the control on top of the form is the second tab position — which is not what you would expect. The tab position of controls should be sequential, beginning with the top-left corner of the form and moving left to right down the form. Sometimes, though, you may want to tab through a form in some other order. Visual FoxPro allows you to tab however you want.

Try displaying the tab order of your form after you finish placing all the controls in the form. To do so, choose View⇨Tab Order. Visual FoxPro displays the tab number alongside each control, as shown in Figure 11-19. Choose View⇨Tab Order again to hide the tab numbers.

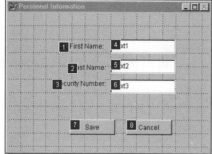

Figure 11-19:
Numbers
alongside
the controls
indicate the
tab order of
the controls.

If you don't like the tab order, change it by altering the value of the
`TabIndex` property of each control. Here's how you make this change:

1. **Select the first control that you want to change.**

2. **Click the Properties button in the Form Designer toolbar to display
   the Properties window.**

3. **Click the All tab.**

4. **Click the `TabIndex` property (see Figure 11-20).**

5. **Type a new tab number in the text box at the top of the dialog box.**

Another way to change the tab order is to click the tab numbers displayed
for each control. With successive clicks, the numbers cycle from 1 to the
number of controls that you have in the form. By adjusting only the controls
that are out of order, you can get your tab orders in order quickly.

You may need to change the tab order for some or all the controls in the
form after you review the current tab order.

Figure 11-20:
Change the
setting of
the
`TabIndex`
property to
change the
order in
which the
control is
selected.

Running the Form

How about seeing how your form looks with real data in the form? Click the exclamation-point button in the Visual FoxPro toolbar. A dialog box asks whether you want to save any changes that you made in the form. Click Yes.

If you haven't saved the form yet, Visual FoxPro automatically displays the Save As dialog box, giving you an opportunity to save the form. If you've already saved the form, the form appears on-screen.

All the controls in the form become functional when the form appears on-screen. If you don't like the way that a control works or how the form works, you can close the form and return to the Form Designer to modify the form.

You can close the form by clicking the Close button (the X) in the top-right corner of the form and then choosing Close from the drop-down menu.

Another way that you can run the form is to issue the DO FORM command in the Command Window. Follow these steps:

1. **Press Ctrl+F2 to display the Command Window.**

   If you have the Properties window on top of the Command Window, click the Close button to close the Properties window.

2. **Type** DO FORM, **followed by the name of your form.**

3. **Press Enter.**

Suppose that you created a form called myform. You can run the form by typing DO FORM myform and then pressing the Enter key. You must include the full directory path to tell Visual FoxPro where to find the form on your disk.

You also can run the form by choosing Form⇨Run Form.

Chapter 12

Adding Controls to a Form

• •

In This Chapter

▶ Making things happen by using a command button

▶ Displaying information in a list box

▶ Drawing shapes in the form

• •

*T*he hallmark of a Windows program is the graphical user interface (GUI), which consists of the buttons and bows used to put the program through its paces. All right, there really aren't any bows; I got a little carried away. But information is presented in a Windows application in many other fancy ways. *GUI* sounds very techie, but it's simply a means of allowing you to click buttons to make Visual FoxPro do something useful and to make selections from lists that you can scroll.

You can take advantage of the work that Bill Gates, Steve Jobs, and their folks did and use their graphical user interface in your forms. (No letters, please. I know that Xerox created the first GUI, but Apple and Microsoft developed the idea.)

Controls are things like labels, buttons, and list boxes. I could go on here, but you read all about the rest of them in this chapter.

In this chapter, I explore all the controls in detail and show you how to use the more popular controls in your form. You find out how to:

✔ Choose the appropriate control for the job

✔ Change the control to meet your needs

✔ Connect controls to your database

If you're not sure how to add a control, refer to Chapter 11.

Label Control

The Label control is used to display text that you don't want someone who is using the form to change. Text typically appears in the following ways:

- ✔ As a caption above Check Box controls
- ✔ Below a graphics control to describe graphs that you place in the form
- ✔ Any other place in the form where you need to provide instructions

The capital letter *A* appears on the Label button in the Form Controls toolbar that represents the Label control. I show you how to place the Label control in a form in Chapter 11.

 The Label control has many properties, some of which decide the color of the label, the text of the label, and what font Visual FoxPro uses for the text. You can see more properties by clicking the Label control to make the label active and then clicking the Properties button in the Form Designer toolbar. (Refer to Chapter 11.)

The following sections talk about the label properties that you'll find most useful. You can accept the default settings for the rest of the properties. You can explore these properties in the future by using Visual FoxPro's help system.

Label text

Probably the first thing that you want to do after placing a label in a form is change the default text of the label to something more appropriate. Here's how you do it:

1. **If you haven't placed a Label control in your form, do so now.**

   If you need help with this step, refer to Chapter 11.

2. **Click the Label control.**

   Small boxes called size boxes surround the control.

3. **Click the right mouse button to display a shortcut menu.**

4. **Choose <u>P</u>roperties.**

   Visual FoxPro displays the Properties window.

5. **Click the All tab of the Properties window.**

6. Click the Caption property.

The current text of the label appears in the text box below the tabs in the Properties window.

7. Type the text that you want to appear in the Label control.

8. Press Enter.

The new text appears in the Label control, as shown in Figure 12-1.

Figure 12-1:
Text
entered for
the Caption
property
becomes
the text of
the label.

9. Choose Format➪Size➪To Fit.

Visual FoxPro readjusts the size of the Label control to fit the Caption.

Alignment of text

A few more label properties enhance the appearance of the labels that you put in your forms. The Alignment property, which appears in both the All tab and the Layout tab of the Properties window, tells Visual FoxPro where to place the text within the space that you reserved for the label.

Suppose that you enter the caption First Name for a label. Visual FoxPro automatically places the caption at the left side of the space reserved for the label in the form. The label First Name, however, can appear too far to the left of the data that the label identifies, as shown in Figure 12-2. The information is contained in a Text Box control, which I show you how to use in the section "Text Box Control," later in this chapter. You can change the Alignment property to Right to move the text closer to the data.

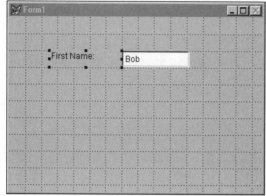

At other times, the label is positioned above the data, such as the case of first names listed in a column. You probably want the caption to be centered over the data, so you can change the Alignment property to Center.

Here's how to change the Alignment property:

1. **Click the label to make the label active.**

2. **Click the Properties button in the Form Designer toolbar to display the Properties window.**

3. **Click either the All tab or the Layout tab.**

4. **Double-click the Alignment property until you find the alignment value that you want to use for the label.**

   Each time you double-click, the alignment value changes in the Alignment property.

Label border

You can create a border by using the BorderStyle property. You can find the BorderStyle property in both the All tab and the Layout tab of the Properties window.

The BorderStyle property has two possible values:

- None
- Fixed Single

Double-click the BorderStyle property to specify whether you want a border for the label. Each time you double-click, the value of the BorderStyle property automatically changes in the Properties window. Visual FoxPro immediately displays the border or removes the border from the label.

See-through label background

Another useful label property is BackStyle. The name doesn't describe the property well, but the function of the property becomes obvious when you see how the property is used with a label.

Visual FoxPro blocks out the area in the form where you position the label. You really can't see this area unless you click the label to display the size boxes or put a border around the label. The label area blends with the background of the form because the background of the label and the background of the form are the same color — except for the label caption, which stands out against the form.

Simply put, you can see through the label when the BackStyle property is set to Transparent. But you can make the label area stand out by setting the BackStyle property to Opaque; then Visual FoxPro displays the background color of the label.

Here's a little experiment you can try with the Form Designer. The followering steps make the background color of the Label control and the form the same color:

1. **Start a new form.**

   Refer to Chapter 11.

   Visual FoxPro displays grid lines in the blank form.

2. **Place a label in the form.**

   Don't worry about the label caption; just use the default caption.

3. **Resize the label so that you can see more than the caption.**

4. **Click the Properties button in the Form Designer toolbar to display the Properties window.**

5. **Click the All tab or the Layout tab.**

6. **Scroll down to the BackStyle property.**

   By default, the value of the BackStyle property is Opaque. Notice that you can't see the grid lines through the label. Actually, the grid lines are below the label. The label's default background color, which is gray (just like the background color of the form), covers the grid lines. You see the contrast between the background colors better when you change the color of the label.

7. **Double-click the BackStyle property to change the value to Transparent.**

   The value of the BackStyle property automatically changes to Transparent in the Properties window. Now you can see the grid lines through the label.

Label color

A Label control has two categories of color:

✔ Foreground
✔ Background

The *foreground color* is the color of the caption. The *background color* is the color of the rest of the label.

In Chapter 11, I show you how to choose a foreground and background color for the form. You use the same technique to select the colors for the Label control.

ForeColor is the foreground property, and BackColor is the background property. Both properties appear in both the All tab and the Layout tab of the Properties window. Here's how you select a color for the label:

1. **Click the label to make the label active.**

2. **Click the Properties button in the Form Designer toolbar to display the Properties window.**

3. **Double-click either the ForeColor or BackColor property.**

   Visual FoxPro displays the Color dialog box, which is a color chart.

4. **Click the color that you want to use.**

5. **Click OK.**

   Visual FoxPro paints the Label control in the color that you choose.

Label fonts

The final label properties that I talk about in this chapter determine the font used to display the caption. In Chapter 11, I show you several properties that determine the style and size of the characters that are used in the form. The same properties are available for the Label control.

You change the FontName and FontSize properties by double-clicking them in the All or Layout tab in the Properties window. Each time you double-click, the value of the property changes. Many values are available for the FontName and FontSize properties. Each time the value changes, Visual FoxPro changes the font of the caption of the label.

Double-clicking a property in the Properties window changes the value of the property and applies the changes to the control in the form. Double-clicking a property is a good way to see whether you like the changes before making a final selection. Actually, *final* is too strong of a word; you can change the font any time you want by double-clicking a font property.

Using the combo box below the tabs in the Properties window may be an easier way to choose values for these properties. The combo box contains a list of values. Click the value that you want to use; Visual FoxPro changes the label accordingly.

The other font properties described in Chapter 11 consist of true and false values. Double-click the property, and the value changes from true to false or from false to true in the Properties window. The results appear in the caption of the Label control in the form.

Text Box Control

The Text Box control is probably one of the most-used controls in a form. The Text Box control contains a single line of text that can be entered or changed by someone who uses the form.

The text that appears in a text box usually is the contents of a field in a table of a database. So you use a Text Box control to enter, display, and change information that is stored in a database.

 The *ab* button in the Form Controls toolbar represents the Text Box control. Click the button and then place the text box in the form (refer to Chapter 11), using the same technique that you use to place any control in the form. The Text Box control automatically appears in the form.

The size boxes surround the word Text1, which is the default text of a text box. Text displayed in a text box is called the *text-box value,* which you find in the Properties window. I discuss this value in "Assigning a field to a text box," later in this chapter.

Alignment, color, and font for a text box

Some of the same properties that you use with a Label control are available for a Text Box control. You can use the Alignment property to position the text within the space that you reserved in the form for the text box.

Alignment choices include Left, Right, and Center. The Text Box control also has an option called Automatic, which allows Visual FoxPro to determine the alignment for the text.

You can add spice to a text box by changing the foreground color (black by default) and background color (gray by default). You also can specify whether the background is see-through. Change the ForeColor, BackColor, and BackStyle properties of a Text Box control just the way that you change the same properties for a Label control.

Don't forget to play around with the font properties for a text box. The font properties are the same as those that are used for the Label control. You can make text appear in fancy type of all sizes and styles.

Maximum number of characters

A Text Box control accepts practically all characters that are entered at the keyboard. Simply type away; the characters are placed in the text box.

Sometimes, you want to restrict the number of characters that someone can enter in a text box — when the information is going to be stuffed into a field in a table of your database, for example.

A field can hold a maximum number of characters, based on the width of the field when you created the table. I show you how to create a field in Chapter 2.

To have Visual FoxPro stop someone from entering too many characters in a text box, follow these steps:

1. **Click the Text Box control in the form to make the text box active.**

2. **Click the Properties button in the Form Designer toolbar.**

   Visual FoxPro displays the Properties window.

3. **Click the All tab or the Data tab.**

   Visual FoxPro displays the properties associated with the tab.

4. Click the `MaxLength` **property to highlight it.**

5. **In the text box at the top of the window, enter the maximum number of characters for the Text Box control.**

Assigning a field to a text box

Most times, you want to associate a text box in your form with a field in a table of the database. At other times, you want the value to be stored in the text box but not placed in a field — when you want to personalize instructions in the form, for example.

When someone begins to use your form, you can ask for the person's first name. The person enters his or her name in a text box. The name then becomes associated with the `Value` property of the Text Box control. You can refer to the `Value` property any time you want to use the person's first name.

Suppose that someone wants to see a person's first name and last name. You can create a form and place two labels and two text boxes in the form. One label has the caption First Name, which appears to the right of the text box that contains the person's first name. The other label has the caption Last Name and is positioned to the right of the other text box that contains the person's last name.

In the following steps, I show you how to associate the text boxes with the first-name and last-name fields in the database.

1. **Select a database and a table.**

   I show you how to do this in Chapter 11.

2. **Click the Text Box control to make the text box active.**

3. **Click the Properties button in the Form Designer toolbar to display the Properties window.**

4. **Click either the All tab or the Data tab.**

5. **Click the** `ControlSource` **property.**

6. **Click the combo box located below the tabs of the Properties window.**

   You see the list of fields in the table that is associated with this form.

7. **Select the field that you want to assign to the text box.**

Status bar help

Everyone needs a little help every now and then, and this holds true for someone who is entering information in a text box. You know what data you expect to find in the text box, but that doesn't necessarily mean that the person who is using your form knows the data.

You probably notice that whenever you place the mouse pointer on a control, such as a toolbar button, Visual FoxPro displays a brief description of the control in the status bar. You can place your own text for the Text Box control in the status bar by using the `StatusBarText` property. Here's how you enter the text.

1. **Click the Text Box control to make the text box active.**
2. **Click the Properties button in the Form Controls toolbar to display the Properties window.**
3. **Click either the All tab or the Layout tab.**
4. **Click the `StatusBarText` property.**
5. **In the text box, enter the text that you want to display in the status bar.**

Text Box Builder

Try using the Text Box Builder whenever you want to enhance a text box that you place in a form. The Text Box Builder enables you to set values for some frequently used text-box properties without having to use the Properties window.

To use the Text Box Builder:

1. **Make sure that a table is associated with the form (refer to Chapter 11).**
2. **Place a text box in the form (refer to Chapter 11).**
3. **Right-click the text box to display a shortcut menu, shown in Figure 12-3.**

Figure 12-3:
The
shortcut
menu
appears
when you
right-click
the text box.

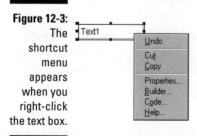

4. Choose <u>B</u>uilder to display the Text Box Builder, shown in Figure 12-4.

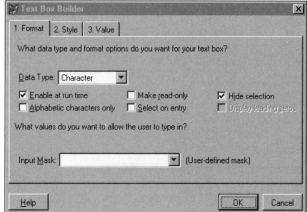

Figure 12-4:
The
Text Box
Builder.

5. Click the Format tab, if the Format tab isn't displayed.

The Format tab contains a few text-box options. The only two options that you need to change are <u>D</u>ata Type and Input <u>M</u>ask.

6. Click the down-arrow button next to <u>D</u>ata Type to display a drop-down list.

Your choices are Character, Date, Logical, and Numeric.

7. Choose the data type that best matches the data that will be entered in the text box.

Make sure that the data type is the same as the field type of the field, if a field is assigned to the text box. (Refer to Chapter 2, which shows you how to set the field type for fields in your tables.)

8. Click the down-arrow button next to Input <u>M</u>ask to display a list of common formats for the information entered in the text box, as shown in Figure 12-5.

9. Select the format that best suits the data entered in the text box.

The list contains common formats, such as for a telephone number. The capital *A* in the list represents any letter of the alphabet; the pound sign (#) and 9 represent digits.

Visual FoxPro inserts the format characters (#, 9, A, and hyphens) into the text box. You don't need to use an input mask for a text box.

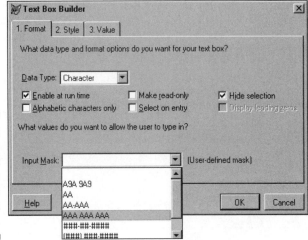

Figure 12-5:
The drop-
down list
shows
common
input mask
formats.

10. **Click the Style tab of the Text Box Builder (see Figure 12-6).**

The Style tab enables you to set special effects, borders, and character alignment for the text box. You set special effects and borders by selecting the appropriate radio buttons; you set the alignment by making a choice from the Character Alignment drop-down list. You can have Visual FoxPro size the text box automatically by clicking the Size text box to fit check box. All properties in the Style tab are optional.

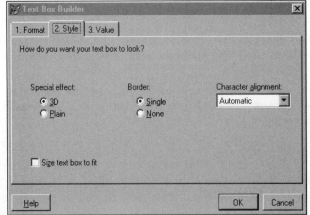

Figure 12-6:
The Style
tab of the
Text Box
Builder.

11. **Click the Value tab to assign a field to the text box (see Figure 12-7).**

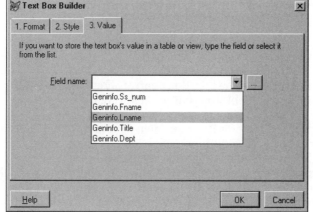

Figure 12-7:
The Value
tab of the
Text Box
Builder.

12. **Click the down-arrow button next to Field name to display a list of available fields.**

13. **Choose a field to assign to the text box.**

If you don't see a list of fields, you haven't assigned a table to the form. Refer to Chapter 11.

14. **Click OK.**

Visual FoxPro applies the changes to the text box.

Read-only data

At times, you're willing to display data in a field of a form, but you don't want anyone to change the data. Visual FoxPro makes the information read-only if you set the ReadOnly property of the text box accordingly. Here's how you do it:

1. **Click the Text Box control in the form to make the text box active.**

2. **Click the Properties button in the Form Designer toolbar to display the Properties window.**

3. **Click the All tab or the Data tab.**

4. **Double-click the ReadOnly property.**

The ReadOnly property in the Properties window changes from false to true.

5. **Double-click the ReadOnly property again.**

The ReadOnly property changes back to false. A true value means that data can be seen in the text box but not changed. A false value means that the data can be seen and changed.

Edit Box Control

The Edit Box control contains multiple lines of text that can be entered, displayed, and changed, similar to the to the way you perform the same tasks using the Text Box control. (Refer to the section "Text Box Control," earlier in this chapter.) The Edit Box control is represented in the Form Controls toolbar by the button that has a lowercase *a*.

 When you position the Edit Box control in the form, Visual FoxPro displays a vertical scroll bar in the edit box.

An Edit Box control is practically the same as a Text Box control, except for the number of lines that a user can enter in the control. You'll find that the Text Box control handles most of your need to collect and display information. On some occasions, however (such as when you want to enter a memo), you need more than one line and therefore need an Edit Box control.

The properties of the Edit Box control are nearly identical to those of the Text Box control, so I don't rehash the information. Simply review the section "Text Box Control," earlier in this chapter, to find out how to set the most common properties of the Edit Box control.

You also can change the properties of the Edit Box control by using the Edit Box Builder (see Figure 12-8), which is similar to the Text Box Builder. The major difference is the Format tab, which has a few options that do not appear in the Format tab of the Text Box Builder.

I suggest that you don't change the properties listed in the Format tab because the default settings work well for most forms that you build.

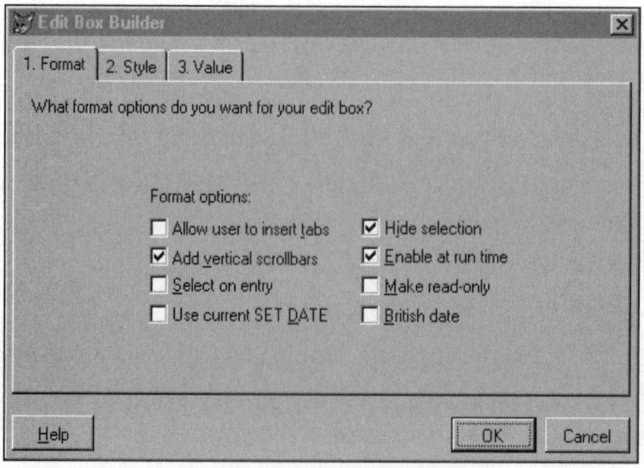

Figure 12-8: The Edit Box Builder.

Command Button Control

 The Command Button control creates the familiar OK, Cancel, and other buttons that appear in Windows programs. The Command Button control is represented by the rectangle button in the Form Controls toolbar.

When you have a Command Button control positioned in the form, you can reset various properties that affect the appearance and function of the command button.

Some properties, such as the Caption property, are familiar because the same properties are used for the Label control and the Text Box control. The Caption property, for example, sets the text that appears on the button. You can align the text, change the color of the text and background of the command button, and change the font of the text by using the same properties that you use with the Text Box control.

Pictures on the command button

You've probably noticed that pictures rather than words identify command buttons in some Windows programs. Pictures appear on command buttons in the Form Controls toolbar in Visual FoxPro, for example.

Two kinds of pictures are used with a Command Button control. One picture is used when the button is selected; another picture is used when the button is deselected. You can determine which picture is used for a command button by using the Picture and DownPicture properties. Here's how you assign a picture to a Command Button control:

1. **Click the Command Button control in the form to make the command button active.**

2. **Click the Properties button in the Form Designer toolbar to display the Properties window.**

3. **Click the All tab or the Layout tab.**

4. **Double-click the Picture property or the DownPicture property to display the Open dialog box.**

5. **Choose the file containing the picture that you want to assign to the command button.**

   You must supply the picture file. You can use any picture file with the file extension .BMP (such as FOX.BMP) as a picture for a command button. If you assign a picture file to the Picture property but not to the DownPicture property, the picture file used for the Picture property is used for both.

Command Button Code Window

A command button dresses up a form, but the real purpose of placing a command button in the form is to make something happen when the button is clicked. You click the OK command button in the Open dialog box, for example, to tell Visual FoxPro to open the file that you selected.

Practically anything that you can imagine can occur when a command button is clicked, but you must do a little work to make things happen. The person who created the Open dialog box in Visual FoxPro, for example, had to tell Visual FoxPro exactly what to do when the OK button is clicked.

If you want a command button to do something, you, too, must give Visual FoxPro explicit instructions to follow when the command button is clicked. (See Chapter 13.) The instructions that you give Visual FoxPro consists of special words, called *commands,* that the program recognizes.

You enter commands in the Command Button control's Code window. Here's how you display the Code window for the Command Button control:

1. **Click the Command Button control in the form to make the Command button active.**

2. **Right-click the Command Button control to display the shortcut menu.**

3. **Choose Code to display the Code window, shown in Figure 12-9.**

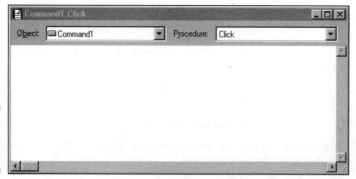

Figure 12-9:
The Code
window.

At the top of the Code window are two combo boxes. The left combo box is titled O*b*ject, and the name of the command button appears in the combo box. *Objects* are things such as forms, controls, reports, queries, a database, and tables.

The right combo box, titled P̲rocedure, displays the word Click. Instructions that you write in the Code window become the Click procedure. A *procedure* is a set of instructions identified by a name. In this case, the procedure's name is Click. The name has a special meaning to Visual FoxPro because the name is associated with an event. An *event* is something that happens when your form, database, table, or any other part of Visual FoxPro is displayed on-screen.

Clicking the command button is an event. Right-clicking the command button is another event. Drop down the P̲rocedure list, and you see all the events that can occur for a command button. (See Figure 12-10.)

Figure 12-10: The Procedure list contains all the events that can occur for a command button.

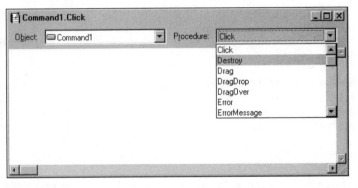

Each event is assigned a procedure, which contains the instructions that Visual FoxPro is to follow when the event occurs. So when you click the OK command button in the Open dialog box, Visual FoxPro reads the Click procedure that is assigned to the OK command button for the Open dialog box.

You can use many commands to tell Visual FoxPro what to do when someone clicks a command button; I show you a few in Chapter 13. Writing commands can be tricky, however, so you may want to put off writing commands until you become comfortable with using Visual FoxPro.

Default OK and Cancel

You need to use two Command Button control properties each time you place command buttons in your form: the Default property and the Cancel property.

You probably notice that each time a dialog box appears in a Windows program, the dialog box contains at least two command buttons: OK and Cancel. The OK command button is used to accept data that is entered in the dialog box; the Cancel command button is used to void the data. In each case, the dialog box closes when either button is clicked.

A form is like a dialog box in that it should have at least two command buttons. One of the command buttons should have the caption OK; the other, the caption Cancel.

You cancel the OK and Cancel command buttons the same way, but they have different captions. Also, you set the `Cancel` property to true by double-clicking the property. The `Cancel` property enables the user to activate the Cancel button by pressing the Esc key.

You must provide all the commands that Visual FoxPro follows when either button is clicked.

At least one command button should be set as the default command button. The default button is selected automatically when someone presses the Enter key. When the Open dialog box appears, for example, the OK command button has a dark border, which indicates that it is the default button.

Here's how you designate a command button as the default button:

1. **Click the Command Button control in the form to make the command button active.**

2. **Click the Properties button in the Form Designer toolbar to display the Properties window.**

3. **Click the All tab or the Other tab.**

4. **Double-click the `Default` property to change the false value to true.**

5. **Double-click the property again to change the true value back to false.**

   A true value means that the command button is the default button.

Command Group Control

 The Command Group control displays several command buttons in the form and groups these buttons within a border. You click the button to place a Command Group control in the form.

Visual FoxPro displays two command buttons in a form by default, but you can create as many command buttons in a command group as you require.

Although you can set the properties for a Command Group control directly, using the same methods that you use with the Command Button control, the easiest way to modify the Command Group control is to use the Command Group Builder. Here's how to display the Command Group Builder:

1. Place a Command Group control in the form (refer to Chapter 11).

2. Click the Command Group control to make the control active.

3. Right-click the control to display a shortcut menu.

4. Choose Builder to display the Command Group Builder, shown in Figure 12-11.

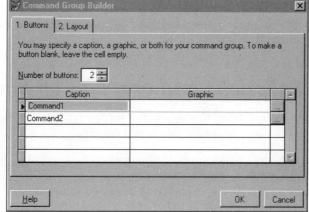

Figure 12-11:
The
Command
Group
Builder.

You can change the number of buttons that appear in the control or use text or graphics to identify buttons by using features located in tabs (see the following sections).

The Command Group Builder contains all the properties that you need to make a Command Group control a working part of your form.

The Command Group Builder has two tabs: Buttons and Layout. The Button tab defines the number of buttons and captions for the buttons. The Layout tab determines the layout of the button in the form.

Setting the number of buttons

You can decide how many command buttons appear in the Command Group control. You can insert any number of command buttons, but use your common sense — don't insert too many buttons, or you will only confuse someone who uses your form.

To set the number of command buttons in a command group:

1. **Place a Command Group control in the form (refer to Chapter 11).**
2. **Click the Command Group control to make the control active.**
3. **Right-click the Command Group control to display a shortcut menu.**
4. **Choose Builder to display the Command Group Builder.**
5. **Increase (or decrease) the number in the <u>N</u>umber of buttons drop-down list.**

   Visual FoxPro inserts a new command button into the form (or removes a command button from the form).

Placing captions and graphics on buttons

Command buttons are listed in a grid in the Button tab (refer to Figure 12-11). The grid contains two columns: Caption and Graphic.

Visual FoxPro uses the name of the command button as the default caption. You should change the caption by selecting the current caption and then entering new text. The new text appears in the Caption column.

You can use a graphic instead of text to identify the command button. You must supply the graphic in the form of a graphic file. Select the Command Button control and then double-click the Picture property in the Properties window to display the Open dialog box. Select the picture file and then click OK. Visual FoxPro inserts the name of the file into the Graphic column of the grid.

Using the Layout tab of the Command Group Builder

You can use the Layout tab (see Figure 12-12) to set three Command Group button options: Button layout, Spacing between buttons, and Border style.

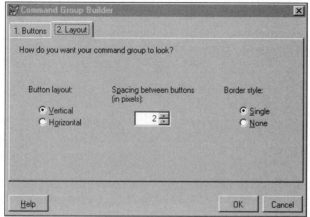

Figure 12-12:
You can
use the
Layout tab
options
to set the
layout of
buttons
in the
Command
Group
control.

The Button layout choices are Vertical and Horizontal. Select Vertical,
and Visual FoxPro stacks the command buttons, as shown in Figure 12-13.
Choose Horizontal, and Visual FoxPro lays the command buttons end to end,
as shown in Figure 12-14.

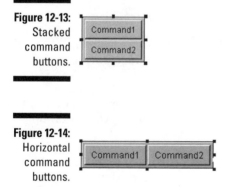

Figure 12-13:
Stacked
command
buttons.

Figure 12-14:
Horizontal
command
buttons.

A spinner is used to adjust the spacing between buttons. The number
represents the number of pixels that separate the buttons. (A *pixel* is a small
piece of your form; don't worry about pixels.) Simply change the spinner
number and look at the position of the command buttons. If you like what
you see, stop. If you don't like what you see, continue spinning.

Visual FoxPro associates the command buttons in a Command Group control. You can have Visual FoxPro group the command buttons by placing a single border around the group. To insert a border around the group, choose Single. If you don't want the border, choose None.

Option Group Control

The Option Group control consists of two or more radio buttons. When you select one radio button in the group, all the others turn off automatically.

 The Option Group button in the Form Controls toolbar places an Option Group control in the form. Visual FoxPro starts you off with two buttons, but you can use whatever number of buttons you require.

You can change the various features of the Option Group control by using the Properties window, but you should avoid doing so until you become proficient with using Option Group controls. The Option Group Builder is a better and faster way to customize the Option Group controls in your form. Here's how you start the Option Group Builder:

1. **Place an Option Group control in the form (refer to Chapter 11).**

2. **Click the Option Group control to make the control active.**

3. **Right-click the control to display a shortcut menu.**

4. **Choose Builder to display the Option Group Builder, shown in Figure 12-15.**

The Option Group Builder is similar to the Command Group Builder (refer to "Command Group Control," earlier in this chapter), but the Option Group Builder has an additional tab: Value.

You use the Button tab to insert and remove group buttons and to set the captions of the buttons. You can place graphics on buttons (refer to "Placing captions and graphics on buttons," earlier in this chapter). The only difference is that you must select the Graphical radio button to display the Graphic column.

The Layout tab is identical to the Layout tab of the Command Group Builder. (Refer to "Using the Layout tab of the Command Group Builder," earlier in this chapter.)

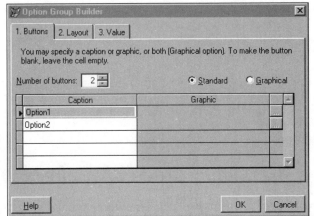

Figure 12-15:
The Option
Group
Builder.

The third tab of the Option Group Builder is Value, which identifies the field that will be used as the value of the option group. Drop down the Field name list and click the field that you want to use to contain the value of the Option Group control. If you don't see a list of field names, you haven't selected a table for the form. Assign a table to the form (refer to Chapter 11) and then assign a field name to the option group.

You can't assign just any field to an Option Group control. The field has to have the right kinds of values in it. The field has to contain numbers, and the highest number can be no greater than the number of buttons in the Option Group control. The first button is selected when the value in the field is 1, the second button is selected when the value in the field is 2, and so on.

Check Box Control

You use the Check Box control to record a choice between two possible conditions. A question in a form may be "Do you drive a car?" You can record the answer in a Check Box control. A check in the box means yes; no check means no. So if a Check Box is associated with a field, the field should be a Logical field type (refer to Chapter 2). A Logical field type has two possible values, such as yes and no or true and false.

You place a Check Box control in a form by clicking the check-mark button in the Form Controls toolbar. You can use as many Check Box controls in a form as you need. Each check box is independent of the other check boxes, so you must place each one in the form separately.

Notice that a check box appears to the right of the text that describes the check box. The text is called the caption. You can change the caption by using the Caption property, which I show you how to change for the Label control in the section "Label text," earlier in this chapter.

You can alter many properties other than the Caption. Many properties are the same ones that you change for the Text Box control (refer to "Text Box Control," earlier in this chapter), including text and background colors and fonts.

Using a picture in place of a check mark

A Check Box control seems to use a check mark to indicate that the check box is selected. You can be fancy, however, by using a picture instead of the traditional check mark. As is true of all pictures that are used in a form, you must supply the picture.

If you decide to use a picture in place of a check mark, you need two kinds of pictures for the Check Box control: a picture for when the check box is selected, and another picture for when the check box is deselected. If you assign a Picture property but not a DownPicture property, the picture assigned to the Picture property is used for both the Picture property and the DownPicture property.

The Picture property tells Visual FoxPro which picture to use when the check box isn't selected. This picture replaces the blank check box. The DownPicture property tells Visual FoxPro which picture to use when the check box is selected. This picture replaces the checked check box. To change these properties:

1. **Click the Check Box control in the form to make the check box active (refer to Chapter 11).**

2. **Click the Properties button in the Form Designer toolbar to display the Properties window.**

3. **Click the All tab or the Layout tab.**

4. **Double-click the Style property and change the value to <u>G</u>raphical.**

5. **Double-click the Picture property or the DownPicture property to display the Open dialog box.**

6. **Choose the file that contains the picture you want to assign to the check box.**

   You must supply the picture file. You can use any picture file with the extension .BMP (such as FOX.BMP) as a picture for a check box.

Adding check-box special effects

Another property that you may want to modify is SpecialEffect. Don't become overly excited; you aren't able to perform the special effects that you see in the movies. The special effects for the Check Box control only change the appearance of the check box from a plain square to a three-dimensional look.

Here's how you make the change:

1. **Click the Check Box control in the form to make the check box active (refer to Chapter 11).**

2. **Click the Properties button in the Form Designer toolbar to display the Properties window.**

3. **Click the All tab or the Layout tab.**

4. **Double-click the SpecialEffect property.**

   The special effect changes from 3-D to Plain. (See Figure 12-16.)

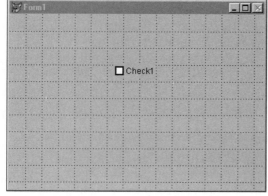

Figure 12-16:
Keep the check box plain by using the Plain Style property.

5. **Double-click the property again.**

   The 3-D special effect appears again. (See Figure 12-17.) You also must make sure that the Style property in the All or Layout tab is set to Standard. If not, double-click the Style property to change the value to Standard.

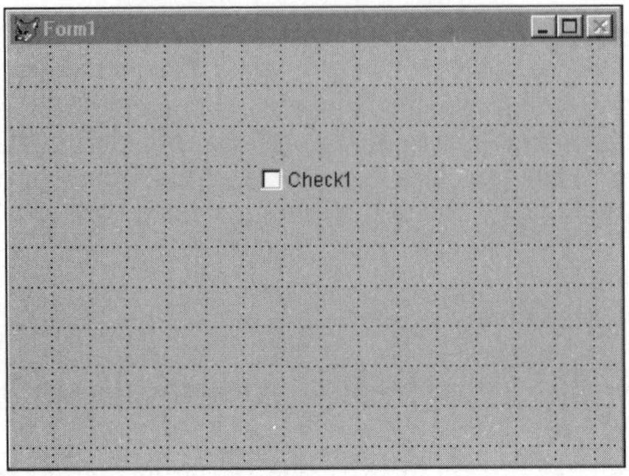

Figure 12-17:
Make a
check box
fancy by
using a 3-D
special
effect.

Combo Box Control

The Combo Box control enables the person who uses the form to enter a value or chose a value from a drop-down list. You use a combo box when you set properties for controls in your form, such as when you choose the font for a Text Box control.

 The button that represents the Combo Box control appears to the right of the Check Box button in the Form Controls toolbar.

The best way to set the properties for the Combo Box control is to use the Combo Box Builder. Here's how to start the Combo Box Builder:

1. **Place a Combo Box control in the form (refer to Chapter 11).**

2. **Click the Combo Box control to make the control active.**

3. **Right-click the control to display a shortcut menu.**

4. **Choose Builder to display the Combo Box Builder shown in Figure 12-18.**

In the following sections, I show you how to assign a table to the combo box and determine the combo-box style.

Using the List Items tab of the Combo Box Builder

The Combo Box Builder has four tabs: List Items, Style, Layout, and Value. I begin with the List Items tab, which you use to fill the combo box's drop-down list with values. You can fill the list in three ways:

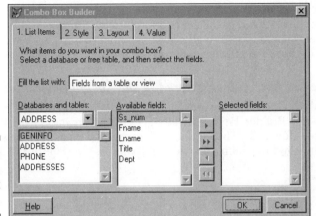

Figure 12-18:
The
Combo Box
Builder.

✔ With values from a table

✔ With values entered in the Combo Box Builder

✔ With values stored in an *array,* which is a place in your computer's memory where values can be stored temporarily until you turn off your computer or close Visual FoxPro

You tell Visual FoxPro which way you want to fill the list by choosing a value from the Fill the list with drop-down list in the Combo Box Builder dialog box. In this section, I show you how to fill the list with values stored in a table and how to enter values straight into the Combo Box Builder. Filling the list from an array is a little too complicated for now, and you won't use arrays until you master the more advanced features of Visual FoxPro.

Filling the list from values in a table

The drop-down list of a combo box contains values that are selected by the person who uses the form. Visual FoxPro stuffs the selected value into the text area of the combo box. The values that appear in the drop-down list can be values that were previously entered in a field of a table.

If you've assigned a database to the form, the name of the database already appears in the combo box of the Combo Box Builder, along with a list of tables contained in the database and the available fields.

If you haven't assigned a database to the form, click the button that appears to the right of the Databases and Tables list in the List Item tab of the Combo Box Builder; Visual FoxPro displays the Open dialog box. Choose the database that you want to use for the combo box; then click OK to return to the Combo Box Builder. Visual FoxPro displays the names of the tables and available fields in the Combo Box Builder.

Double-click the names in the Available fields list to use the field(s) in the combo box's drop-down list. Visual FoxPro moves the selected fields to the Selected fields list, and you're all set. Visual FoxPro fills the combo box with the values of these fields when you run the form.

Filling the list from values entered in the Combo Box Builder

You can enter values directly into the combo box's drop-down list by using the Combo Box Builder. First, choose Data entered by hand from the Fill the list with drop-down list. The List Items tab changes dramatically, showing columns and rows in which you can enter values. (See Figure 12-19.)

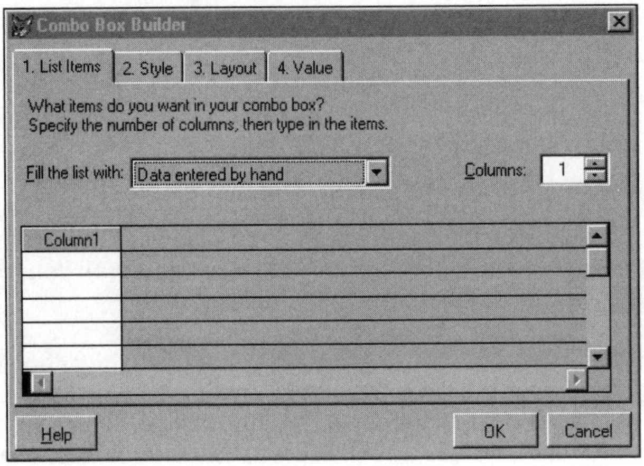

Figure 12-19: The List Items tab displays columns and rows in which you can enter values.

The List Items tab contains a drop-down list that you use to tell Visual FoxPro the number of columns that you want in the Columns area. The default setting (1 column) is sufficient for most of your forms because you rarely use more than a one column list.

Place the insertion point in the first row of the column and begin entering values. Each row is a separate value in the drop-down list. When you complete the list, Visual FoxPro is ready to stuff those values into the drop-down list.

Entering values by hand versus by field value

You may be scratching your head, wondering whether entering values by hand or by field value is better for placing values in a combo box's drop-down list. The answer is that it depends on the situation. Values entered by hand become part of the combo box and of the form, whereas values in a table are part of the database. In most cases, changing a value in a database is easier than changing the form.

Following are a few guidelines that can help you make the best choice:

✔ If the information in the drop-down list **changes frequently,** consider placing those values in a table. A list of customer numbers and names, for example, changes often and should be stored in a table rather than entered in the drop-down list by hand.

✔ If the information in the drop-down list **doesn't change often,** enter those values in the drop-down list by hand. Abbreviations of state names, for example, are values that aren't going to change.

✔ If the information in the drop-down list **is used by other parts of the form or by other forms, reports, and queries,** store the information in a table. Otherwise, you'll have the same information stored in more than one place — a nightmare to maintain.

Using the Style tab of the Combo Box Builder

Options in the Style tab, shown in Figure 12-20, allow you to decide how the combo box appears in the form and how the combo box is used by the person who uses your form.

Here's how to set the style for a combo box:

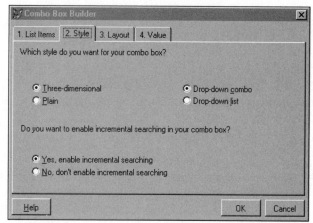

Figure 12-20: The Style tab of the Combo Box Builder.

1. **Select the appropriate radio button to specify whether you want the combo box to be three-dimensional or plain.**

   I always select Three-dimensional to give the combo box a professional appearance.

2. **Select the appropriate radio button to specify whether you want the text box to appear as part of the combo box or whether you want to display the drop-down list.**

   • Select Drop-down combo if you want the traditional combo box, which includes the text box in which someone who uses your form can enter a value.

   • Select Drop-down list if you want all the selections to be made from the drop-down list.

3. **Turn incremental searching on or off by selecting the appropriate radio button.**

   Each time you enter a letter in the text portion of the combo box, Visual FoxPro searches the values in the drop-down list, trying to match the letter. So if you type M, the old fox looks for the first occurrence of *M* as the first letter of values in the drop-down list and then displays the value in the text box of the combo box. Visual FoxPro continues the process as each letter is entered.

Using the Layout tab of the Combo Box Builder

Many options aren't in the Layout tab because the Layout tab is used to change the width of the column of the drop-down list or to hide a column.

You may want to adjust the column width to make the drop-down list more appealing. Here's how to adjust the width:

1. **Make sure that you've assigned fields to the Combo Box control by using the List Items tab in the Combo Box Builder.**

   Refer to the section "Using the List Items tab of the Combo Box Builder," earlier in this chapter.

2. **Display the Combo Box Builder (see Combo Box Control Step 1) and then click the Layout tab.**

   The field name that you selected in the List Items tab appears as a column heading.

3. **Move the mouse pointer to the right side of the column until the mouse pointer changes to a line with arrows at both ends.**

4. **Hold down the left mouse button and drag the mouse pointer to the new position.**

5. **Release the mouse button.**

   The column width changes.

The other option in the Layout tab is a check box that tells Visual FoxPro to adjust the combo box width to display all the columns of the value list. Check the check box if you want all the columns of the drop-down list to be displayed at the same time. If you don't check the check box, only part of the values in the list are displayed. The user must use the horizontal scroll bar to see the other values.

Using the Value tab of the Combo Box Builder

The Value tab of the Combo Box Builder, shown in Figure 12-21, tells Visual FoxPro what value in the drop-down list you want to store in a table and which field of the table you want to receive the value.

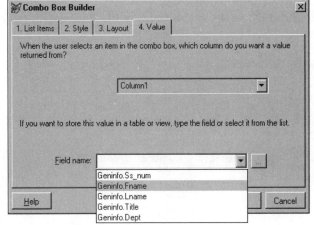

Figure 12-21:
The Value
tab of the
Combo Box
Builder.

Earlier in this chapter (refer to the section "Combo Box Control"), I show you how to enter more than one column of information in a drop-down list. You can enter the data manually or assign fields of a table to the drop-down list by using the Combo Box Builder.

Use the bottom combo box of the Value tab to choose the field in which the value will be stored. If you don't see any field names, you haven't assigned a table to either the form or the combo box. Click the button that appears to the right of the Field name combo box to display the Open dialog box, in which you can select the database.

List Box Control

The List Box control is just like a Combo Box control, except that a List Box control doesn't permit a user to enter text in the control. Instead, the person who uses your form must choose an item that appears in the list box. The list box displays items in a scrollable list.

 The button that represents the List Box control appears to the right of the Combo Box button in the Form Controls toolbar.

The best way to set the properties for the List Box control is to use the List Box Builder. Here's how to start the List Box Builder:

1. Place a List Box control in the form (refer to Chapter 11).

2. Click the List Box control to make the control active.

3. Right-click the control to display a shortcut menu.

4. Choose Builder to display the List Box Builder, shown in Figure 12-22.

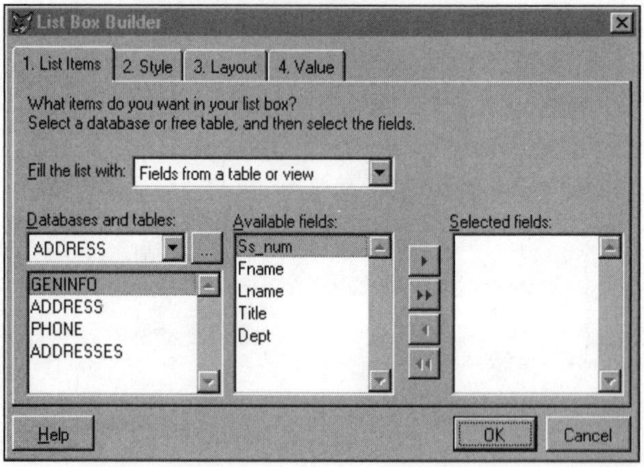

Figure 12-22:
The List Box
Builder.

The List Box Builder is nearly identical to the Combo Box Builder. In fact, the two dialog boxes are the same except for the Style tab. The Style tab of the List Box Builder does not have the Drop-down combo and Drop-down list options.

Refer to the section "Combo Box Control," earlier in this chapter, if you have questions on how to change features of the list box.

Grid Control

At times, you want to display information from a database in a spread-sheetlike grid in your form, similar to the way that data looks when you browse a table. I show you how to browse a table in Chapter 3.

 You can easily display information in rows and columns by using the Grid control. The button that represents the Grid control is just below the Combo Box button in the Form Controls toolbar.

The best way to set the properties for the Grid control is to use the Grid Builder. Here's how to start the Grid Builder:

1. Place a Grid control in the form (refer to Chapter 11).

2. Click the Grid control to make the control active.

3. Right-click the control to display a shortcut menu.

4. Choose Builder to display the Grid Builder, shown in Figure 12-23.

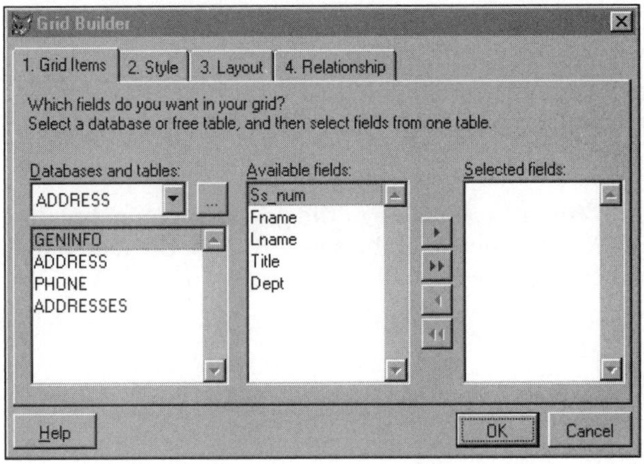

Figure 12-23:
The Grid
Builder.

You use the Grid Builder to assign fields to the grid and choose a style for the grid. The Grid Builder consists of four tabs: Grid Items, Style, Layout, and Relationship.

The Grid Items tab is identical to the List Items tab of the Combo Box Builder; you use this tab to select the fields that will be displayed in the grid. If you selected a database for the form, Visual FoxPro displays the available fields. If you didn't, you assign a database by using the Grid Builder. Use the same technique that you use to assign a database to a Combo Box control. (Refer to the section "Combo Box Control," earlier in this chapter.)

The Style tab, shown in Figure 12-24, determines the style of the grid. The Style tab is fun to use because it shows you a sample of how the grid is going to look in your form. Visual FoxPro changes the sample style to match the style that you choose from the Style list.

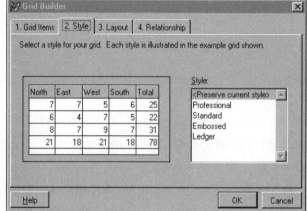

Figure 12-24:
The Style
tab of the
Grid
Builder.

Visual FoxPro has four grid styles: Professional, Standard, Emboss, and Ledger. I simply click a style and then look at the way that Visual FoxPro changes the style in the sample. When I find the style that I like, I move on to the Layout tab.

The Layout tab contains a sample of the grid that you're building. (See Figure 12-25.) Columns heads in the same grid are the field names that you selected for the grid. Rows are filled with actual data that is stored in the field.

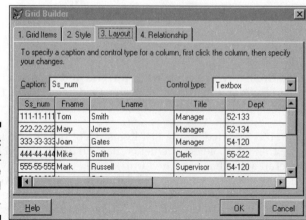

Figure 12-25:
The Layout
tab of the
Grid
Builder.

The purpose of the Layout tab is to fine-tune the appearance of the grid. When you select a column, the name of the field appears in the <u>C</u>aption text box. You can enter your own caption by highlighting the field name and then entering the new caption.

You also can change the control type that is used to display the information in the grid. I suggest that you use the default control type until you become a whiz at using the Grid Builder.

You also can change the width of the columns in the grid. Use the same technique that you use to change the width of the columns in the Combo Box Builder. (Refer to the section "Using the Layout tab of the Combo Box Builder," earlier in this chapter.)

You can use the Relationship tab to join multiple forms. You don't need to use any options in the Relationship tab until you create complex forms for your database.

Line Control

Try dressing up your form with lines. A line in the right place can add a professional touch to the overall appearance of the form. Don't go overboard by drawing lines everywhere you find an open space in a form. Instead, use your common sense and position a line when you think it will help to organize information in the form.

 The button that represents the Line control appears in the Form Controls toolbar.

You can change the length or slope of the line, or the angle of the line, by clicking the size boxes and resizing the line. I show you how to resize controls in Chapter 11.

The Line control's Properties window contains a host of properties. You probably will use only two of those properties: `BorderStyles` and `BorderWidth`. The `BorderStyles` property determines the style of the line that appears in your form. The `BorderWidth` property determines the thickness of the line.

Here's how to set the `BorderStyles` property:

1. **Click the Line control to make the line active (refer to Chapter 11).**

2. **Click the Properties button in the Form Designer toolbar to display the Properties window.**

    3. Click the All tab or the Layout tab.

    4. Click the `BorderStyles` property.

    5. Choose a line style from the combo box at the top of the Properties window, shown in Figure 12-26.

       Visual FoxPro changes the style of the Line control in the form.

Figure 12-26:
Choose a
line style
from the
combo box
in the
Properties
window.

You set the line width almost the same way that you set the style of the line, except that you click the `BorderWidth` property in Step 4 and enter a number in the text box in Step 5.

Don't try to measure the line width — you'll be just wasting your time. Instead, increase the value of the number to increase the line width. Keep increasing the number until you find the width that you need. (Decreasing the number decreases the width of the line, but you probably figured that out already.) Visual FoxPro automatically adjusts the width of the Line control in the form accordingly.

Shape Control

You use the Shape control button in the Form Controls toolbar to place squares, rectangles, or circles in your form. These elements are perfect for enhancing the appearance of the form.

You don't get a choice of shapes in the toolbar; every Shape control starts out as a square. You change a square to a rectangle by clicking the control and resizing the square with the size boxes. Changing a square into a circle, though is tricky, and the size boxes won't help you at all. You need to set the `Curvature` property of the Shape control. You can find the `Curvature` property in the All tab or Layout tab of the Properties window. The `Curvature` property's value is a number. Without getting into sophisticated measurement, I'll say that the higher the number, the more the corners of the square (or rectangle) become curved.

 You need to practice changing the `Curvature` property's value a few times before you get the hang of creating a circle from a square. Try changing the value to 60, and see whether you like what Visual FoxPro draws in your form (see Figure 12-27). Lower the value to 30, and notice the difference (see Figure 12-28). The maximum number that you can enter is 99.

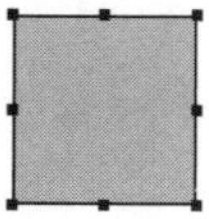

Figure 12-27:
The Shape control with the `Curvature` property's value set to 60.

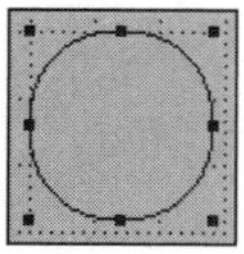

Figure 12-28:
The Shape control with the `Curvature` property's value set to 30.

More than a few properties control various aspects of the Shape control. I find that I always need to change five of these properties. I never touch the other properties, and you'll probably have the same experience.

The `Curvature` property, which I discuss in the preceding section, is one of the five properties that I use frequently. The other four are `BorderStyle`, `BorderWidth`, `FillStyle`, and `FillColor`.

You set the BorderStyle and the BorderWidth properties the same way that you set these properties for the Line control. Review the section "Line Control," earlier in this chapter, for more information about these properties.

The FillStyle property determines the pattern that is used to fill the shape. You can choose Horizontal and have Visual FoxPro fill the shape with straight horizontal lines, for example.

Locate the FillStyle property in the All tab or the Layout tab of the Properties window, and drop down the list at the top of the dialog box to see the complete list of fill styles. Try each style and see whether you like the results.

If you become confused and want to get back to where you started, choose Transparent. Visual FoxPro removes all fill from the shape and allows the background color of the form to flow through the shape.

The FillColor property sets the color for the shape. Click the FillColor property in the All tab or Layout tab of the Properties window; Visual FoxPro displays the Color dialog box. You saw the Color dialog box in Chapter 11. You choose the color for the Shape control the same way that you choose the color for the form.

Chapter 13

Making Controls Do Something

*P*robably the most enjoyable part of Visual FoxPro is building a form for your database. The form is the face of your database, which you dress up by adding an assortment of controls to display and collect data.

In Chapter 11, I show you how to create and position controls in a form, but you're likely to wonder how you make the controls work with your database. That's the point of this chapter, which shows you how to make the controls in your form work with your database.

Displaying the Value of a Field

A table can hold a large number of records, but you can use only one record at a time. The record that you are currently using is called the *current record*. Visual FoxPro makes the first record of the table the current record when you open the table. The current record is identified by a right arrow in the left margin of the table, as shown in Figure 13-1. You can see the cursor when you click the table.

You can refer to the value of a field in the current record by specifying in a control in a form the name of the table and the name of the field. Geninfo.fname, for example, tells Visual FoxPro that you want the value of the fname field of the current record in the geninfo table.

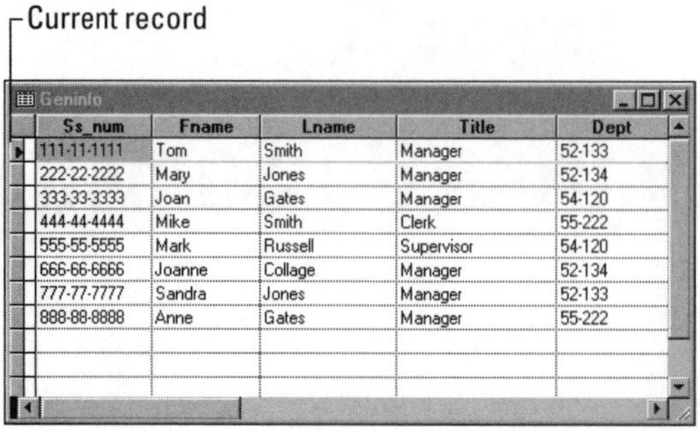

Current record

Figure 13-1:
The right
arrow in the
left margin
of the table
indicates
the current
record.

Ss_num	Fname	Lname	Title	Dept
111-11-1111	Tom	Smith	Manager	52-133
222-22-2222	Mary	Jones	Manager	52-134
333-33-3333	Joan	Gates	Manager	54-120
444-44-4444	Mike	Smith	Clerk	55-222
555-55-5555	Mark	Russell	Supervisor	54-120
666-66-6666	Joanne	Collage	Manager	52-134
777-77-7777	Sandra	Jones	Manager	52-133
888-88-8888	Anne	Gates	Manager	55-222

Assigning a Field Value to a Control

You can assign a field in a table to a control by using the `ControlSource` property of the control. (Refer to Chapters 11 and 12 for more information on controls.) In this section, I show you how to assign a field by using the Text Box control because you use the Text Box control most of the time.

To assign a field by using the Text Box control:

1. **Display the Form Designer and place a Text Box control in the form for each field that you want to display.**

   Chapter 11 explains how to display the Form Designer and shows you how to place controls in a form.

2. **Click the Data Environment button in the Form Controls toolbar.**

   This button is the second one in the toolbar. When you click it, Visual FoxPro displays the Add Table or View dialog box and the Data Environment dialog box.

3. **In the Add Table or View dialog box, double-click the table names that contain the fields you want to assign to the controls.**

4. **Click the Close button after you select all the tables that you need.**

   The Add Table or View dialog box disappears. The Data Environment dialog box remains on-screen.

5. **Click the Properties button on the Forms Toolbar to display the Properties window.**

6. **In the form, select the Text Box control to which you want to assign the field.**

   Small boxes surround the Text Box control.

7. **Click the** `ControlSource` **property in the All tab of the Properties window to assign a field to the Text Box control.**

8. **Click the down-arrow button of the combo box located below the tabs.**

   Visual FoxPro displays a list of available field names, as shown in Figure 13-2.

Figure 13-2: A list of all available fields that you can assign to the Text Box control appears in the combo box.

9. **Select the field name in the Property window that you want to assign to the Text Box control.**

   The name of the table and the name of the field appear in the property window alongside the `ControlSource` property.

10. **Click the Run button in Visual FoxPro toolbar to run the form.**

    The value of the first record in the table of the field you selected appears in the form in the Text Box control.

11. **Choose File⇨Close to close the form that is running.**

    You return to the Form Designer.

Moving to the Next Record

In this section, you place a command button in the form to instruct Visual FoxPro to move to the next record in the table. Follow these steps:

1. **Display the Form Designer and create a command button with the caption Next.**

   Refer to Chapter 11 if you need help with displaying the Form Designer or creating a command button.

2. **Right-click the Next command button to display a shortcut menu.**

3. **Choose Code to display the Code window.**

4. **Enter the following commands in the Code window:**

```
SKIP
IF EOF()
GO TOP
ENDIF
FORM1.REFRESH
```

5. **Click the Run button in the Visual FoxPro toolbar to run the form.**

   The value of the next record in the table of the field that you selected appears in the form in the Text Box control.

6. **Choose File⇨Close to close the form.**

   You return to the Form Designer.

The SKIP command tells Visual FoxPro to move to the next record in the table. There is always a chance that the next record is the end of the table, so you ask Visual FoxPro whether the table has any more records by using the EOF() function. (A *function* is a hunk of instructions that Visual FoxPro already knows how to perform.) The EOF() comes back with a true or false answer, indicating whether you've hit the end of the table.

When Visual FoxPro reaches the last record, the GO TOP command tells it to jump to the first record.

When Visual FoxPro moves to the next record, the value of the Text Box control changes to the value of the assigned field of the record because you told Visual FoxPro to refresh the value when you used the FORM1.REFRESH command.

Moving to the Preceding Record

If you can tell Visual FoxPro to go to the following record, you also can tell it to move to the preceding record. Here's how you tell Visual FoxPro to move back one record in the table:

1. **Display the Form Designer and create another command button with the caption Previous.**

   Refer to Chapter 11 if you need help with displaying the Form Designer or creating a command button.

2. **Right-click the Previous command button to display a shortcut menu.**

3. **Choose <u>C</u>ode to display the Code window.**

4. **Enter the following commands in the Code window:**

```
SKIP -1
IF BOF()
GO BOTTOM
ENDIF
FORM1.REFRESH
```

5. **Click the Run button in the Visual FoxPro toolbar to run the form.**

   The value of the previous record in the table of the field that you selected appears in the form in the Text Box control.

6. **Choose <u>F</u>ile⇨<u>C</u>lose to close the form.**

   You return to the Form Designer.

The SKIP-1 command tells Visual FoxPro to move to the preceding record in the table. The preceding record, however, could be the beginning of the table, which means that the current record is the first record in the table and that there is no preceding record to move to. So after giving the SKIP-1 command, use the BOF() function to see whether you're at the beginning of the table.

The BOF() function performs almost the same task as the EOF() function (refer to the preceding section), but the function returns true if you've reached the beginning of the table and false if you're not at the beginning of the table.

If you're at the beginning of the table, you immediately tell Visual FoxPro to move to the bottom of the table by issuing the GO BOTTOM command.

When you reach the preceding record, the FORM1.REFRESH command makes the value of the Text Box control reflect the value of the assigned field in the record.

Moving to the Bottom of the Table

If you read the preceding section, you can probably write the command to tell Visual FoxPro to move to the last record of the table. To do so:

1. **Display the Form Designer and create another command button with the caption Bottom.**

   Refer to Chapter 11 if you need help with displaying the Form Designer or creating a command button.

2. **Right-click the Bottom command button to display a shortcut menu.**

3. **Choose Code to display the Code window.**

4. **Enter the following commands in the Code window:**

   ```
   GO BOTTOM
   FORM1.REFRESH
   ```

5. **Click the Run button in the Visual FoxPro toolbar to run the form.**

   The value of the last record in the table of the field that you selected appears in the form in the Text Box control.

6. **Choose File⇨Close to close the form.**

   You return to the Form Designer.

Appending a New Record to the Table

Inserting a new record into a table is a two-step process called *appending* a record to the table. First, you open a blank record at the bottom of the table. Then you stuff values into the blank record. Here's how you append a new record:

1. **Display the Form Designer and create another command button with the caption Append.**

   Refer to Chapter 11 if you need help with displaying the Form Designer or creating a command button.

2. **Right-click the Bottom command button to display a shortcut menu.**

3. **Choose Code to display the Code window.**

4. **Enter the following commands in the Code window:**

   ```
   APPEND BLANK
   FORM1.REFRESH
   ```

5. **Click the Run button in the Visual FoxPro toolbar to run the form.**

   The value of the record in the table of the field that you selected appears in the form in the Text Box control.

6. **Choose File⇨Close to close the form.**

   You return to the Form Designer.

When you click the Append command button, Visual FoxPro executes the APPEND BLANK command and inserts a new record at the end of the table. The FORM1.REFRESH command tells Visual FoxPro to replace the value of the Text Box control with the value of the field in the new record that is assigned to the Text Box control. That field has no value, of course, because you haven't entered information in the new record. The Text box is empty. When you enter information in the field, Visual FoxPro automatically saves the information to the table.

Deleting a Record

You can delete any record displayed in your form by issuing the DELETE command. Create another command button in the form and set the caption to Delete.

A record is marked for deletion when the DELETE command is issued. When you enter the command SET DELETED ON in the Command Window (you display the Command Window by pressing Ctrl+F2), Visual FoxPro treats records that are marked for deletion as though they do not exist in the database.

Entering the command SET DELETED OFF in the Command Window displays all the records, including those that are marked for deletion. In Chapter 4, I show you how to remove records marked for deletion from your table and how to recall those records.

For now, simply mark records for deletion by using a Delete command button in your form. Follow these steps:

1. **Display the Form Designer and create another command button with the caption Delete.**

   Refer to Chapter 11 if you need help with displaying the Form Designer or creating a command button.

2. **Right-click the Delete command button to display a shortcut menu.**

3. **Choose Code to display the Code window.**

4. **Enter the following commands in the Code window:**

```
DELETE
SKIP
IF EOF()
GO TOP
ENDIF
FORM1.REFRESH
```

     5. Click the Run button in the Visual FoxPro toolbar to run the form.

     The current record is deleted and the value of the next record in the table of the field that you selected appears in the form in the Text Box control.

     6. Choose File⇨Close to close the form.

     You return to the Form Designer.

The DELETE command tells Visual FoxPro to mark the current record for deletion. Next, Visual FoxPro moves to the next record and checks to see whether it has reached the end of the table; if so, the program moves to the top of the table. When a record is made current, Visual FoxPro refreshes the value of the field to the Text Box control in the form.

Part IV
Reports, Labels, and Graphs

The 5th Wave   By Rich Tennant

Life in Mousepad Land:
The Drive-In Theater

Well, the special
effects are great,
but there's not
much of a story.

In this part . . .

Some whiz kids see the world slowly evolving into a paperless society, in which all information is communicated electronically. (I'm sure that printer manufacturers disagree, however, as do those people who like to say, "The check is in the mail.")

For now, however, you need to print information on paper in the form of reports and mailing labels, and you need to mail-merge information into form letters. You also need to display some information as a graph rather than a series of boring numbers.

Visual FoxPro can print reports and mailing labels, handle mail merges (with the help of your word processor), and convert drab numbers to pretty, informative graphs of various shapes and sizes. In Part IV, you find out how to do all these tasks.

Chapter 14

Creating Reports and Labels

● ●

In This Chapter

▶ Using the Report Designer

▶ Linking a report to a database

▶ Displaying the results of a query in a report

▶ Creating mailing labels

▶ Choosing the right label for the job

▶ Merging data into a form letter

● ●

There's an old saying that you can't take it with you. Well, old sayings sometimes are wrong, especially when you're talking about information that you've stuffed into your database. Granted, you can't take the information stored in your database to the great beyond, but you can take the data anywhere you want down here.

Like most people who use Visual FoxPro all the time, you want to jot down — on paper — information that pops up on-screen as a response to a query or from a simple browse of the data in the tables of your database.

Put down the pencil and take the paper and shove it — into your printer, that is. Visual FoxPro can write the information on the paper for you in the form of a report. In this chapter, I show you how to create custom reports with Visual FoxPro.

Creating a Quick Report

Sometimes, you're in a rush to produce a report that contains information from a database. You don't have time to let your creative juices flow; you need the report now, and you have no time to waste.

If you find yourself in a bind, Visual FoxPro can do the work for you by creating a quick report. A quick report isn't fancy, but it does contain all the data that you want to see from the tables that you assigned to the report.

Here's how to produce a quick report:

1. **Choose File⇨New to display the New dialog box.**

2. **Select the Report radio button.**

3. **Click the New file button.**

   Visual FoxPro displays the Report Designer.

4. **Choose Report⇨Quick Report.**

   Visual FoxPro displays the Open dialog box.

5. **In the Tables in Database list, double-click the name of the table that you want to use for the report.**

   Visual FoxPro displays the Quick Report dialog box, shown in Figure 14-1.

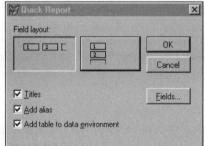

Figure 14-1:
The Quick
Report
dialog box.

6. **In the Field layout section, choose a layout style.**

   The Horizontal button is selected by default; you can select the Vertical button if you want.

7. **Choose Fields to display the Field Picker dialog box, shown in Figure 14-2.**

8. **In the All fields list, double-click the fields that you want to place in the report.**

   Visual FoxPro moves those fields to the Selected fields list.

9. **Double-click the field names in the Selected fields list to remove the fields from the report (in case you selected the wrong field in Step 8).**

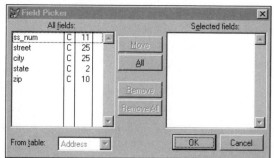

Figure 14-2:
The Field
Picker
dialog box.

10. **Click OK to return to the Quick Report dialog box.**

11. **Click OK to display the quick report in the Report Designer.**

12. **Choose Report⊳Run Report to run the report**

Creating a Customized Report

Most of your reports will be quick reports until you want to move up to the better life — or at least to fancier reports, in which you control everything that appears in them. In that case, you'll want to create customized reports. A customized report requires you to make more decisions about the way that Visual FoxPro displays the information in your database.

How do you decide whether to use a quick report or a customized report? Suppose that your boss asks you for a list of all the people who work in your department. Don't bother designing a customized report; use a quick report (assuming that the names of all the employees are in your database). If your boss asks for a weekly employee attendance report, however, you should create a customized report because you'll use the same report each week.

In a customized report, you tell Visual FoxPro which database and tables or views to use in the report, and you choose the fields to be included in the report. You also make many more choices. In the section "Creating a Report," later in this chapter, I show you how to make those choices smart ones.

Using the Report Designer

You assemble a customized report from objects by using the Report Designer. The Report Designer displays a model of the report, which you use to get the report looking just the way that you want.

The model report, which appears in the center of the Report Designer, is divided into bands. The default bands are

- ✔ Page Header
- ✔ Detail
- ✔ Page Footer

You can include additional bands in the report; I show you how to do that in the section "Creating a Report," later in this chapter.

Objects such as labels and fields are placed in the form in the appropriate band. Labels that are to appear at the top of every page are placed in the Page Header band, fields typically are placed in the Detail band, and page numbers that are to appear at the bottom of every page are placed in the Page Footer band.

Creating a Report

You see computer-generated reports when you see bills in the mail, bank statements, and various kinds of printed information at work. Any printed document containing information that is produced by a computer can be called a *report*.

A report is composed of various objects, such as labels and other controls. (I talk about controls in Chapter 12.) Here are the objects that you use in your Visual FoxPro reports:

- ✔ **Labels:** A *label* is text that is not available in the database, so you must type the text in the report where you want the text to appear.
- ✔ **Fields:** A *field* is data in a database that Visual FoxPro automatically places in a report.
- ✔ **Shapes:** *Shapes* are lines, rectangles, and rounded rectangles that you can use to dress up your reports.
- ✔ **Pictures:** *Pictures* are photos, logos, and other images that increase the professional appearance of the report.

You create a report by using the Report Designer, which displays a blank copy of the report divided into sections called *bands*. A band shows you where the titles, data, and summary information appear in the report. You find more information on report bands in the section "Using the Report Designer," earlier in this chapter.

You place objects in the report by clicking the buttons in the Report Controls toolbar that represent the objects and then dragging the objects into the report. When you're satisfied with the way that the report looks, you can have Visual FoxPro assemble all the data from the database and print the data in the report.

The easiest way to create a report is to open a database and tell Visual FoxPro which tables or views of the database you want to use for the report. In Chapter 7, I show you that a view is a combination of several tables of a database.

Technically, a report does not have to be linked to a database because you can create a report that does not contain any data. You can enter only labels and no fields in a report; Visual FoxPro prints the text of the labels on the page.

In this chapter, you stick with using a report to display both labels and fields because you'll create similar reports most of the time. Here's how you create a report:

1. **Open the database that you want to use for the report.**

   Visual FoxPro displays the Database Designer.

2. **Choose File⇨New to display the New dialog box, select Report, and then click the New file button**

   Visual FoxPro displays the Report Designer, shown in Figure 14-3.

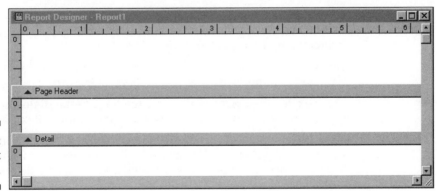

Figure 14-3:
The Report
Designer.

3. **Click the Data Environment button in the Report Controls toolbar.**

   Visual FoxPro displays the Data Environment dialog box. (See Figure 14-4.)

Figure 14-4:
The Data
Environment
dialog box.

4. **Right-click anywhere in the Data Environment dialog box to display a shortcut menu and then choose <u>A</u>dd.**

   Visual FoxPro displays the Add Table or View dialog box, shown in Figure 14-5.

Figure 14-5:
The Add
Table or
View dialog
box.

5. **In the <u>T</u>ables in database area, double-click the tables that you want to include in the report and then click Close.**

   The Add Table or View dialog box closes. The Data Environment dialog box and the Report Designer remain open on-screen.

6. **Choose <u>F</u>ile⇨Page Set<u>u</u>p to display the Page Setup dialog box, shown in Figure 14-6; when you finish setting the options, click OK.**

   Note: Before you begin to place objects in the report, you should make sure that the page is the size and style that you require for the report. You can choose the number of columns that appear in the report and set the margin.

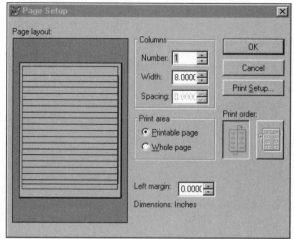

In this dialog, you can change several settings:

- **Use the Number spinner to change the number of columns, if necessary.** You can click the spinner arrows or simply type the number that you want in the text box. The default number of columns (1) is sufficient for most reports, so you may not need to change the value in the Number spinner.

- **Use the Left margin spinner to set the left margin.** You can set the margin at 0.5 inch, 1 inch, or whatever you want.

- **Determine the right margin by subtraction.** Subtract the Left margin and Width settings from 8.5 (the width, in inches, of a standard sheet of paper). The difference is the right margin. If you want the margin to be wider or narrower, spin the Width down or up.

7. Click the Report Controls Toolbar button.

Visual FoxPro displays the Report Controls toolbar, shown in Figure 14-7. This toolbar contains buttons for objects that you can use in your report.

8. **Choose Report⇨Title/Summary to display the Title/Summary dialog box, shown in Figure 14-8; select the Title band check box and then click OK to return to the Report Designer.**

Visual FoxPro displays a Title band in the Report Designer.

9. **Click the Label button in the Report Controls toolbar and then click the spot in the Title band where you want the title text to begin and enter text.**

You also can place labels elsewhere on the report by repeating this step.

You can enter no more than 256 characters.

Note: A *label* is any text that you want to type in the report. In this context, the term *label* refers to the text that identifies a field rather than the text that you affix to a sticky piece of paper.

10. **Click the label whose font you want to change and then choose Format⇨Font to display the Font dialog box, shown in Figure 14-9; using the list boxes, select the Font, Font Style, and Size options that you want to use and then click OK to close the Font dialog box.**

You also can select color for the characters that you type in the report and specify underline or strikethrough formatting effects. (Strikethrough formatting is a line placed horizontally across the character; you probably won't need to use it.)

11. **Click the label whose text you want to align and then choose Format⇨Text Alignment to display the Text Alignment submenu, shown in Figure 14-10.**

Choose Left, Center, or Right to align text within the space reserved for the label, as follows:

- **Left:** Places the first letter of the label on the left side of the space reserved for the label

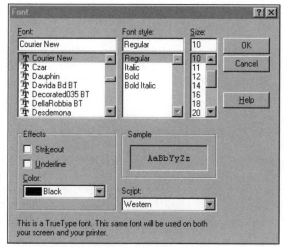

Figure 14-9:
The Font
dialog box.

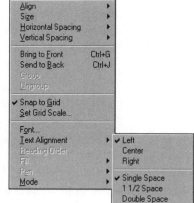

Figure 14-10:
The Text
Alignment
submenu.

- **Center:** Places the text in the center of the space reserved for the label

- **Right:** Places the last letter of the label on the right side of the space reserved for the label

You also can click Single Space, 1¹/₂ Space, or Double Space to set the spacing of the lines of text within the space reserved for the label.

12. Click the label whose mode you want to change and choose Format➪Mode to display the Mode submenu.

You use the Mode submenu to specify whether the background of the label is opaque or transparent, as follows:

- *Opaque* means that the background of the report (in most cases, the color of the paper on which the report is printed) does not show through the background of the label. Suppose that the paper is white and that the background color of the label is green. If the mode of the label is set to opaque, the background color of the label prints as green (assuming that the report is printed on a color printer).

- *Transparent* means that the background of the report blends through the background of the label. If the mode of the label is set to transparent, the background color of the label is the same color as the background of the report — in this example, white.

Choose Opaque (to prevent the background of the label from blending with the background of the report) or Transparent (to allow the background of the report to be used as the background of the label).

13. **In the Data Environment dialog box, click the field of the table that you want to place in the report; then drag the field name to the report and release the mouse button.**

    Be sure that you link a database and a table or view to your report before you attempt to position a field object in a report. If you don't, you won't find any table in the Data Environment dialog box.

    The field appears in the report.

    Visual FoxPro uses the default font, style, and mode to display the field in the report. You can change these settings by using the techniques that I show you in Steps 24–33.

14. **Choose Report⇨Title/Summary to display the Title/Summary dialog box (refer to Figure 14-8, earlier in this chapter) and select the Summary band check box; click OK to return to the Report Designer.**

    The Summary band contains information that appears at the end of the report, such as a grand total or a count of items that appear in the report.

    Visual FoxPro displays a Summary band in the Report Designer.

15. **Click the Field Control button (the *ab* button) in the Report Controls toolbar and place the Field Control on the report where you want calculations to appear such as the total value of a field in all the records of a table.**

    Typically, you'll place the calculation in the Summary band. Visual FoxPro displays the Report Expression dialog box. (See Figure 14-11.)

16. **Click the button (the button with three dots) to the right of the Expression text box to display the Expression Builder; in the Fields list box, double-click the field name that you want to use in the calculation and then click OK to return to the Report Expression dialog box.**

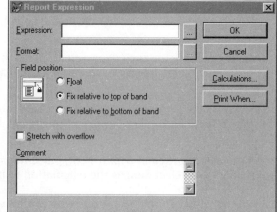

Figure 14-11:
You use the
Report
Expression
dialog box
to create a
calculated
field.

17. Click the Calculations button and then select the radio button that represents the type of calculation that you want to perform on the field; click OK to return to the Report Expression dialog box.

Visual FoxPro displays the Calculate Field dialog box, shown in Figure 14-12.

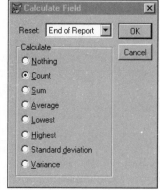

Figure 14-12:
The
Calculate
Field
dialog box.

To decide what radio button represents the type of calculation that you want to perfect, check out the following list:

- To find the number of employees in each department of the company, place the department number field in the group band (see the section "Grouping Data in a Report," later in this chapter) and select Count as the calculation to perform.

- To find the average salary for each department, place the salary field in the group band and select Average as the calculation to perform.

- To find the highest salary for each department, place the salary field in the group band and select Highest as the calculation to perform.

- To find the lowest salary for each department, place the salary field in the group band and select Lowest as the calculation to perform.

- To find the total salary for each department, place the salary field in the group band and select Sum as the calculation to perform.

18. **Click the button to the right of the Format box (the button with three dots) and select the Numeric radio button (see Figure 14-13); click OK to return to the report.**

    Visual FoxPro displays the Format dialog box.

Figure 14-13:
Click the
Numeric
radio button
to see the
format
options for
numeric
calculations.

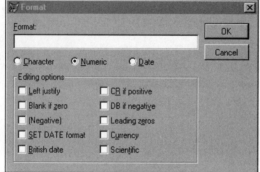

The Editing options in the Format dialog box display the format options for the numeric value of the calculation. These options are self-explanatory. Currency is the option that you'll use most of the time if you're calculating currency; the result appears with a dollar sign and a decimal point.

19. **Choose File⇨Save As to display the Save As dialog box where you enter the name for the report and then click Save to save the report.**

20. **Choose Report⇨Run Report to run the report.**

Working with Objects in a Report

Placing controls on a report is a rather straightforward process. However, you can easily become frustrated when you try to arrange controls in some kind of order on the report such as placing the Field control containing the first name next to the Field control that contains the last name.

Here are some shortcuts and tools that you can use to make aligning controls on the report a snap.

Aligning objects by using grid lines

Placing the first few objects in the report goes smoothly, but soon, you'll find yourself having a difficult time lining up the objects. Your hand-eye coordination sometimes isn't enough to align objects just the way you want.

If you have a little problem, try using grid lines in the report. Grid lines, which don't appear in your printed report, divide the report into a tic-tac-toe-like grid that you can use as a guide for positioning objects. You can drag objects to the same vertical grid line to align the objects, for example.

To display grid lines in a report, choose View⇨Grid Lines. Choose the command again to turn off the grid lines.

To change the number of lines used in the grid:

1. **Choose Format⇨Set Grid Scale.**

   Visual FoxPro displays the Set Grid Scale dialog box, shown in Figure 14-14.

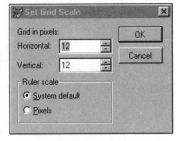

Figure 14-14:
The Set
Grid Scale
dialog box.

2. **Use the spinners or type the numbers to change the vertical and horizontal scale of the grid.**

   The default scale is just fine for most of your reports.

Don't worry about trying to measure the grid; experimenting produces the best results. Change the settings and then look at the grid. If you don't like what you see, change the settings again.

3. Click OK to return to the Report Designer.

Even better than simply using grid lines as guidelines is having Visual FoxPro place objects on the grid lines for you automatically. This feature is called *snapping* the object to the grid line. All you need to do is to drag the object close to the grid line and release the mouse button; Visual FoxPro aligns the object with the grid line.

To turn on the feature that automatically snaps objects to the closest grid line, choose Format⇨Snap to Grid. Choose Format⇨Snap to Grid again to turn off the feature.

Aligning objects by using position markers

Another way to position objects in a report is to use the position markers, which appear in the bottom-left corner of the Report Designer dialog box, shown in Figure 14-15. Position markers identify the location of the mouse pointer in the report and the location of the selected object.

Position markers indicate how objects are aligned in the report, as follows:

- ✔ Objects that have the same vertical position marker are stacked one on top of another.
- ✔ Objects that have the same horizontal position marker are aligned horizontally.

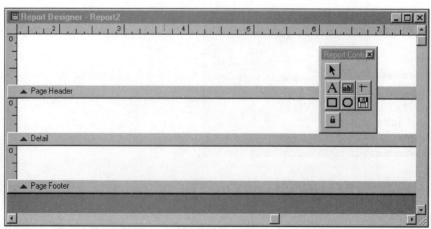

Figure 14-15:
Position markers display the exact position of selected objects in the report.

To turn on the position markers, choose <u>V</u>iew⇨Sho<u>w</u> Position. To turn off the position markers, choose <u>V</u>iew⇨Sho<u>w</u> Position again.

Aligning objects by using the Layout toolbar

You can align objects by using grid lines and position markers, and undoubtedly, you'll do a good job. An easier way to align objects in a report, however, is to use the Layout toolbar.

The Layout toolbar is nearly identical to the Layout toolbar that you use to align controls in a form. (I show you how to use the Layout toolbar in Chapter 11.) Select all the objects in the report that you want to align and then choose an alignment style by clicking the appropriate button the Layout toolbar. Visual FoxPro handles the rest of the alignment job.

Here's how to align objects in a report the easy way:

1. **Click the Report Controls Toolbar button in the Report toolbar.**

    Visual FoxPro displays the Report Controls toolbar. (Refer to Figure 14-7 earlier in this chapter.)

2. **Click the Layout Toolbar button.**

    Visual FoxPro displays the Layout toolbar, shown in Figure 14-16.

Figure 14-16:
The Layout toolbar.

3. **In the report, select the objects that you want to align.**

4. **Click the Alignment button.**

    Visual FoxPro aligns the objects for you.

Moving an object in a report

Here's how to move an object in a report:

1. **Click the Select Object button in the Report Controls toolbar.**

2. **Drag the label, field, or other object that you want to move to the new location.**

3. **Release the left mouse button.**

You can easily position any object in the report by dragging it with the mouse. At times, however, the grid lines interfere with the process, and you find yourself in a tug of war with Visual FoxPro. You move the object away from the grid line, and the program drags the object back to the grid line. You'll wonder whether the program has gone mad. No. Visual FoxPro is just doing what you told it to do.

If you run into this problem while you're repositioning objects in a report, choose Format⇨Snap to Grid to turn off the snapping feature. (Refer to the section "Aligning objects by using grid lines," earlier in this chapter.)

Resizing an object in a report

An object that you place in a report takes up space. In a sense, you reserve a specific amount of space in the report for the object when you place the object in the report. You can increase or decrease this space by resizing the object. Follow these steps:

1. **Click the Select Object button in the Report Controls toolbar.**

2. **Click the object to select it.**

   Visual FoxPro displays size boxes around the object.

3. **Drag one of the size boxes.**

   The object changes size according to the mouse movement.

4. **When the object is the size that you want, release the left mouse button.**

Deleting an object from a report

Don't worry if the report doesn't come out the way that you intended. Any object that you place in a report, you can easily delete.

You get only one chance to change your mind when you delete an object from a report. To place a deleted object back in the report, choose Edit⇨Undo immediately, before you do anything else. If you forget to choose Edit⇨Undo, you'll have to replace the object in the report yourself.

Here's how you delete an object:

1. **Click the Select Object button in the Report Controls toolbar.**

2. **Click the object that you want to delete.**

3. **Press the Delete key.**

   Visual FoxPro removes the object from the report.

Adding Color to a Report

You can add color to the objects that you place in a report, but keep in mind that you need a color printer to see the result in the printed report.

Each object can have two colors:

✔ Foreground, which is the color used for text and lines

✔ Background, which is the color used for everything that is not text or lines

You have a choice of 16 colors. Choosing a color is a breeze; simply click a color in the Color Palette.

Here's how to tell Visual FoxPro what color you want to use for an object:

1. **Click the Report Controls Toolbar button in the Report toolbar.**

   Visual FoxPro displays the Report Controls toolbar.

2. **Click the object in the report that you want to color.**

3. **Click the Color Palette Toolbar button in the Report Controls toolbar.**

   Visual FoxPro displays the Color Palette, shown in Figure 14-17.

Figure 14-17:
The Color
Palette.

4. **Click the first button, which is the Foreground Color button (the *T*), to choose foreground color, or click the second button, which is the Background Color button (the paint can), to choose background color.**

5. **Click the color that you want to use.**

   Visual FoxPro applies the color to the selected object.

Placing Shapes in a Report

You can spice up your report by placing shapes in key locations in the report, such as the first page. Use your creative talents to find the location that will make the reader of your report say, "Wow!"

You can place three kinds of shapes in a report:

  ✔ Line

  ✔ Rectangle

  ✔ Rounded rectangle

Click the button in the Report Controls toolbar that represents the shape you want to use; then put the shape in position in your report. You can move and resize the shape by using the same method that you use to move any object in your report.

Placing a line in a report

You place a line in your report the same way as you place a line in a form:

1. **Click the Report Controls Toolbar button in the Report toolbar.**

   Visual FoxPro displays the Report Controls toolbar.

2. **Click the Line button.**

3. **Click the spot in the report where you want the line to begin.**

4. **Holding down the left mouse button, drag the mouse to stretch the line in the report.**

5. **When the line is the length that you want it to be, release the mouse button.**

Placing a rectangle in a report

Here's how you place a rectangle in your report:

1. **Click the Report Controls Toolbar button in the Report toolbar.**

   Visual FoxPro displays the Report Controls toolbar.

 2. **Click the Rectangle button.**

3. **Click the spot in the report where you want the top-left corner of the rectangle to be.**

4. **Holding down the left mouse button, drag the mouse to position the rectangle in the report.**

5. **When the rectangle is the size that you want it to be, release the mouse button.**

Placing a rounded rectangle in a report

Here's how you place a rounded rectangle in your report:

1. **Click the Report Controls Toolbar button in the Report toolbar.**

   Visual FoxPro displays the Report Controls toolbar.

 2. **Click the Rounded Rectangle button.**

3. **Click the spot in the form where you want the top-left corner of the rounded rectangle to be.**

4. **Holding down the left mouse button, drag the mouse to position the rounded rectangle in the report.**

5. **When the rounded rectangle is the size that you want it to be, release the mouse button.**

Enhancing shapes in a report

You can enhance a shape to make your report more attractive by:

- ✔ **Adding color.** I show you how to add color to an object in "Adding Color to a Report," earlier in this chapter.

- ✔ **Using patterns to fill the shape.** You can use a bunch of interesting patterns, such as slanted and horizontal lines.

✔ **Changing the thickness of the line.** You can have Visual FoxPro use a solid line or one made up of dots and dashes.

✔ **Making the shape see-through.** The see-through look is determined by the mode setting.

Changing the fill of a shape

To change the pattern that fills a shape, follow these steps:

1. **Click the shape to select it.**

2. **Choose Format⇨Fill to display the Fill submenu.**

3. **Click the fill style that you want to use.**

You'll probably find that no fill (the default setting) works fine with most shapes that you place in a report. Avoid using a fill that is too busy, so that you don't distract the reader of your report from the information in the report.

Changing the pen used to draw a shape

The thickness of the line that is used to draw the shape is determined by the pen that Visual FoxPro uses to draw the shape in the report. No, the program doesn't use a ballpoint pen. In Visual FoxPro, *pen* is another name for the thickness of the line and the kind of line that is drawn.

To change the pen used for a shape, follow these steps:

1. **Click the shape to select it.**

2. **Choose Format⇨Pen to display the Pen submenu.**

3. **Click the pen style that you want to use.**

The 1-point pen style (the default setting), which produces a thin line, is acceptable for most shapes ion the report. Be careful not to make lines too thick, because they won't look right in the report.

Changing the mode used to draw a shape

You can change the mode of a shape to make it transparent or opaque. To change the mode of a shape:

1. **Click the shape to select it.**

2. **Choose Format⇨Mode to display the Mode submenu.**

3. **Click Opaque or Transparent.**

Opaque (the default setting) is fine for most reports.

Placing Pictures in a Report

 A *picture* is a special file that usually has the extension .BMP. If you search your disk, you'll probably come up with one or two pictures. You should even be able to find one called FOX.BMP, which is the picture of the fox logo.

You also can scan your own pictures by using a *scanner,* which is something like a copy machine. Instead of copying the picture onto paper, however, a scanner copies the picture into a file on your computer.

Placing a picture in your report is a snap when you have the picture file loaded on your disk. Follow these steps:

1. **Click the Report Controls Toolbar button in the Report toolbar.**

   Visual FoxPro displays the Report Controls toolbar.

 2. **Click the Picture/OLE Bound Control button.**

3. **Click the spot in the report where you want the picture to appear.**

   Visual FoxPro displays the Report Picture dialog box, shown in Figure 14-18.

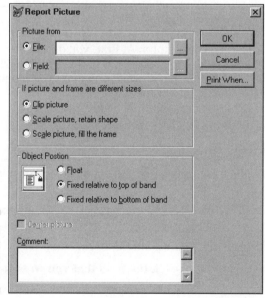

Figure 14-18:
The Report
Picture
dialog box.

4. **In the Picture From section at the top of the dialog box, select the button that appears to the right of the File text box (the button with three dots).**

   Visual FoxPro displays the Open dialog box.

5. **Click the name of the picture file that you want to use.**

6. **Click OK.**

   You return to the Report Picture dialog box.

7. **Click OK.**

   The picture appears in the report.

Grouping Data in a Report

You can group information in a table or a view by values in a field of a report. Suppose that you want to see all the information in the table grouped by department. Visual FoxPro can do the work for you. You see all the information about the department in the report, with the groups separated by blank lines.

Two new Group bands are automatically inserted into the report — one for a group header and one for a group footer. These new Group bands allow you to place group heading information in the header and group summary information and calculations in the footer. At first, you don't have room to place an object in the new bands. To make room in the group header or footer, just point to the band and drag down. If you make too much room, you can point to the band again and drag up.

Here's how you group data in a report:

1. **Choose Report⇨Data Grouping.**

   Visual FoxPro displays the Data Grouping dialog box, shown in Figure 14-19.

2. **Click the button with three dots to the right of the Group Expressions list box.**

   Visual FoxPro displays the Expression Builder.

3. **In the Fields list box, double-click the field that you want to use to group records in the report.**

4. **Click OK to return to the Data Grouping dialog box.**

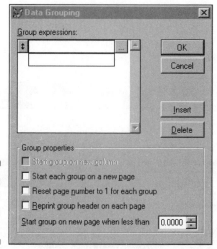

Figure 14-19:
The Data
Grouping
dialog box.

5. Choose grouping options at the bottom of the dialog box.

I suggest that you accept the default settings suggested by Visual
FoxPro, because I rarely need to change them. You can, however,
choose the following options:

- **Start each group on new page:** This option causes each group to
  start on a new page so that groups are not mixed in the same
  page. If you don't choose this option, each group follows the
  preceding group in the same page.

- **Reset page number to 1 for each group:** This option treats each
  group as a separate report by starting the paging numbering over
  again. If you don't choose this option, pages of the report are
  numbered sequentially.

- **Reprint group header on each page:** This option prints the group
  header on each page in which the group appears. If you don't
  choose this option, the group header is printed one time (when
  the group is first printed).

6. Click OK to return to the report.

Visual FoxPro inserts a Group band into the report, as shown in
Figure 14-20.

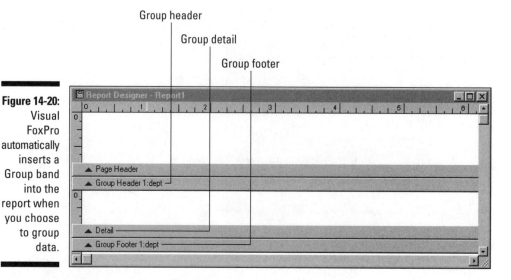

Group header

Group detail

Group footer

Figure 14-20:
Visual
FoxPro
automatically
inserts a
Group band
into the
report when
you choose
to group
data.

Changing the Font in a Report

The way that the text appears in a report is determined by the default font that Visual FoxPro uses. If you don't like the font, style, or size of the type, change the default settings.

I avoided changing the default font settings when I started to use Visual FoxPro; instead, I changed the font settings individually for all labels and field objects in the report. You don't have to make font changes the hard way, like I did; you can achieve the same result by changing the default settings. Follow these steps:

1. **Choose Report⇨Default Font.**

   Visual FoxPro displays the Font dialog box, shown in Figure 14-21.

2. **In the appropriate drop-down lists, select the Font, Font style, and Size options that you want to use.**

3. **Click OK to change the default font and return to the Report Designer.**

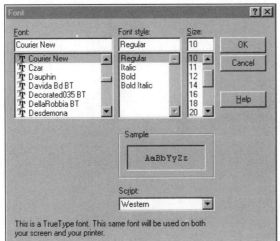

Figure 14-21:
The Font
dialog box.

Linking a Query to a Report

In Chapter 10, I show you how to use a query to ask Visual FoxPro to answer questions about information in your database. You can send the result of a query to a report.

You also can use a report as the destination for the result of a query. Follow these steps:

1. Create a new query or open an existing query.

See Chapter 10 if you're now sure how to create or open a query. The Query Designer appears.

2. Choose Query⇨Query Destination.

Visual FoxPro displays the Query Destination dialog box.

3. Click the Report button.

Visual FoxPro enlarges the Query Destination dialog box to display the options shown in Figure 14-22.

4. Click Open Report.

Visual FoxPro displays the Open dialog box.

5. Click the name of the report that will use the query.

6. Click OK to return to the Query Destination dialog box.

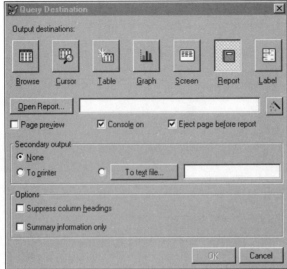

Figure 14-22:
The Report
button
enlarges
the Query
Destination
dialog box.

7. **Click OK to return to the Query Designer.**

Visual FoxPro sends the result of the query to the specified report the next time that the query is run.

8. **Click the Close button (the X) to close the Query Designer.**

Using Print Preview

You're about ready to print your report, but before you waste paper and kill a few trees, you should see what the report will look like. Visual FoxPro shows you a miniaturized version of the report whenever you choose File⇨Print Preview. Follow these steps:

1. **Display the report on-screen.**

2. **Choose File⇨Print Preview.**

Visual FoxPro shows you how your report will look when you print it. (See Figure 14-23.)

3. **Click the buttons in the Print Preview toolbar, shown in Figure 14-24, to turn pages of the report.**

4. **When you're ready to print, click the Print button in the Print Preview toolbar.**

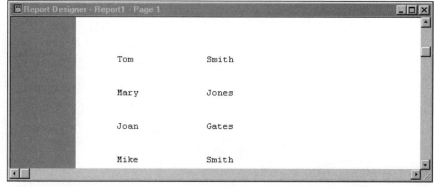

Figure 14-23:
Print
Preview
gives you
an idea of
how your
report will
look when
it's printed.

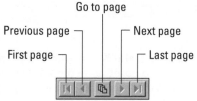

Figure 14-24:
The Print
Preview
toolbar.

Printing a Report Quickly

If you can't take the time to preview your report on-screen, you can simply send it to the printer. You can choose File⇔Print, but there's a faster way to print. Follow these steps:

1. **Right-click anywhere in the report.**

   Visual FoxPro displays the Print dialog box, shown in Figure 14-25.

2. **Choose the print options that you want to use, as follows:**

   • **Print range:** Visual FoxPro prints all the pages of your report by default. If you want to print only certain pages, click the Page button in the Print Range section of the Print dialog box; then type the page numbers that represent the range of pages that you want to print.

   • **Number of copies:** In the Copies section, you can choose the number of copies that you want to print.

   • **Collation:** Also in the Copies section, you can specify whether you want Visual FoxPro to collate the printed pages. Suppose that you want two copies of a three-page report. If you choose Collate,

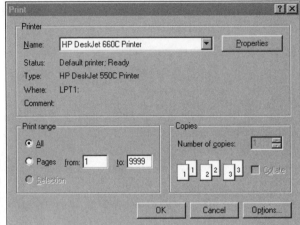

Figure 14-25:
The Print
dialog box.

Visual FoxPro prints pages 1, 2, and 3 of the first copy, followed by pages 1, 2, and 3 of the second copy, and so on. If you don't choose Collate, Visual FoxPro prints three copies of page 1, followed by three copies of page 2, and so on.

3. Click OK to print the report.

Creating and Printing Mailing Labels

Most people take for granted the fact that you can stick a label into a printer and get a perfectly centered name and address. But creating a good-looking mailing label is tricky and can be one of the most frustrating experiences that you'll ever have.

Fortunately, you don't have to spend hours adjusting text so that names and addresses fit squarely inside the label; Visual FoxPro handles the alignment chores for you. All you need to worry about is where to place the name and address (or any other information you want to use) on one label. The program then follows your layout and prints the mailing list on the labels.

Visual FoxPro can produce flawless mailing labels because it already knows the size of the label and the number of labels in a sheet of labels. No, Visual FoxPro can't see the labels that you stuffed into the printer. Instead, the Avery label company provided a list of product numbers and the corresponding specifications for its labels. (You don't have to use Avery labels, but you're sure to get perfect results if the label that you use meets the specifications of the corresponding Avery label.)

Don't worry about the specifications; Visual FoxPro reads those specifications. Your job is to find the product number of the label you're using on the package of labels that you purchased. Enter that product number in the New Label dialog box, and Visual FoxPro goes to work aligning the labels.

Your first step in creating mailing labels is deciding what kind of label to use for the mailing list. Your label choice may determine how easy creating mailing labels will be.

Visual FoxPro shows you a list of Avery product numbers that correspond to the company's labels.

Some label manufacturers cross-reference their product numbers to Avery product numbers. Look at the product literature that came with the labels you're using to see whether the manufacturer provides a cross-reference. If so, choose the corresponding Avery product number.

You can create your mailing list by creating a table (refer to Chapter 1) that contains names and addresses. Then you can then link the table to the labels in this section of this chapter.

Here's how you select a label type for your mailing list:

1. **Choose File⇨New to display the New dialog box.**

2. **Select the Label radio button.**

3. **Click the New file button.**

   Visual FoxPro displays the New Label dialog box, shown in Figure 14-26.

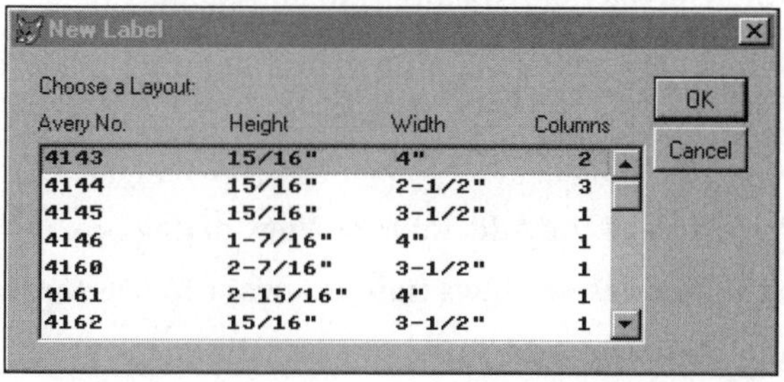

Figure 14-26:
The
New Label
dialog box.

4. **Click the appropriate Avery product number.**

5. **Click OK.**

   Visual FoxPro displays the Label Designer, shown in Figure 14-27.

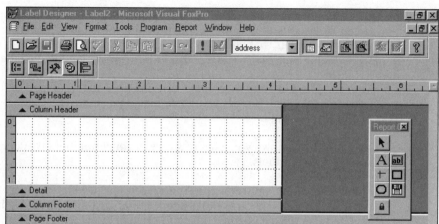

Figure 14-27:
The Label
Designer.

The Label Designer is the same as the Report Designer, which I describe earlier in this chapter. The menus and toolbars are the same, so I don't go into too much detail on how to use the Label Designer. The entire page in the Label Designer represents one label; therefore, any object that you place in the page appears in every label that Visual FoxPro prints.

6. **Open the database that contains the table or view that you want to use.**

7. **Right-click anywhere in the Label Designer to display a shortcut menu.**

8. **Choose Data Environment.**

   Visual FoxPro displays the Data Environment dialog box.

9. **Right-click anywhere in the Data Environment dialog box to display a shortcut menu.**

10. **Choose Add.**

   Visual FoxPro displays the Add Table or View dialog box.

11. **Double-click the tables or views that you want to use for the label.**

12. **Click Close to close the Add Table or View dialog box.**

   The Label Designer and the Data Environment dialog box remain on-screen.

13. **Place objects in the label.**

   The objects that you can place in a label are the same objects that you can place in a report, so I don't repeat the steps here; for details, refer to the section "Creating a Report," earlier in this chapter.

14. **Choose File⇨Print.**

    The Print dialog box appears.

15. **Click OK to print the labels.**

Grouping Labels

Labels can be grouped according to values that you specify. Suppose that you want to print mailing labels for all employees, but you want to produce sets of labels, with each set containing labels for the employees in one department. You can tell Visual FoxPro to group the labels by department number (assuming that the department number is in the database). The department number itself does not have to appear on the labels; that number is simply used as the value for grouping the labels.

You group labels the same way that you group reports. Refer to the section "Grouping Data in a Report," earlier in this chapter.

Linking a Query to a Label

You can have Visual Fox filter out unwanted names and addresses by creating a query. (I show you how to create a query in Chapter 5.) Each time the query is run, the result of the query is printed on labels.

Here's how to link a query to your labels:

1. **Choose File⇨New (to create a new query) or File⇨Open (to open an existing query).**

2. **Choose Query⇨Query Destination.**

    Visual FoxPro displays the Query Destination dialog box.

3. **Click the Label button.**

    Visual FoxPro enlarges the Query Destination dialog box, as shown in Figure 14-28.

4. **Click the magic-wand button that appears below the Label button.**

    The Label Wizard appears, as shown in Figure 14-29.

5. **Provide the information that Visual FoxPro needs to create the labels.**

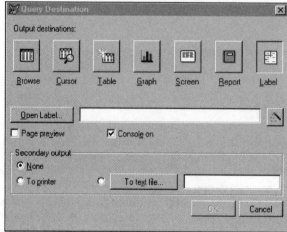

Figure 14-28:
Click the
Label
button to
send the
result of the
query to
your labels.

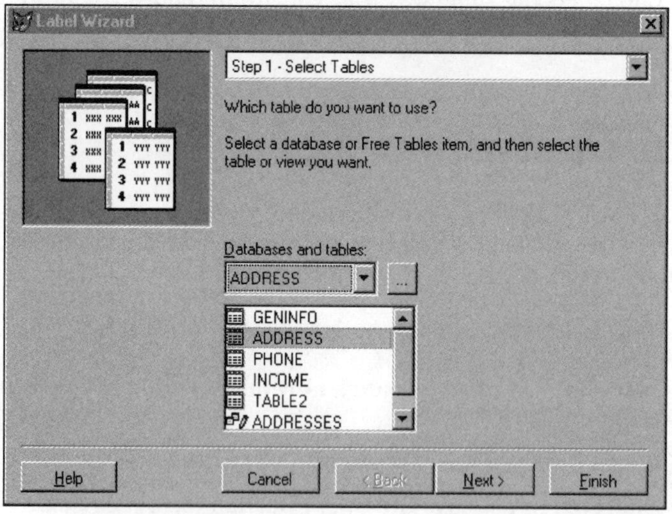

Figure 14-29:
The Label
Wizard.

The wizard displays a series of dialog boxes, each of which asks you for information about how you want to see the labels. The wizard's questions are easy to answer.

6. Click OK to return to the Query Destination dialog box.

7. Click OK to return to the Query Designer.

Printing Labels

The steps that you use to print a report also work for printing labels that you create with the Label Designer. Refer to the section "Printing a Report Quickly," earlier in this chapter. You can

- ✔ Preview the labels by choosing File⇨Print Preview
- ✔ Print the labels by choosing File⇨Print
- ✔ Print labels fast by choosing Report⇨Quick Report

Performing a Mail Merge

A *mail merge* consists of using information that is stored in your database for form letters. You could use mail merge to personalize letters to all employees by writing the text of the letter in a word processor and then using special codes in the letter to represents fields in a table. When you print the form letter, the text of the letter is printed, with values from fields in the table being substituted for the special codes in the letter.

Many word processors require you to enter data, represented by special codes in the form letter, in a word-processor table. A word-processor table is a spreadsheetlike grid in which columns are fields and rows are records.

Instead of using a word-processor table, you can use some or all of the fields in a table of your database. The actual merging of the data, however, is performed by your word processor. If you don't have a word processor, such as Microsoft Word for Windows, you won't be able to use Visual FoxPro's mail-merge capabilities.

Here's how you perform a mail merge in Visual FoxPro:

1. **Choose File⇨Open to display the Open dialog box.**

2. **Choose the database file that you want to use.**

3. **Click OK.**

   Visual FoxPro displays the Database Designer.

4. **Choose Tools⇨Wizards⇨Mail Merge.**

   Visual FoxPro displays the Mail Merge Wizard, shown in Figure 14-30.

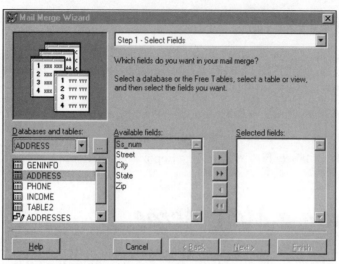

Figure 14-30:
The Mail
Merge
Wizard
walks you
through the
process of
merging
information
in your
table with a
form letter.

Chapter 15

Making Data into a Graph

*W*henever I see a bunch of numbers displayed in a spreadsheetlike grid in a form or report, I lose the real meaning of the series of numbers. Sure, I can read the numbers, but the message that they're sending gets lost.

If you're like me — confused by numbers — stay tuned; I have something to show you that will make your life easier. In this chapter, I show you how to create a graph from the numbers in a table. A graph gives you a picture of data in a way that practically anyone can understand — without being a genius in math.

Changing Data into a Graph

Remember from your school days when the teacher gave you a sheet of graph paper and showed you how to plot a series of numbers? That's all you do in this chapter. You supply the series of numbers; Microsoft Graph, with the aid of Visual FoxPro, plots those numbers on a graph.

Microsoft Graph is distributed with Visual FoxPro and other Microsoft programs, so you probably have it on your computer. You can't run it directly, though; Microsoft Graph can be called only by another program — in this case, Visual FoxPro.

Most sophisticated programs, such as Microsoft Word for Windows and Microsoft Excel, are capable of displaying a series of numbers as a graph. But Word and Excel don't draw graphs, and neither does Visual FoxPro. Word, Excel, Visual FoxPro, and other Windows programs call on Microsoft Graph to do all the plotting.

Understanding Basic Graphing

You can use any numeric value in a field of a table as data for a graph. Visual FoxPro allows you to specify the field that contains the data for the graph and the characteristics of the graph, such as style, which are saved in a special file on your disk called a Microsoft Graph file. Later, Visual FoxPro calls Microsoft Graph to read the specifications from the file and draw the graph in a form or a report.

Suppose that you insert your income for the past ten years into a field in a table. Say that you want your income to be plotted on a graph, displaying how your income has increased or decreased over those ten years. The graph appears as a big *L*. The vertical line of the graph is the *vertical axis,* and the horizontal line of the graph is the *horizontal axis.*

The vertical axis contains a series of values, and all the values in the field fall within that series. Suppose that over the past ten years, your salary increased from $30,000 to $50,000. The values that appear in the vertical axis of the graph start with $30,000 and end with $50,000. (Don't worry about setting the ranges for the vertical axis of your graph. Visual FoxPro determines the range based on the data in the field.)

The horizontal axis contains each occurrence of the data. In the case of your income, a marker on the horizontal axis represents each year's income. Visual FoxPro places another marker in the graph for the value of each year's income. A line connects the markers, creating a graphic representation of the data.

Creating a Graph

You can create the specifications for a graph by using either the Graph Wizard or a query.

I use the Graph Wizard to create most of my graphs because I already know the data that will be displayed in the graph. You'll probably use the Graph Wizard for most of your graphs, too.

The Graph Wizard prompts you to answer questions that Visual FoxPro requires to build the specifications for the graph. Although this book doesn't tell you explicitly how to use all wizards (how to use them is rather obvious), I make an exception in the case of the Graph Wizard because some terms in its dialog boxes can be confusing.

Using the Graph Wizard to create specifications

Here's how you use the Graph Wizard to create specifications for a graph:

1. **Choose Tools➪Wizards➪All.**

   Visual FoxPro displays the Wizard Selection dialog box, shown in Figure 15-1.

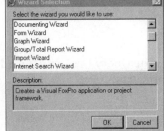

Figure 15-1: The Wizard Selection dialog box.

2. **Select Graph Wizard as the wizard that you'll use.**

   Notice that a description of the chosen wizard appears in the Description area of the Wizard Selection dialog box.

3. **Click OK.**

   Visual FoxPro displays the first Graph Wizard dialog box, shown in Figure 15-2. All you need to do to create a graph is follow the steps in the Graph Wizard.

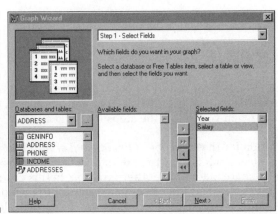

Figure 15-2: The Graph Wizard prompts you for the information needed for the graph and then creates the graph for you.

The Graph Wizard prompts you to select tables and fields for the graph, along with the style to apply to the graph. The answers to these questions are obvious, so I don't give you the answers.

Make sure that you give the graph a different filename than the one suggested by the Graph Wizard; otherwise, your new graph overwrites the graph that you saved under the suggested filename.

Using a query to create specifications

Creating graph specifications from a query is similar to creating graph specifications by using the Graph Wizard. Here's how you do it:

1. **Create a query.**

   Refer to Chapter 10, if necessary. The Query Designer should be on-screen, with your query already defined.

2. **Choose Query➪Query Destination.**

   Visual FoxPro displays the Query Destination.

3. **Click the Graph button.**

   Nothing visual happens when you click the button, but Visual FoxPro prepares the query behind the scenes.

4. **Click OK to close the Query Destination dialog box and return to the Query Designer.**

5. **Click the exclamation point button in the Visual FoxPro toolbar to run the query.**

   Visual FoxPro automatically runs the Graph Wizard at the end of the query. Refer to the preceding section to see how to use the Graph Wizard to complete the graph specifications.

Displaying a Graph

You can use a graph in a form or report by using the *OLE Bound control*, such as an Excel spreadsheet. Visual FoxPro automatically places the graph in the form or report when you follow the steps in this section.

OLE is the abbreviation for the term *object linking and embedding*. The concept sounds confusing but is easy to understand. OLE enables your forms and reports to share pieces of another program. In this case, the other program is Microsoft Graph, and the piece that you want to include is a graph. The OLE Bound control assigns an object to a particular place in your form or report.

Remember that you use Visual FoxPro to write the specifications for the graph. Microsoft Graph is the program that creates the graph. A graph in this example is an object of Microsoft Graph, which *embeds,* or places, the graph in a form or report.

Here's how you embed a graph in a form or a report:

1. **Create a form or report.**

   I show you how to create a form in Chapter 11 and a report in Chapter 14.

2. **Click the Data Environment button in the Forms toolbar.**

   Visual FoxPro displays the Add Table or View dialog box and the Data Environment dialog box.

3. **In the Add Table or View dialog box, click the Other button.**

   The Open dialog box appears.

4. **Double-click the table that contains your graph.**

   The Open dialog box closes, and the table appears in the Data Environment dialog box. Notice that the field name *olegraph* is the only field name in the table.

5. **Click Close to close the Add Table or View dialog box.**

6. **From the Data Environment dialog box, drag the field of the table that contains your graph to the form or report.**

   The OLE Bound control associated with your graph automatically appears in the form or report, as shown in Figure 15-3.

7. **To see the graph, run the form or report by clicking the exclamation point button in the Visual FoxPro toolbar.**

Figure 15-3:
The OLE
Bound
control
appears
when you
drag the
olegraph
field into
your form
or report.

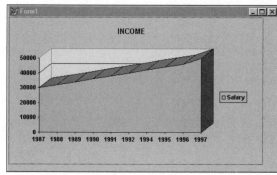

Part V
Things That Make a Big Difference

In this part . . .

FoxPro was one of the first databases designed for personal computers, and it has a long, successful history of serving corporations as an important business tool. With the passage of time, thinking of FoxPro as being old and outdated is easy to do. You remember the saying that you can't teach an old dog (or an old fox) new tricks?

Guess what? Visual FoxPro isn't an old fox; it's a sly fox. Visual FoxPro has built-in, cutting-edge technology that you can incorporate into your databases, forms, and reports. I'm talking about features that excite today's nerds. I'm talking about network computing, client/server computing, putting your database on the Internet, building your own controls from those created by Bill Gates' whiz kids, using ActiveX controls in your forms and reports, building macros, and organizing projects.

Best of all, you can include fancy features as part of your Visual FoxPro form without going through all the hassles that you expect from complex technology. Simply put, you don't have to be a nerd to use these features with your database, forms, and reports. In Part V, I show you how easy it is to use these features.

Chapter 16

Networking, Remote Computing, and the Internet

In This Chapter

▶ Using Visual FoxPro on a local-area network

▶ Retrieving information from a client/server database

▶ Building a database for the Internet

*Y*ou've probably heard about someone cracking the password that allowed her to gain access to government secrets — from her home at the other end of the country. Makes you wonder whether anything is safe these days.

Computer security is breached on occasion in real life — and all the time in the movies — because computers are connected to other computers. The link between computers is called a *network*, and in this chapter, I explore ways that Visual FoxPro can be used on a computer network. (I don't show you how to break into the Pentagon's computers, however.)

I talk about three types of computer networks in this chapter:

✔ Local-area networks (LAN)

✔ Client/server

✔ The Internet

Connecting Computers

Remember when your schoolteacher punched a hole in the bottom of two paper cups and tied them together with a string? A couple of kids pulled the string taut; then one of them spoke into one cup and the other listened in the other cup. A miracle had occurred: The teacher had made two cups and a string into a telephone.

Actually, the teacher created a small network that consists of two computers (cups) that are joined by a cable (string). Computer networks are more sophisticated than cups and a string, of course, but the same basic process occurs. One computer (cup) sends another computer (cup) information electronically over a cable (string) that can transmit the information over a distance. This setup is a simple computer network.

Each computer connected to the cable has an address, just like each house on a street has an address. Special network software acts like a traffic cop, making sure that each piece of information reaches the correct computer.

Understanding servers

At least one computer connected to the network is designated as the center of the network. That computer is called a *server*. Think of a server as being the computer that is used to store information shared by the other computers in the network. A server frequently is the computer that runs the network, although more than one server can be connected to the network, with only one of those servers actually running the network.

Computers that talk to the server over the network are called *clients*. You've probably seen the term *client/server* used in the press (and heard it used by the geeks in your office). The term is used to describe a computer network. Simply put, clients (computers like your PC) are connected to a server (such as a shared hard disk) through cables called a network. Sometimes, the server on a network is referred to as a *file server*.

You store your programs and your database on the hard disk inside your computer. You can store programs and a database on a floppy disk or a CD-ROM, of course, but most people use a hard disk.

Only your computer can get to the information stored on your hard disk. A friend can't access your data if your friend's computer and your computer aren't connected. You probably don't want a friend snooping around your hard disk, anyway.

You *do* want to share information, however, if you and the rest of your friends are working on the same project, such as building the FoxPro database that's going to make all of you millionaires. You can share information such as programs and a database by creating a *local-area network* (LAN), which is a bunch of computers connected by a cable.

At the center of the network is a file server that runs the LAN and stores all the files that you want to share on the file server's hard disk. A file server is little more than a shared hard disk. You can place your files on the file server, and someone else whose computer is connected to the network can use those files. You don't have to use sneaker net to exchange files. (You're using _sneaker net_ when you load your file onto a floppy disk, put on your sneakers, and run the disk over to your friend so that she can use your file.)

Whenever you or your friends want to run a program or look at data in a database, you tell your computer to look for those files on the file server's hard disk. The hard disk usually is identified as the F drive (or another letter) when you log into the network. You then refer to the server's hard disk by that letter, just as you refer to your computer's hard disk as C.

Suppose that you create a database containing the names and addresses of all the businesses in your area. The database is stored on the file server's hard disk. Whenever you want to locate the address of a business, you tell Visual FoxPro to use the database located on the file server.

Some people consider a file server to be different from a client/server, although both a file server and client/server are computers connected to other computers in a network. The difference between a file server and client/server is a bit technical, but you'll have no problem understanding the concept.

When you query your database located on your hard disk, your computer goes to work, obeying Visual FoxPro's instructions to do the following:

- ✔ Open the database.
- ✔ Compare the search criteria with information in the database.
- ✔ Display records that match the search criteria.

When you query a database located on a file server, your computer performs the same work, with one important exception: Records from the database travel from the file server along the cable to your computer; then your computer compares the records with the search criteria.

When you query a database located on a client/server, your computer sends the search criteria to the client/server and asks the client/server to find the matching record. The client/server then goes to work comparing records in the database. Your computer sits backs and waits for the client/server to send the matching record.

Understanding conflicts among computers

A computer network enables you and your friends to share resources. Although I've been talking about sharing only programs and data, a network also allows you to share printers and modems. Because this book talks about databases, I don't discuss those other shared resources.

You may have problems sharing practically everything. Remember the fights that ensued when you and a friend tried to grab the same toy? Similar problems — minus the bruises — occur when more than one computer tries to the use the same record from the database at the same time. The nerd term for this situation is *contention*. In some cases, no computer receives the record because of the conflict.

Contention occurs by chance, similar to lightning strikes. People get hit by lightning, but the conditions must be perfect for the strike to occur. The same is true of contention. You experience contention infrequently when you use a file server and even less often when you use a client/server. Client/server software has a better opportunity to prevent the perfect conditions from occurring because the client/server performs all the processing.

Although contention occurs infrequently, a common problem is for a person to lose changes made in a record shared on a file server because the changes are overwritten by another person.

Suppose that you want to change the department number of John Smith. You open the database and display the record in the table that contains John Smith's department number. You make the change in the record and close the table, and Visual FoxPro saves the changes to the database.

A problem arises, however, when someone else wants to change information in John Smith's record at the same time that you're changing the department number. Only one person can make changes in the same record at the same time.

Here's what happens behind the scenes:

1. You request a copy of John Smith's record from the file server.

2. The file server sends you the copy, which you change. You make changes in the copy of the record, not the record itself.

3. Another person requests a copy of John Smith's record from the file server.

4. The file server sends the other person a copy, which he changes. That person makes changes in the copy of the record, not the record itself.

5. You save your changes to the file server, overwriting the current record. Now the permanent copy of John Smith's record reflects your changes.

6. The other person saves his changes to the file server, overwriting the current record. Now the permanent copy of John Smith's record reflects his changes. The other person's changes overwrite your changes.

Resolving conflicts

Client/server software prevents common conflicts among computers because computers request information from the database and the client/server does all the searching and updating of records. The client/server knows to update and save the record before making other changes in the record.

File-server software does not prevent common conflicts among computers unless each computer takes necessary precautions when its user records changes.

Visual FoxPro automatically locks a table whenever a record in the table is being updated, such as when you:

 ✔ Insert a new record into the table.

 ✔ Save a record in the table.

 ✔ Delete a record from the table.

 ✔ Remove deleted records from the table.

 ✔ Modify the field specifications of the table.

Don't feel that Visual FoxPro takes care of conflicts for you; it prevents conflicts from occurring only when it updates the table.

When you want to insert a new record into a table, save a record in the table, or delete a record from a table, you give Visual FoxPro a command. The program locks the table while the record is being updated; then it immediately unlocks the table. No one can use the table while the table is locked.

No lock is placed on the table while you're making changes in the record, however. You can make changes in the record while you are viewing a copy of the record. The actual changes occur only when you tell Visual FoxPro to close the table or save the table. Other computers still have access to the table while you're making the changes in the record.

Locking and unlocking a table

You can prevent conflicts from occurring by locking the table before you begin making changes. The other computers can access other tables of the database but not the table that you're using until you stop using the table.

You must remember to release the lock on the table, though; otherwise, other computer users will hunt you down like a fox.

Here's how you lock tables:

1. **Press Ctrl+F2 to display the Command Window.**
2. **Type** SET EXCLUSIVE ON.
3. **Press Enter to lock all the tables that you're going to use.**

   Any time you open any table by choosing File⇨Open, Visual FoxPro automatically locks the table.

4. **Open the table that you require and make changes in one or more records.**
5. **Choose File⇨Close to close the table.**

   The Command Window remains open.

Here's how you unlock tables:

1. **Press Ctrl+F2 to display the Command Window.**
2. **Type** SET EXCLUSIVE OFF.
3. **Press Enter to remove the lock from all the tables that you're going to use.**

   Visual FoxPro automatically unlocks tables that are open or are opened after you press Enter.

You should follow two general rules to prevent conflicts whenever you use a database that is located on a file server:

- ✔ If you're going to view data and not change data, type **SET EXCLUSIVE OFF** and press Enter in the Command window before you open the table. Visual FoxPro automatically locks tables when you open the table and prevents anyone except you from looking at the table. You don't need to lock out other users, however, if you are not changing data in the table.

- ✔ Refresh the data that you see on-screen frequently by pressing F5. Although you aren't changing the data, someone else could be changing it without locking the table. Therefore, the data on-screen won't reflect changes made in the permanent record by the other person unless you refresh your screen. Refreshing tells Visual FoxPro to go back to the table and get you a fresh copy of the information.

You can lock individual records by using the RLOCK() command before you open the record; using the UNLOCK() command removes the locks. I don't go into detail on how to use RLOCK() and UNLOCK() because the SET EXCLUSIVE command is easier to understand and use.

Solving network performance problems

Sharing information in a network requires all the people who are using the network to have consideration for one another. The first consideration is to avoid hogging the database by locking tables and records unnecessarily.

Performance is another concern. All the computers in the network are using the same resource — usually the file server. So while you're asking for a large file or a large number of records from the file server, it ignores other requests.

To reverse the situation a little, the time that you must wait for the file server to send you a file depends on how many requests are ahead of your request. If you wait too long, you'll complain to the system administrator (the person who is responsible for the network) about the network's lack of performance.

The problem occurs when someone makes an unreasonable request of the file server. Here are a couple of ways to avoid causing performance problems on the network:

✔ **Avoid using index files to sort data in tables.**

Suppose that you always want to see records in a table by a person's department name, last name, and first name. You can sort the records in the table or leave the records in data-entry order and use an index. Sorting the table increases the performance of the network.

An index requires a two-step process. First, Visual FoxPro opens and reads the index; then it opens and reads the table. A sorted table, however, requires only one step: Visual FoxPro opens and reads the table.

✔ **Make changes in records during off-peak times, if possible.**

Everyone else must wait until you change and save the copy of the record. Performance improves for everyone if you make changes when few, if any, other users need to see information in the table.

I suggest that you don't worry too much about performance until you experience long wait times or hear that other users are having long wait times. If performance falls off, call your system administrator.

Accessing a Remote Database

A client/server is similar to a file server, except that the client/server does most of the work with the database.

Suppose that you need all the information about XYZ Co., and the information is stored in a database on a client/server. You use Visual FoxPro to place your request in the proper format and send the request to the client/server's database. Your computer waits for the client/server to extract and send you the information that you requested. The entire search is performed outside your computer.

The database on the client/server does not have to be a Visual FoxPro database. You can use Visual FoxPro to access practically any database supported by the Microsoft Open Database Connectivity driver (ODBC), such as a Paradox database or a SQL database.

Suppose that your company has a SQL database located on a client/server, and you want to query the database. You can do so by using Visual FoxPro if the database is supported by ODBC. (Your system administrator can tell you whether it is.)

Connecting to a remote database

You must connect your computer to a remote database before you can access data from it. Follow these steps:

1. **Create or open an existing database.**

2. **Choose File⇨New to display the New dialog box.**

3. **Select the Connection radio button.**

4. **Click the New file button to display the Connections dialog box.**

   The Connections dialog box contains several options, but you need to deal with only four: Data Source, User ID, Password, and Database. (The Data Source list displays all the remote databases that you can use with Visual FoxPro.) I suggest that you consult your system administrator to determine the settings for the connection.

- <u>D</u>ata Source is the remote computer to which you want to connect.

- <u>U</u>ser ID is the user ID that lets you log onto the remote computer.

- <u>P</u>assword is the password that is used to log onto the remote computer.

- Da<u>t</u>abase is the name of the database on the remote computer that contains the data you need.

5. **Click <u>V</u>erify Connections to link with the remote computer.**

   The Select Database dialog box opens, allowing you to select the remote computer and database by using the same technique that you use to open a file from the Open dialog box.

Finding data in a remote database

After you make the connection to the remote database, you can search the database for information by using the Query Wizard. Follow these steps:

1. **Choose <u>T</u>ools⇨<u>W</u>izards⇨<u>Q</u>uery.**

   Visual FoxPro displays the Wizard Selection dialog box, shown in Figure 16-1.

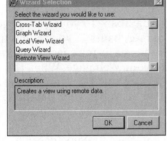

Figure 16-1:
The Wizard
Selection
dialog box.

2. **Choose Remote View Wizard to start the Remote View Wizard; click OK.**

   Note that the wizard's description also appears in the dialog box.

3. **Click <u>C</u>onnections to display the connection to the remote database.**

   The remaining Remote View Wizard settings are obvious, so I don't go into too much detail here. You're asked to select the remote database and then choose the tables and fields to which you want to connect. You're then asked to choose the fields that you want to use to sort records as well as an expression to filter out unwanted records. You make your choices from lists displayed on-screen.

4. Click <u>F</u>inish to send your request to the remote database.

The information is returned to your computer from the remote database and displayed on your screen.

Putting Your Data on the Internet

By now, you've probably heard about the Internet revolution, and you may have explored the Internet yourself. I assume that you know how the Internet works and know how to create a Web page. If you're preparing to build your own page on the Net or to enhance your existing page with database capabilities, read on.

In this section, I show you how to give the world access to your Visual FoxPro database. The program can build the page, database, and database connection for you.

If you'd like more information about the Internet, check out *The Internet For Dummies,* 4th Edition, by John R. Levine, Carol Baroudi, and Margaret Levine Young (IDG Books Worldwide, Inc.) for a complete discussion.

Adding a database to your Web page

You can allow visitors to your Web page to search information in your database if you link your Visual FoxPro database to your Web page. Suppose that you want to provide a directory of merchants in your community. Anyone who is looking for a good place to eat or purchase hardware supplies can use a computer to connect to your Web page. When the visitor connects, he enters in a text box the service that he wants to use and then clicks the Search button. The Web server searches your database and returns to the visitor information about appropriate merchants.

You can use Visual FoxPro to provide database lookup access to any visitor to your Web page. Before you become too excited, however, I have to tell you about the restrictions:

- ✔ The Web server must be a Windows NT or Internet Information Server with HTTP (Hypertext Transfer Protocol) service, which is used to send your Web page to your visitors' computers. Check with your Web-site service provider to see whether its Web server qualifies.

- ✔ A licensed copy of Visual FoxPro 3.0b or later must be installed on the Web server. Don't try to install a copy of Visual FoxPro on the server yourself unless you have the approval of the Web server provider; the Web server may not be compatible with your version of Visual FoxPro.

> ✔ Searches are limited to exact matches. You can't search for values that are greater than or less than the search criteria. Neither can you process a partial search, such as finding all last names that begin with the letters *Sm*.

Creating your search page

Typically, your database Web page is one of several pages that comprise your Web site. A Web site usually has an opening page from which visitors can jump to other pages in your Web site, one of which is the search page. The *search page* is the place where the visitor enters search criteria. Here's how you create a search page:

1. **Create the database and tables that you want to place on your Web site.**

   Refer to Chapters 1 and 2 if you need to brush up on how to create databases and tables.

2. **Place data in the database.**

   This data is the information that visitors to your Web site will search.

3. **Choose Tools⇨Wizards to display the Wizards submenu.**

4. **Choose All to display the Wizard Selection dialog box (refer to Figure 16-1).**

5. **Select the Internet Search Wizard; click OK.**

   The Internet Search Wizard steps you through each phase of building the database Web page.

6. **Enter a title and description for the page.**

   The title can be something like "Where to Shop in My Town." The description can be something like "Welcome to my shopping guide. Enter the type of service that you need in the box; then click the Search button. Information about merchants is displayed on-screen."

7. **Choose a background image and a header image.**

   An *image* is an electronic picture, such as the Visual FoxPro logo. You can purchase commercial pictures from your local computer store or through mail-order houses. The *background image* is the electronic picture that appears as the background of the page, and the *header image* is the electronic picture that appears between the title and the header.

   I find that trying different electronic pictures as the background image and the header image is the best way to decide which pictures are best for your page.

8. **Identify the fields that will be returned to the visitor and displayed on the visitor's screen.**

   These fields make up what is called the *return page*. You also determine the electronic pictures to be used as the background image and header image on the return page.

   Visual FoxPro displays returned information in the form of a grid; columns are the fields that you selected, and rows are records of information. The wizard asks you to decide how many records you want to display in the return page. The default value is ten records, which probably is sufficient for most return pages.

9. **Click Finish.**

   Visual FoxPro prompts you to enter the file name for the search page.

10. **Click OK.**

    Visual FoxPro creates the search page for you.

Placing your search page on the Web server

The Internet Search Wizard creates three files, which you copy to your Web server. Your Web site provider can help you move the files into the proper directory on the Web server. The wizard generates the following files (replace *<myfile>* with the names that you gave the .HTM file):

 ✔ *<myfile>*.HTM, which contains the search page

 ✔ *<myfile>*.IDC, which contains the database connector file

 ✔ *<myfile>*.HTX, which contains an extension of the .HTM file

Note: The .HTM file contains your search page; the other files are used to connect to your database.

When you copy these files to the Web server (which must have the proper copy of Visual FoxPro and compatible server software), you're almost ready for your first visitor.

The final step is to link the search page to your home page (or another appropriate page) of your Web site. The *home page* is the first page that the visitor sees when she enters your Web site.

Behind the scenes on your Web server

If you're like me, you want to know a little of what actually happens when someone uses your search page. I'll share what I have found:

1. **A visitor enters** http://www.mypage.com **in his browser (replacing** www.mypage. com **with the address of your Web site).**

2. **The browser calls your Web site.**

3. **The Web server sends your home page to the browser.**

4. **The visitor jumps to your search page, enters search criteria, and then sends the search criteria to your Web server.**

5. **The Web server runs Visual FoxPro, which creates a file called a common gateway interface (CGI).**

This file contains commands that handle communications between your search page and Visual FoxPro.

6. **The CGI file writes your visitor's request to a file and then tells Visual FoxPro to read the file.**

7. **Visual FoxPro searches the database and creates a return page that contains the result of the search.**

8. **Visual FoxPro tells the CGI file that the return page is ready to be shipped to the visitor.**

9. **The CGI file sends the return page to the browser.**

10. **The browser displays the return page and the result of the search on-screen.**

Chapter 17

Classes and ActiveX

● ●

In This Chapter

▶ Creating classes

▶ Using your own classes with forms and reports

▶ Using ActiveX with forms and reports

● ●

*T*he hottest way to add features to your Visual FoxPro application is to use classes and ActiveX, which don't have anything to do with school or a television series. Classes and ActiveX can enhance the performance of Visual FoxPro. Best of all, these new features are built into your copy of Visual FoxPro, and you can incorporate classes and ActiveX into your forms and reports right now.

In this chapter, I show you how to use classes and ActiveX.

Creating Classes

A *class* is an object, such as a command button, that you place in a form. (Refer to Chapter 11.) An object has a specific look and feel. A command button, for example, is a rounded rectangle that has text or a picture on top. When you place the mouse pointer on the button and click the left mouse button, the command button appears to be indented; then some action takes place, such as displaying the next record in the table.

The people who built Visual FoxPro decided how an object looks and operates, but they stopped short of making the final version of the object for you. For example, when you place a command button in a form, you must change the caption of the button and add instructions to make the command button do something when you click the button. These final touches make the command button a complete part of your form.

Understanding inheritance

More than a decade ago, programmers had to write all the instructions necessary to create the image of an object on-screen and give the object all the functionality required to make it a working part of the program. As you can imagine, creating objects took an enormous amount of time. Fortunately, programmers got smarter and decided to build most of these objects in advance; then they used copies of the objects whenever they needed the objects for a form.

The original object and all its basic functions are called a *class,* and a copy of the class is called an *instance* of the class. Each instance has the features that appear in the class. An instance of a class is said to *inherit* those features from the class. Furthermore, an instance can have its own features that enhance the features inherited from the class.

You may be a little confused by these definitions, so here's an example. Suppose that Mom and Dad have three kids. You can say that Mom and Dad are a class and that each kid is a different instance of Mom and Dad. Each kid has the some of the same features as Mom and Dad, such as two arms and two legs. Each kid also develops skills that are different from Mom's and Dad's. One kid may be a doctor; another, a lawyer; and the third, a stockbroker. The kids enhanced the features that they inherited from Mom and Dad.

Making your own class

You use classes every time you build a form or report. Each control that you place in a form or report is an instance of a class. A copy of the Check Box control, for example, is an instance of the CheckBox class.

You enhance the features of an instance of a class when you change the caption or size of an instance or add commands, such as displaying the next record.

Visual FoxPro also enables you to create your own class. You need to create a class only if you want to really get fancy with your forms and reports, so if you're not so inclined, skip this section and read the section on ActiveX.

The first question that comes to mind when you hear about classes is "Why would I ever want to create my own class?" The answer is obvious when you begin to build many forms for your database. You'll find yourself making the same changes in the same objects over and over again — a waste of time.

Typically, for example, you'll always want five command buttons in your forms, rather than the two command buttons that appear by default when you place a Command Group control in a form. You'll want the five buttons to have the captions Save, Next, Previous, OK, and Cancel, as well as the related commands that allow you to move through a table quickly.

So you read about classes and discover that you can create your own class, based on the Command Group control that the Visual FoxPro people built. Instead of inserting three command buttons each time, you can change the Command Group control one time and save your version of the Command Group control as your own class. Whenever you need to place the Command Group control in a form, you can use your version of the Command Group control instead of the Visual FoxPro Command Group control.

Creating your own class

In this section, I show you how I created my version of the Command Group control. Creating your own class isn't difficult; you can use the same steps for any Visual FoxPro control. Remember that any change you make in the control while building the class becomes a feature of your class.

Here's how to create your own class:

1. **Choose <u>F</u>ile⇨<u>N</u>ew to display the New dialog box.**

2. **Select the Cl<u>a</u>ss radio button.**

3. **Click the <u>N</u>ew file button.**

   Visual FoxPro displays the New Class dialog box, shown in Figure 17-1.

   The dialog box asks for three pieces of information, the first of which is the name of your new class.

4. **In the Class <u>N</u>ame box, type the name of your new class.**

   I named my class mycommandbuttons.

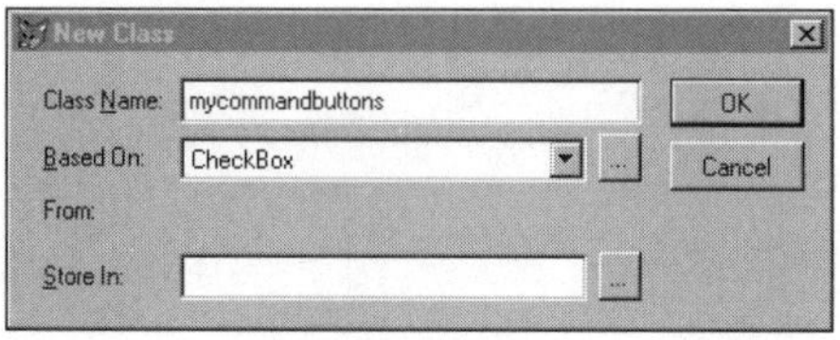

Figure 17-1:
The
New Class
dialog box.

Class <u>N</u>ame:	mycommandbuttons
<u>B</u>ased On:	CheckBox
From:	
<u>S</u>tore In:	

5. **From the Based On combo box, select the existing control or class that is the basis for your new class.**

All the controls that are available for you to place in a form appear in the Based On list, along with the names of any classes that you've built. I suggest that you base your new class on an existing control because you'll be enhancing the existing Visual FoxPro control most of the time. I chose CommandGroup. (See Figure 17-2.)

Figure 17-2:
Choose the
basis for
the new
class.

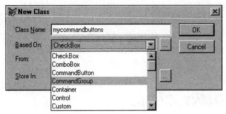

6. **In the Store In box, enter the path of the library that you'll use to store your new class.**

A *library* is like a database of classes. I prefer to save all my classes in the same library, which I call mylibrary. Click the button to the right of the Store In box to display the Save As dialog box, if you're unsure of the library name or path to the library. This dialog box is the same one that appears each time you save a file for the first time.

7. **Click OK.**

Visual FoxPro displays the Class Designer, shown in Figure 17-3, which contains the control that you specified as the basis for your new class.

Figure 17-3:
Use the
Class
Designer to
create your
own class.

8. Modify the control.

Use the techniques in Chapter 11 to modify a control in a form. I changed the button count from 2 to 5, using the `ButtonCount` property, and I changed the captions to Next, Previous, Save, OK, and Cancel. (See Figure 17-4.) I also inserted the necessary instructions for moving around the table into the Code window of each of the buttons.

9. Choose File⊅Save to save your new class in the specified library.

Figure 17-4:
The new
class.

10. Close the Class Designer by clicking the Close box (the *X* in the top-right corner of the window).

Using your own class

The process of inserting an instance of your own class into a form or report is straightforward. In this section, I show you how to place an instance of your own class in a form. The instance of your class becomes a control in your form. I assume, of course, that you've already created a class and stored the class in a library. (Refer to "Creating Classes," earlier in this chapter.) You can place an instance of your own class in your forms and reports by using the same technique. Follow these steps:

1. Create a form.

If you don't know how to create a form, refer to Chapter 11.

2. Display the Form Controls toolbar by clicking the Form Controls button in the Form Designer toolbar.

 3. Click the View Classes button.

Visual FoxPro displays the shortcut menu shown in Figure 17-5.

Figure 17-5:
The View
Classes
button
displays
this
shortcut
menu.

4. **Choose Add.**

   Visual FoxPro displays the Open dialog box.

5. **Double-click the name of the library where you stored your own class.**

   The classes that you have in your own class library, as shown in Figure 17-6, replace the standard Form Controls toolbar. These classes are your customized controls. Don't worry — you can re-display the standard Form Controls toolbar. (I show you how when you finish placing your control in the form.)

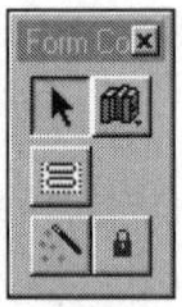

Figure 17-6:
Your
classes
appear.

6. **Click your control in the Form Controls toolbar and place the control in the form.**

   The button of your control is the same as the button of the control in the Form Controls toolbar. If you place the mouse pointer on the button, Visual FoxPro displays the name of your control on-screen.

7. **Click the View Classes button in the Form Controls toolbar to display the shortcut menu.**

8. **Choose Standard.**

   The standard Form Controls toolbar replaces your classes.

Tapping into ActiveX

Suppose that you want to include a feature in your program — a telephone dialer, for example. Instead of figuring out how to write all the instructions to create a telephone dialer, you need only find someone who has already built a telephone dialer as a control. After exchanging a few bucks, you have the control, ready to be included into your program.

Microsoft took the concept of building a program from controls a bit further. The company developed a standard for building controls — *ActiveX* — and encouraged programmers and software manufacturers to build ActiveX controls as a way to make money. ActiveX is a standard that enables you to easily include in your Visual FoxPro form ActiveX controls purchased from vendors other than Microsoft.

Furthermore, an ActiveX feature is included in Microsoft software such as Visual FoxPro. This feature allows you to include any ActiveX control in your forms and reports easily. A few ActiveX controls come with Visual FoxPro.

ActiveX controls appear in the Form Controls and Report Controls toolbars. You click the control that you need and then place the control in the form or report, just as you do with the standard Form or Report Controls toolbar. Here's how you place an ActiveX control on your form:

1. **Create a form or report.**

   If you don't know how to create a form or report, refer to Chapter 11 or Chapter 14. For this example, use a form because you'll be using ActiveX controls in forms more than in reports.

2. **Click the View Classes button in the Form Controls toolbar to display the shortcut menu.**

3. **Choose ActiveX Controls.**

   Visual FoxPro displays the ActiveX toolbar, shown in Figure 17-7. This toolbar has neat buttons, such as the Progress control that you saw when you installed Visual FoxPro. (The Progress control is the line that grows as the installation process proceeds.)

   Each ActiveX control has a Properties dialog box, a Code window, and other windows that you find for buttons in the standard Form Controls toolbar.

Figure 17-7:
The ActiveX
toolbar.

4. Change properties and add code as necessary.

Refer to Chapter 11 if you need help with this step.

You can check Visual FoxPro's online help system for tips on using a particular ActiveX control.

5. Click the View Classes button to display the shortcut menu.

6. Choose Standard to return to the standard Form Controls toolbar.

Chapter 18

Creating a Macro

• •

▶ Creating a macro

▶ Recording a macro

▶ Loading a macro

▶ Editing a macro

• •

*T*ired of typing a whole bunch of keys each time you want to do something, such as opening a file? Then store those keystrokes into one key
by creating a macro. When you run the macro, Visual FoxPro automatically
does all the steps you programmed in the macro.

Macros allow you to streamline your work and cut down on repetitive
keystrokes. In this chapter, you find out how to take advantage of macros
and how to create shortcuts that get your work completed quickly.

Deciding When a Macro Is Useful

Consider a *macro* a shortcut to typing several keys or choosing several
menu commands. Say that you always use the Import Wizard to take information from a file other than a Visual FoxPro table and insert the information into a Visual FoxPro database. Normally, you'd choose Tools⇨Wizard
and then select Import to display the Import Wizard dialog box. However,
you can reduce your work by creating a macro. Rather than choose those
commands, you can use hot keys and build a macro to start the Import
Wizard from the keyboard. You then assign the macro to a set of keys, such
as Ctrl+I. Each time you want to run the macro, you simply enter the macro's
assigned key combination.

Macros can't do everything

Macros, brilliant as they may be, do have a few limitations:

✔ **You can't save mouse movements to a macro.** For example, when you run the Import Wizard, you can choose Tools from the menu by pointing and clicking the mouse instead of pressing Alt+T on the keyboard. You can't, however, use the mouse to build a macro, although you can use the Alt+T key combination to save a macro.

✔ **You can't save keystrokes in response to a dialog box.** Say that you want to create a macro that not only displays the Open dialog box, but automatically enters the name of the file you want open into the Open dialog box. You can save the Alt+F+O keystrokes — as in File⇨Open to display the Open dialog box — to a macro. However, you can't save the name of the file to the macro.

Recording a Macro

The easiest way to create a macro is to let Visual FoxPro build it. Recording a macro is similar to recording your voice by using a tape recorder. Everything said while you record is encoded onto the tape. You can then replay your tape to relive those fond moments. Like a tape recorder, a macro records your keystrokes. Then when you call the macro, it automatically performs the action.

To record a macro:

1. Choose Tools⇨Macros.

The Macros dialog box, shown in Figure 18-1, appears. You can use this dialog box to record, save, delete, and edit macros.

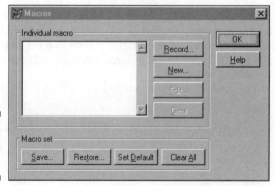

Figure 18-1:
The Macros
dialog box.

2. Click Record.

The Record Macro dialog box, shown in Figure 18-2, appears.

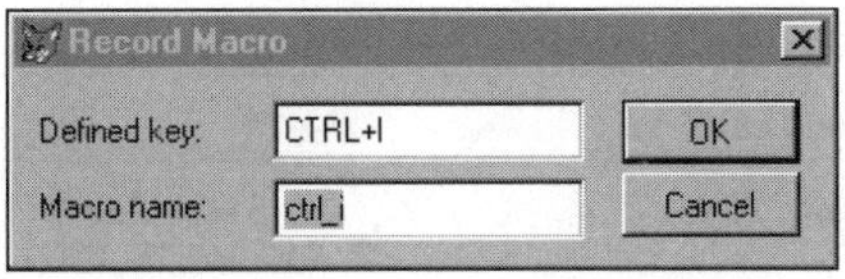

Figure 18-2:
The Record
Macro
dialog box.

Record Macro	✕
Defined key:	CTRL+I	OK
Macro name:	ctrl_i	Cancel

3. In the Defined key text box, enter the keys that you want in the macro.

I typed Ctrl+I, which I'll use to bring up the Import Wizard. (Although I picked Ctrl+I for my macro, you can choose any key.)

Visual FoxPro automatically uses the selected keys as the macro name. You probably don't want to change the macro name because the name chosen by Visual FoxPro serves as a reminder of the key used to run the macro.

When you type your macro, keep in mind that keys must begin with Alt or Ctrl. You can also choose function keys, identified on your keyboard as F1 . . . F12, to run a macro by simply selecting the function key that you want to use. You don't need to select another key as you do when you use the Alt or Ctrl keys.

You may temporarily overwrite an existing shortcut, such as Ctrl+S for Save an open file, when you assign the same key combination to run your macro. So if you use Ctrl+S, Visual FoxPro runs your macro instead of saving your file. However, the next time you run Visual FoxPro, the shortcut key is restored until you load your macro into memory. (See the section "Loading Your Macro into Memory," later in this chapter.) Table 18-1 lists common existing shortcuts.

Table 18-1	Common Existing Shortcuts
Press these keys	_To choose this command_
Alt+F	File
Alt+E	Edit
Alt+V	View
Alt+O	Format
Alt+P	Programs

(continued)

Table 18-1 *(continued)*

Press these keys	To choose this command
Alt+W	Windows
Alt+H	Help
Ctrl+N	New File
Ctrl+O	Open File
Ctrl+P	Print
Ctrl+S	Save
Ctrl+Z	Undo
Ctrl+R	Redo
Ctrl+X	Cut
Ctrl+C	Copy
Ctrl+V	Paste
Ctrl+A	Select All
Ctrl+F	Find
Ctrl+G	Find Again
Ctrl+L	Replace
Ctrl+D	Do
Ctrl+F1	Cycle through windows
Ctrl+F2	Display the Command Window
F1	Help

4. Click OK to begin recording.

Visual FoxPro displays a message, shown in Figure 18-3, that reminds you that every keystroke is being stored in the macro.

Figure 18-3:
A macro
is being
recorded.

Recording ctrl_i. Choose Macro from Tools menu to stop.

5. Enter the keystroke you want stored to the macro.

For example, I typed

- Alt+T

- W

- I

Visual FoxPro displays whatever dialog box your command causes to appear. You need to close the dialog box because you do not want to run that command. After you close the dialog box, you still see the message box that reminds you that you're still recording the macro.

6. Choose Tools➪Macro.

Make sure that you use the mouse rather than the keyboard.

The Stop Recording Macro dialog box, shown in Figure 18-4, appears. If you can't complete Step 6, check out the sidebar called "What to do when Visual FoxPro won't let you close the dialog box," later in this chapter.

Figure 18-4:
The Stop
Recording
Macro
dialog box.

7. Click OK in the Stop Recording Macro dialog box to stop recording keystrokes.

You don't need to change any of the default options in the Stop Recording Macro dialog box. As soon as you click OK, the Stop Recording Macro dialog box disappears.

8. Choose Tools➪Macro to display the Macros dialog box, as shown in Figure 18-5.

The name of the macro you just recorded appears in the Individual macro list box.

9. Click Save.

The Save Macros dialog box, shown in Figure 18-6, appears.

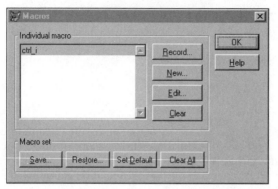

Figure 18-5:
The Macros
dialog box.

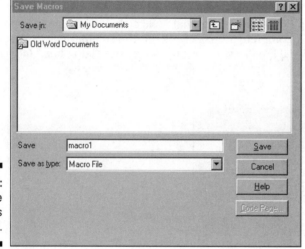

Figure 18-6:
The Save
Macros
dialog box.

10. In the Save text box, enter the name of the file where the macro will be stored.

The filename must follow the Visual FoxPro naming rules. (See Chapter 1.) You can accept the default settings of the Save in and Save as type areas.

11. Click Save.

The Save Macros dialog box closes, leaving the Macros dialog box on-screen.

12. Click OK to close the Macros dialog box.

Your macro awaits you.

What to do when Visual FoxPro won't let you close the dialog box

When you're recording a macro, you may find yourself in this situation: You entered the last keystroke you want to store in the macro and the dialog box you want displayed when you run the macro appears on-screen. However, Visual FoxPro won't let you choose Tools⇨Macro to stop recording your keystrokes.

Here's the problem: Some dialog boxes, such as the Form Designer, don't require you to choose an option in the dialog box; you can choose options from the menu bar while the dialog box is on-screen. In that case, you can choose Tools⇨Macro to stop recording your keystrokes.

However, other dialog boxes, such as those displayed by the Import Wizard, require you to choose an option in the dialog box; you can't do anything outside the dialog box, such as choosing options from the menu bar. So you can't choose Tools⇨Macro to stop recording your keystrokes.

Here's the solution: Use the mouse to close the dialog box (click the Close button (X) in the dialog box) and then choose Tools⇨Macro to stop recording your keystrokes. Clicking the Close button isn't stored in the macro because macros don't record actions completed with the mouse.

Testing Your Macro

After recording a new macro and saving the macro to a file, you can test to see whether Visual FoxPro does what you want when you run the macro.

To test your macro, simply choose the keys that run your macro. If you're not sure which keys to use, then choose Tools⇨Macro to display the Macros dialog box. The Individual macro list contains the names of the macros. Those names are usually the keys you need to run the macro.

If the macro doesn't work, then delete the macro (see the section "Deleting a Macro," later in this chapter) and record the macro again (see the preceding section).

You can make your macro run efficiently by storing only keystrokes that you require in the macro. You can easily forget that every keystroke you press while recording a macro is stored in the macro. So if you pressed the wrong key and then the correct key, the macro records both keys. Each time you run the macro, Visual FoxPro enters the wrong key and the correct key when you really intended for Visual FoxPro to enter only the correct key. If you have wrong keys in your macro, then be sure to re-record the macro.

Loading Your Macro into Memory

When you create a macro, the macro remains in memory until you load another macro file into memory or close Visual FoxPro.

Each time you want to use a macro, you must load the file containing the macro into memory. Here's how you do it:

1. **Choose Tools⇨Macro.**

   The Macros dialog box appears.

2. **Click Restore.**

   The Restore Macros dialog box, shown in Figure 18-7, appears.

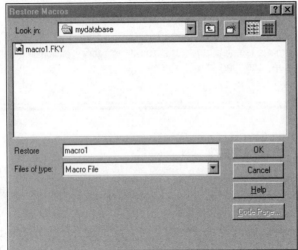

Figure 18-7:
The Restore
Macros
dialog box.

3. **In the Restore text box, enter the name of the file that contains the macros you want loaded into the memory.**

4. **Click OK.**

   Your macro is loaded.

Automatically Loading Macros

You're likely to forget to load your macro file each time you start up Visual FoxPro. If so, you'll press the keys that run your macro, but nothing will happen.

You can avoid loading the macro file yourself by designating the macro file as the default macro file. Whenever you start Visual FoxPro, Visual FoxPro automatically loads the default macro file into memory. Here's how you set the default macro file:

1. **Load the macro into memory.**

   Keep in mind that you're selecting a macro file, not a macro, in this step. A macro file can contain one or more macros. Second, you're not deleting a macro or a macro file. All you're really doing is replacing the default macro file with a new macro file.

   The Macros dialog box appears. (See the preceding section if you're not sure how to load the macro.)

2. **Click Set Default.**

3. **Click OK to close the Macros dialog box.**

   Your macro is now automatically loaded each time you start Visual FoxPro.

Stopping Macros from Loading

Default macros may outlive their usefulness. If so, you may want to stop automatically loading the default macro file each time you run Visual FoxPro. However, unless you tell Visual FoxPro not to load the default macro file, the macros continually load. To stop loading the default macro file:

1. **Load the macro into memory.**

   The Macros dialog box appears. (See the section "Loading Your Macro into Memory," earlier in this chapter, if you're not sure how to load a macro.)

2. **Click Clear All.**

   The names of all the macros in the default macro file are deleted from the Individual macro list box.

3. **Click Set Default.**

4. **Click OK to close the Macros dialog box.**

   No macros will be loaded into memory the next time you start Visual FoxPro.

Changing the Default Macro File

You can easily replace the default macro file with a different macro file if you created separate macro files for different tasks.

To change the default macro file:

1. Choose Tools⇨Macro.

The Macros dialog box appears.

2. Click Restore.

The Restore Macros dialog box appears.

3. In the Restore text box, enter the name of the file you want to use as the new default macro file.

4. Click OK.

5. Click Set Default.

6. Click OK to close the Macros dialog box.

You've now changed your default macro file.

Deleting a Macro

You should maintain your list of macros so that you avoid wasting space on your drive with macros that you no longer use. When you load the macro file into memory, a list of macros that are contained in the file that appears on-screen. This list is where you can delete the macro. Review the list of macros periodically and delete those macros that you no longer need.

To delete a macro:

1. Load the macro into memory.

The Macros dialog box appears. (See the section "Loading Your Macro into Memory," earlier in this chapter, if you're not sure how to load a macro.)

2. Highlight the name of the macro in the Individual macro list box that you want to delete.

3. Click Clear.

Visual FoxPro prompts you to confirm that you want to delete the macro.

4. Click Yes.

The Macros dialog box appears. The name of the macro you deleted no longer appears in the Individual Macro list box.

An inside look at a macro

A macro is similar to a program except you can store only keystrokes in a macro. The keystrokes that are used in a macro are typically shortcut menu keys. In a program, you can store commands and expressions used to control Visual FoxPro without using menus.

As you record a macro, Visual FoxPro automatically converts your keystrokes into macro commands. A *macro command* is the text description of the keystrokes you press during the recording session.

You can see the macro commands for a macro by loading the macro into memory (see "Loading Your Macro into Memory" earlier in this chapter, for more information), highlighting the name of the macro on the Individual macro list box in the Macros dialog box, and choosing Edit. The Edit Macro dialog box appears, listing the macro commands in the Macro content text box.

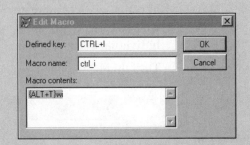

The figure lists the macro I recorded to display the Import. Here's what the macro code means in English:

✔ **{ALT+T}** is the same as pressing the ALT key with the T key, which is used to choose the <u>T</u>ools menu.

✔ **w** is the same as pressing w when the Tools menu is displayed to choose <u>W</u>izard.

✔ **i** is the same as pressing i when the list of wizards is displayed. The i tells Visual FoxPro to start the Import Wizard.

You cannot undo the deletion of a macro. You must re-record the macro if you accidentally delete the macro.

Editing a Macro

If you press a wrong key and then the correct key when you record a macro, Visual FoxPro simulates pressing both keys each time you run the macro. As a result, the macro is running an unnecessary step and the wrong keystroke is also taking up valuable space on your drive.

You can solve this problem in two ways:

✔ **Delete the macro and re-record the macro.**

(See the section "Deleting a Macro," earlier in this chapter.)

✔ **Edit the macro.**

To edit a macro:

1. **Load the macro into memory.**

   The Macros dialog box appears. (See the section "Loading Your Macro into Memory," if you're not sure how to load a macro.)

2. **Highlight the name of the macro that you want to delete in the Individual macro list box.**

   The Edit Macro dialog box, shown in Figure 18-8, appears.

Edit Macro		
Defined key:	CTRL+I	OK
Macro name:	ctrl_i	Cancel
Macro contents:		
{ALT+T}wi		

3. **Highlight the macro command for the wrong key in the Macro contents text box.**

4. **Press the Delete key on your keyboard to delete the macro command for the wrong key.**

   The macro command for the wrong key disappears from the Macro contents text box.

5. **Click OK.**

   The Edit Macro dialog box closes. The Macros dialog box remains on-screen.

6. **Click Save.**

   The Save Macros dialog box appears.

7. **In the Save text box, enter the name of the macro file that contains the macro you edited.**

   You don't need to change the default settings in the Save in and Save as type areas.

8. **Click Save.**

   Visual FoxPro displays a message that asks you whether you want to overwrite the existing macro file.

9. **Click Yes.**

   The Save Macros dialog box closes, leaving the Macros dialog box in view.

10. **Click OK to close the Macros dialog box.**

    Your edits are complete.

Chapter 19

Identifying Parts of a Project

● ●

In This Chapter

▶ Analyzing a system

▶ Identifying data input, data processing, and data output

▶ Creating a project

● ●

*Y*ou can assemble databases, tables, forms, and reports together to computerize any data you manage by hand, such as maintaining employee records or maintaining information about customers.

You can group these components together into a Visual FoxPro project. A project makes it easy for you to track the database, tables, forms, and reports used to computerize manual data maintenance. You can consider a project a Visual FoxPro application, which is sometimes called a computer system.

In this chapter, you find out how to analyze a typical database that you manage by hand and convert the manual process into a Visual FoxPro application.

Analyzing a Noncomputerized System

Before you begin to assemble components for your project, you must perform a detailed analysis of the way the current system manages data. A *system* is a series of steps you perform with information.

If you perform all the steps manually, then the system is called a *manual system*. If the computer performs most of the steps, then the system is called a *computerized system*.

You don't need to be a whiz kid to perform the analysis. Your own common sense is all you need to find out how the task is performed by hand.

Your objective is to analyze the manual system so that you can use Visual FoxPro to create a computerized version of the same system.

Say that you want to computerize the task of maintaining employee records. Also suppose that you enter employee information on a personnel form and stored that form in a file folder in the personnel department's file cabinet.

Your job is to create the database, tables, forms, and reports necessary to computerize the task of maintaining employee records. You begin the computerization process by analyzing the way employee records are maintained using the manual system.

The concept of input output

Every manual system used to manage data has three basic components:

- ✔ Data input
- ✔ Data processing
- ✔ Data output

Data input is the collection of information. Data input is a fancy term for writing information on paper, such as when you fill out an employment application.

Data processing is the term used to describe what you do with the information after it's collected. Simply, data processing occurs when the personnel manager reads information on the employment application.

Data output occurs when information collected during data input is copied onto another piece of paper. Data output happens when the personnel manager copies information from the employment application into a letter sent to the candidate offering a position with the firm.

Identifying data input, data processing, and data output

Your analysis of any manual system begins with finding data input, data processing, and data output of the manual system. Here's how to do the analysis:

1. **Take a piece of paper and label it Data Input; then list all the information that is collected by the manual system.**

The paper will contain all the data input. Typically, one or more forms collect information in a manual system, which makes your job easy. Simply find a copy of the forms and list on the paper all the information, such as first name, last name, and street.

Table 19-1 shows you how your data input sheet would look if you were planning to computerize employee files. You may even have more on your list; I purposely limited the number of data input items so that the table could fit on a page in this book.

2. Determine the number of characters used for each piece of information on your data input list.

You need to know the number of characters for each item on your list when you create tables for the computerized version of the system. You can brush up on how to determine the size of information in Chapter 1 and Chapter 2.

3. Determine the kind of information for each item on your data input list.

Information can be

- Text
- Numbers
- Currency
- Logical, such as yes/no or true/false

Table 19-1	Results of the Data Input Analysis	
Information	*Size*	*Kind*
first name	20	text
middle name	20	text
last name	30	text
salary	6	currency
sex	1	logical

4. Label another sheet of paper Data Processing; then list all the data processing that occurs in the manual system.

Table 19-2 shows you how your data-processing sheet would look if you were planning to computerize employee files. Again, your list will probably be longer than the one shown in Table 19-2.

Typical data processing includes

- Data modification
- Data calculations

Table 19-2	Results of the Data Process Analysis

Data Process
The personnel manager reads the employment application.
The personnel manager calculates the months of employment for previous jobs.
The personnel manager calculates the number of years of continued employment.
During the interview, the personnel manager deletes information and modifies other information based on the responses of the applicant.

5. **Take another piece of paper and label it Data Output; then list all the ways data from the manual system is used.**

Look for reports that contain information maintained by the manual system. Be sure to list the name of each report and all the information that appears on the report. You need this information when you recreate the reports in Visual FoxPro. Table 19-3 contains an abbreviated list of a data output report. You've completed your analysis.

Table 19-3	Results of the Data Output Analysis

Reports	*Data on Reports*
Department Report	first name
	middle name
	last name
	title
	salary
Telephone Directory	last name
	first name
	department name
	telephone number

Identifying data flow

Data flow is the sophisticated way of saying which data is collected first and then what you do with the data after you collect it. Say you want to computerize employee recordkeeping. Before you identify data flow, you should identify the data that needs to be collected, the data processing, and the reports that use the data. (See the section "Identifying data input, data processing, and data output," earlier in this chapter.) Then you're ready to determine the order in which data input, data processing, and data output happens.

Here's how you do it:

1. **Label a new piece of paper Data Input Flow; then list the order in which data needs to be collected.**

2. **Review your data input list and the manual system to decide the order in which the data is collected.**

   If you're computerizing employee records, for example, the typical order in an employment application is first name, middle name, last name, street, city, state, and zip.

3. **Label another new piece of paper Data Processing Flow; then list the order in which data needs to be processed.**

   If you want to see an example of a typical data processing flow, check out the sidebar "If you want to computerize employee records."

If you want to computerize employee records

If you're computerizing employee records, for example, your Data Processing Flow list may look something like the following list:

✔ The applicant must acquire a blank employment application.

✔ After the applicant enters data into the employment application, a member of the personnel staff quickly reviews the data to make sure that all the information is entered in a reasonable way. For example, the staff member may check to make sure that a date is actually entered into the "Date Graduated" portion of the employment application.

✔ The staff member places the employment application in a folder.

✔ The staff member tells the personnel manager that the employment application is ready for review.

✔ The personnel manager reviews the employment application before the interview.

✔ The personnel manager modifies information on the employment application based on responses given by the candidate during the interview.

✔ The employment application is then returned to the folder and filed.

3. **Label another piece of paper Data Output Flow; then list the order in which data flows out of the system and break your list into sections.**

The first section should contain those reports and other data output that must follow a particular order. The other section lists reports and other data output that can be produced on demand.

Keep the following tips in mind when you're determining data output flow.

✔ **Sometimes the order of the data output flow must follow a particular order.** For example, an employment application must be reviewed by the personnel manager before the department manager reviews the employment application. Likewise, the department manager must review the employment application before information on the employment application is sent on to the payroll department.

✔ **Other times the order of the data output flow is not in any particular order.** For example, data from the employee record system is used for the telephone directory and for a roster of employees for each department in the company, among other kinds of reports which are produced on demand.

Identifying Pieces of a Computerized System

A computerized system has the same three basic components found in a manual system: data input, data processing, and data output. You probably recognize the components as a data entry form, a query or some other processing, and a report. Data output also can be a form which displays information on-screen.

Your objective is to find out which Visual FoxPro components you can use to provide the same functionality as the manual system.

Building the database

Use all the data on your Data Input sheet as a reference for creating the database and tables for the computerized version of the system. You must:

✔ Make sure that all the information used in the manual system is included in the database and tables of the computerized system.

✔ Group together information so that similar information is stored in the same table. This process is called *normalization*. (See Chapter 1.)

✔ Create a database and tables to store the data. (See Chapters 1 and 2.)

Building views

Review the Data Input sheet, Data Processing sheet, and Data Output sheet to identify which pieces of data are used together for data input, data processing, and data output.

Here's what you do next:

✔ List all the data for each data group on a piece of paper. Label the paper Data Groups.

✔ Write alongside each piece of data the name of the table where the data is stored.

✔ Create a view for each data group. (See Chapter 4.) You use the view whenever the computerized version of the system performs data input, data processing, and data output.

Building the indexes

Review the Data Input sheet and the Data Output sheet to determine how information in the manual system is recalled and sorted. You must:

✔ Identify data used to recall information, such as a person's Social Security number.

✔ Identify data used to place information in order for reports.

✔ Create an index for each way data is recalled and for each way data is sorted. (See Chapter 3.)

Building forms

Review the Data Input, Data Processing, Data Output, Data Input Flow, and Data Processing Flow sheets to assist you in building the forms for the computerized system. You can use a form for numerous purposes, such as:

✔ Collecting information

✔ Reviewing the data to see whether it's in an acceptable format

✔ Presenting data on-screen

Your data input analysis identifies the way data is collected in the manual system, which usually is with a form. The easiest way to create a form for the computerized system is to try to copy the format of the form used in the manual system. Here are some pointers:

✔ **Use the same labels to identify places to enter data on the computerized form as you use on the manual system's form.** For example, if the manual system's form uses the label "Telephone Number" to show the applicant where to enter the telephone number on the form, then the computerized form also should use the same text for the label.

✔ **Keep the same data flow and data organization on the computerized form as is used on the manual system's form.** For example, the first name typically comes before the middle name and then the last name follows. Everyone who uses the manual system's form is used to seeing data in a particular place on the form. If you use the same data flow and organization, you need to do less re-training when you change to the computerized system's form.

✔ **Where appropriate, build the same data-processing functions used in the manual system into the computerized form.** For example, when an applicant completes an employment application, someone in the personnel department quickly reviews the data to make sure that the required information is included and that the data is in the proper place on the form. The computerized system accomplishes the same validation process by using the data validation features of fields in a table. (See Chapters 1 and 2.)

✔ **Create a computerized form for each form used in the manual system.** (See Chapter 11.) Be sure to take advantage of features available in Visual FoxPro that aren't available in the manual system, such as using a Combo Box control that lets the user choose a correct value from a list of valid entries.

Building reports

Review the data output sheet and the data output flow sheet and determine the reports that need to be created in the computerized system. Typically, you collect copies of reports already used, which can serve as a model for the computerized reports that you create.

Here's what to do:

✔ **Match the data needed for the report you create with the existing report and tables in the database you created.** Typically, you use a view rather than a table. (Most information contained in the report is found in more than one table in the database because you've normalized the data.)

✔ **Examine the report data from the manual system to see whether the data is grouped together or sorted a particular way.** Typically, data is grouped and/or sorted based on the value in one or more fields. You need to know the grouping and sorting criteria so that you can reproduce the report in Visual FoxPro.

✔ **Examine the report to determine whether any data is the result of a calculation of other data on the report.** For example, a field may display total sales of a product, which represents the sum of values in the sales field of the database. You can perform the calculation at the time Visual FoxPro generates the report. (See Chapter 14.)

✔ **Decide whether data on the report is just a selection of the data that is stored in the database.** For example, a report may display account information for accounts that produce revenue of more than $100,000.

If the report contains a selection of data, then identify the selection criteria. Create a query (see Chapter 10) using the same criteria and designate the output of the query to a report.

✔ **Create the report using the techniques in Chapter 14.**

Creating a Project

Databases, tables, forms, reports, and queries that you create for a computerized version of the manual system should be grouped together into a project. A *project* is a way to associate various files (for example, databases, tables, forms, and so on) to a single name, the name of the project.

You can open the project anytime you need to use any component of the project. You also can then open the component directly from the project dialog box, which eliminates the need to hunt around your disk for the files you need.

Making a new project

To make a new project, you simply start a project and add databases, tables, forms, reports, and queries that you've already created to the project. You also can create a new database, tables, forms, reports, and queries directly from the Project Manager. Here's how you add files to the project:

1. **Choose File⇨New.**

   The New dialog box, shown in Figure 19-1, appears.

Figure 19-1:
The New
dialog box.

2. **Select Project from the New dialog box to begin a new project; then click the New file button.**

   The Create dialog box, shown in Figure 19-2, appears.

3. **Enter the name for the project in the Enter text box.**

4. **Click Save.**

   The Project Manager dialog box, shown in Figure 19-3, appears. You use this dialog box to manage your project.

5. **Click the Data tab, shown in Figure 19-4.**

   You use the Data tab to add databases, free tables, and queries to the project.

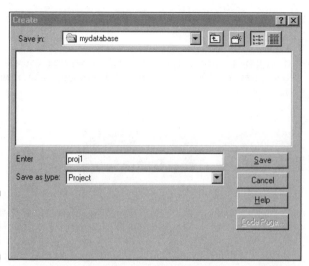

Figure 19-2:
The Create
dialog box.

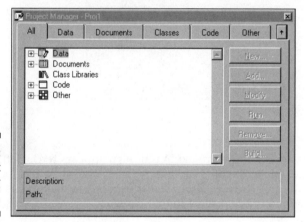

Figure 19-3:
The Project
Manager
dialog box.

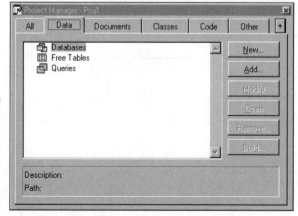

Figure 19-4:
The Data
tab of the
Project
Manager
dialog box.

6. **Highlight the type of file you want to add to the project.**

7. **Click Add.**

   The Open dialog box, shown in Figure 19-5, appears. (You also can click New to create a new file — for example, a database, form, report, or so on — for the project.)

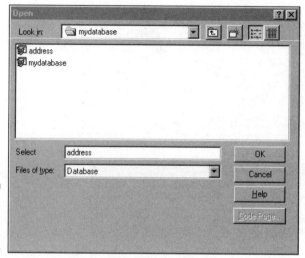

Figure 19-5:
The Open
dialog box.

8. **Click OK.**

   The file is added to the project. A plus sign appears to the left of the type of file you highlighted on the Project Manager dialog box. When you double-click the plus sign, the list expands to display the names of the files added to the project in that category, as shown in Figure 19-6.

Figure 19-6:
Double-
click the
plus sign to
display the
names of
the files
added to
the project
in that
category.

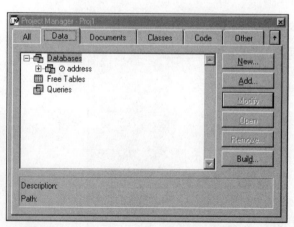

9. **Double-click the filename in the Data tab.**

   Visual FoxPro displays the file.

10. **Click the Document tab to add forms, reports, and labels to the project.**

    Repeat Steps 6-10, using the Document tab rather than the Data tab.

11. **Click Build.**

    The Build Options dialog box, shown in Figure 19-7, appears. You use this dialog box to rebuild the project.

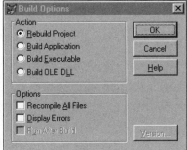

Figure 19-7:
The Build
Options
dialog box.

12. **Select the Rebuild Project radio button and then click OK.**

    Visual FoxPro saves the project to disk and closes the Build Options dialog box. You use the other options in the Build Options dialog box to create a Visual FoxPro application, which can be run on a computer that doesn't have Visual FoxPro installed. Refer to the owner's documentation for more information about creating a Visual FoxPro application. For now, simply rebuild the project.

13. **Click the Close button to close the Project Manager dialog box.**

    You're now finished creating a project.

Part VI
The Part of Tens

The 5th Wave   By Rich Tennant

"HOLD ON, THAT'S NOT A PROGRAM ERROR, IT'S JUST A BOOGER ON THE SCREEN."

In this part . . .

I'm not one for breaking tradition, especially a tradition that has been successful tens of millions of times. So I must close this book of adventures in Visual FoxPro with the classic, anticipated Part of Tens.

You receive enlightenment and excitement far beyond your worldly experiences in this part. (Sorry. I'm close to finishing the book and got a little carried away.) The topics and tidbits in Part VI are well worth the time that it takes you to read these chapters.

Chapter 20

Ten Useful Things to Type in the Command Window

● ●

In This Chapter

▶ Looking behind the scenes of Visual FoxPro

▶ Taking control of Visual FoxPro by giving commands

● ●

*T*hroughout the book, I show you how to create databases, tables, fields, forms, and reports by using designer tools provided by Visual FoxPro. Although these tools offer an intuitive way to put the program through its paces, advanced users of Visual FoxPro type commands in the Command Window to give orders to Visual FoxPro. (Refer to Chapter 7 if you're unfamiliar with the Command Window.)

Typing commands gives you an advantage over using designer tools because controls allow you to control every action of Visual FoxPro, including many actions that cannot be performed through the use of designer tools.

Also, you place commands into a program file, which allows you to issue a sequence of commands without typing each command separately in the Command Window. All you need to do is to have Visual FoxPro read the program file.

This chapter explores ten or so of the most useful commands. You can investigate the other commands (more than a hundred of them) on your own by reading the online documentation and the printed documentation that comes with Visual FoxPro.

USE and BROWSE

The USE command tells Visual FoxPro to open a table that you've already created. Suppose that you want to see all the records in a table named geninfo. Instead of using the Open dialog box, you can type the USE command, followed by the table's name, in the Command Window. (Substitute the name of your table for geninfo, of course.)

```
USE geninfo
```

Nothing happens when you press Enter after typing the USE command; Visual FoxPro simply waits for your next command. Although you told the program that you want to use the geninfo table, you didn't tell it *how* you want to use the table.

To display records in the table, enter the BROWSE command in the Command Window, as follows:

```
BROWSE
```

APPEND BLANK, DELETE, and PACK

The commands APPEND BLANK, DELETE, and PACK are helpful when you work with a table.

When you issue the USE command, Visual FoxPro opens the table, but doesn't display anything on-screen. Think of the table as being open inside your computer. Before you can insert a new record into the table, you must tell Visual FoxPro to make room in the table for the new record. APPEND BLANK inserts an empty record at the bottom of the opened table. After you open space for the new information, you issue the BROWSE command to display the table on-screen. Then you can enter information in fields of the new record.

If you decide to remove a record from the table, enter the DELETE command to mark the current record for deletion. Whenever you enter SET DELETED ON in the Command Window, Visual FoxPro treats records that are marked for deletion as being deleted. Entering SET DELETED OFF tells the program to ignore the deletion marks so that you can use all the records.

Issue the PACK command whenever you want to get rid of records that are marked for deletion. Visual FoxPro rewrites the table, excluding the records that are marked for deletion.

CLOSE

The CLOSE command closes databases, tables, and other objects and removes them from the screen. Use the CLOSE command whenever you want to shut down databases and tables so that you can start over again.

Whenever you use the CLOSE command, you must tell Visual FoxPro what kind of object you want to close. CLOSE ALL TABLES, for example, closes an open table. CLOSE ALL DATABASES shuts an open database. And if you want to close an open form, type CLOSE ALL FORMS in the Command Window.

MODI STRUCT

Collectively, field names, file types, and field sizes of a table are called the *structure of the table*. In Chapter 6, I show you how to use menus and dialog boxes to display and modify the table structure. Here's a way to display and modify the table structure by using a single command:

1. **Enter the** USE **command in the Command Window to tell Visual FoxPro which table you want to modify.**

2. **Enter the** MODI STRUCT **command in the Command Window.**

   Visual FoxPro displays the Table Designer dialog box, in which you make changes. (Refer to Chapter 6.)

3. **Click OK to close the Table Designer and save the changes that you made in the table.**

MESSAGEBOX()

You can display your own message in a message box by using the MESSAGEBOX() command in the Command Window or in a program file.

The MESSAGEBOX() command requires three pieces of information:

- The text to appear in the message box
- The button(s) to appear in the message box
- The text to be the title of the message box

Suppose that you create a program file containing two commands, and the first command displays a form. When you close the form, the program file displays a message box. The title of the message box is "Goodbye," and the message is "Thanks for using my program." You also want an OK button to appear in the message box.

Here's what you need to type in the Visual FoxPro Command Window:

```
DO FORM myform
MESSAGEBOX( Thanks for using my program. , 0,  Goodbye )
```

Notice that all three pieces of information are inserted inside the parentheses, separated by commas. The first piece of information is the text of the message; following that text is the number used to represent the OK button. The title is the last piece of information.

You can use an assortment of buttons in the message box by changing the value of the button number. Stick with using only the OK button until you become proficient in programming Visual FoxPro. You can find more information about the values of button numbers in the online help system.

Besides buttons, you can include various pictures in the message box by using the appropriate numbers. These pictures include

- A stop sign (value 16)
- A question mark (value 32)
- An exclamation point (value 48)

You can use both buttons and pictures in a message box by adding the corresponding numbers. Suppose that you want to show the OK button and the stop sign in the message box. Add the numbers: 0+16.

You can also enter the number 16 in place of 0 in the message box. Other button combinations, however, such as the OK and Cancel button combination, have a value greater than 0. Therefore, you must add the button value and the picture value to determine the number that you place in the message box command.

Here's how to include the "Goodbye" message and the stop-sign picture in the message box:

```
MESSAGEBOX( Thanks for using my program. , 0+16,  Goodbye )
```

Chapter 21

Ten Top Operators

In This Chapter

▶ Compare values by using operators

▶ Join expressions by using operators

▶ Determine the order in which operators are used in an expression

*V*isual FoxPro has many operators that you can use in expressions. I cover ten of the most useful operators in this chapter. You can look up the other operators in the online help system.

Equal (=)

The equal operator asks Visual FoxPro to compare two values and determine whether the value to the left of the operator is equal to the value to the right of the operator. You use the equal operator frequently to compare values, which is why it makes my top-ten list.

If the value on the left side is equal to the value on the right side, Visual FoxPro tells that you the comparison is true; otherwise, it reports the comparison as false.

Here's an example in which Visual FoxPro is asked to compare two values:

```
54 = 54
```

The result is True.

Not Equal (<>)

The not-equal operator asks Visual FoxPro to compare two values and determine whether the value to the left of the operator is not equal to the value to the right of the operator. You use the not-equal comparison many times when you create queries and reports, which makes this operator one that you need to know.

If the value on the left side is not equal to the value on the right side, Visual FoxPro tells you that the comparison is true; otherwise, it reports the comparison as false.

In the following example, Visual FoxPro is asked to determine whether two values are not the same:

```
54 <> 32
```

Because the values are different, the result is True.

Greater Than (>)

The greater-than operator asks Visual FoxPro to compare two values and determine whether the value to the left of the operator is greater than the value to the right of the operator. This operator is an important one to use when you're creating a query in your database.

If the value on the left side is greater than the value on the right side, Visual FoxPro tells you that the comparison is true; otherwise, it reports the comparison as false.

In this example, Visual FoxPro is asked to decide whether 54 is greater than 32:

```
54 > 32
```

Visual FoxPro returns True.

Less Than (<)

The less-than operator asks Visual FoxPro to compare two values and determine whether the value to the left of the operator is less than the value to the right of the operator. I include this operator among the top ten because you almost always need to use it in reports and queries.

If the value on the left side is less than the value on the right side, Visual FoxPro tells you that the comparison is true; otherwise, it reports the comparison as false.

Here's an example in which Visual FoxPro is asked to decide whether 32 is less than 54:

```
32 < 54
```

Visual FoxPro returns True.

Greater Than or Equal To (>=)

The greater-than-or-equal-to operator asks Visual FoxPro to compare two values and determine whether the value to the left of the operator is greater than or equal to the value to the right of the operator. The greater-than-or-equal-to operator makes the top-ten list for helping you simplify the search criteria in a query.

If the value on the left side is greater than or equal to the value on the right side, Visual FoxPro tells you that the comparison is true; otherwise, it reports the comparison as false.

Here's an example in which Visual FoxPro is asked to decide whether 54 is greater than or equal to 32:

```
54 >= 32
```

Visual FoxPro returns True.

Less Than or Equal To (<=)

The less-than-or-equal-to operator asks Visual FoxPro to compare two values and determine whether the value to the left of the operator is less than or equal to the value to the right of the operator. You can streamline a complex query by using this operator rather than a combination of the less-than operator and the equal operator.

If the value on the left side is less than or equal to the value on the right side, Visual FoxPro tells you that the comparison is true; otherwise, it reports the comparison as false.

In this example, Visual FoxPro is asked to decide whether 32 is less than 54:

```
32 <= 54
```

The result is True.

.AND.

The .AND. operator asks Visual FoxPro to compare the results of two expressions and determine whether the expressions on both sides of the operator are true. The .AND. operator is the only way to join two expressions for a query, so the top-ten list wouldn't be complete without it.

If both expressions are true, Visual FoxPro tells you that the comparison is true; otherwise, it reports the comparison as false.

Here's an example in which Visual FoxPro is asked to decide whether 32 is less than 54 and whether 33 is greater than 22:

```
(32 < 54) .AND. (33 > 22)
```

The result is True.

.NOT.

The .NOT. operator asks Visual FoxPro to reverse the logic of the expression. The .NOT. operator makes the top-ten list because you can use it to change the logic of an expression quickly.

If the expression is false, Visual FoxPro tells you that the expression is true; otherwise, it reports the expression as false.

Here's an example in which Visual FoxPro is asked to reverse the logic of an expression:

```
.NOT. (33 > 22)
```

Because 33 is greater than 22, the expression is true, but the .NOT. operator reverses the result to False.

.OR.

The .OR. operator asks Visual FoxPro to compare the results of two expressions and determine whether either of the expressions is true. You can use the .OR. operator to consolidate multiple expressions into one expression. (Any time-saving step makes my top-ten list.)

If one expression is true, Visual FoxPro tells you that the comparison is true; otherwise, it reports the comparison as false.

In this example, Visual FoxPro is asked to decide whether 54 is less than 32 or whether 33 is greater than 22.

```
(54 < 32) .OR. (33 > 22)
```

Only the 33 > 22 expression is true, of course. As long as one of the expressions is true, Visual FoxPro returns True.

Group ( )

The group operator tells Visual FoxPro which operation should be performed first. Visual FoxPro performs operations in order, according to a table called the *precedence table,* which Visual FoxPro uses whenever you tell it to perform an operation. The group operator changes the order of operations.

I'm always getting confused about the order in which Visual FoxPro solves an expression. The group operator allows me to be explicit in the way that I want Visual FoxPro to solve an expression. Removing the confusion for me — and Visual FoxPro — shoots the group operator into the top-ten list.

Suppose that you want Visual FoxPro to solve the following equation, which performs multiplication and addition:

```
10 * 5 + 6
```

What is the result of the equation — 56 or 110? Either value can be correct, depending on the order in which the operations are performed. If multiplication is performed first, the result is 56. If addition is performed first, the result is 110.

Visual FoxPro performs multiplication and division before addition and subtraction. Therefore, the correct answer is 56.

You can tell Visual FoxPro which of the two calculations to perform first by placing parentheses around the expression. Suppose that you want addition to be performed before multiplication. Here's how to do it:

```
10*(5+6)
```

The group operator tells Visual FoxPro to add 5 and 6 and then multiply the result by 10.

Always use the group operator to make sure that both you and Visual FoxPro know how you want an expression to be calculated. Otherwise, you may be disappointed with the result of the calculation.

Chapter 22

Ten Things That Sometimes Go Wrong

In This Chapter

▶ Finding data lost in a table

▶ Joining tables that can't be joined

▶ Getting your Internet search page working

---

*V*isual FoxPro is easy and fun to use, but you'll probably stumble across some common problems. Expect these problems to arise at the worst possible time and drive you into a state of panic.

Try to keep a cool head and remember — Visual FoxPro does only what it is told to do. Someone probably gave Visual FoxPro the wrong instruction.

In this chapter, I discuss the ten most common problems. I also give you my solutions to these problems, of course, so that you don't go crazy when you run into them.

A Window Disappears When You Open Another Window

As you create databases, tables, forms, and reports, you're bound to run into this problem: All of a sudden, most of the windows on-screen disappear. You start to panic, thinking you really messed up. (At least, that's what I thought when I lost the Properties dialog box while I was creating a form — there one second and gone the next.)

Don't fret; nothing is lost. Windows can become hidden by other windows that appear on top of them. If this happens to you, choose the Window menu to see the list of open windows. The window that has a check mark next to its name is the current window. Click the name of the window that you think is lost to make it reappear. Visual FoxPro then moves that window to the top of the stack of windows on-screen.

If you don't see your window listed (if you're missing the Properties dialog box, for example), you can reopen the window by clicking the appropriate toolbar button.

Tables Just Don't Relate

One painful problem is bound to make you yell, "I hate computers!" The problem that I'm referring to occurs when you try to join tables into a view, and Visual FoxPro displays a message box, telling you that the tables can't be joined.

Don't blame the program; the person who entered records in the table caused the problem. As I show you in Chapter 7, you can join two tables to create a view if the tables contain a common field and if all the records of both tables have the same value in the common field. When Visual FoxPro tells you that the tables can't be joined, there's a good chance that one or more values in the common fields don't match.

Suppose that the Social Security number is used as the value in the common field of both tables, meaning that every common field in Table 1 has the same Social Security number as the common field in Table 2. Visual FoxPro matches the value of the Social Security number field in each record of Table 1 to Table 2 when the tables are joined.

If a Social Security number is in a record of Table 1 and not in a record of Table 2, however, Visual FoxPro can't join the tables. The likely reason for the mismatch is that someone entered the Social Security number in Table 1 and not in Table 2. The fix is to enter the missing Social Security number in Table 2.

You Can't Find Data That You Know Is in the Database

Nothing can be more exasperating than data disappearing from a table when you browse the table. Many factors can cause this problem. The most common cause is that you accidentally marked the record for deletion, and Visual FoxPro isn't showing records marked for deletion.

Here's a quick fix:

1. **Press Ctrl+F2 to display the Command Window.**

2. **Type** SET DELETED OFF.

3. **Press Enter.**

4. **Browse the table again.**

   You should see the missing record. The first column of the record probably is dark, indicating that the record is marked for deletion.

5. **Click the column to remove the deletion mark.**

The Search for Data Comes Up Empty

Visual FoxPro uses several methods to find data in your database. The most common method involves using an index. (I show you how to locate information in Chapter 8.)

An index is separate from the table that contains the information you seek. When you ask Visual FoxPro to hunt down information, it searches the index for the search criteria. If no match is found, Visual FoxPro reports that no such data exists.

The data could exist in the table and not in the index, however, if the index wasn't used when information was entered in the table. You can easily bring the index and the table in sync again by choosing Table⇨Rebuild Indexes. You'll be able to find the data the next time that you use the index to search the table.

You Can't Recall Records That Were Deleted

When you choose Table⇨Recall Records, you can unmark records that are marked for deletion. When you choose this command, all the deleted records should appear in the table.

If the deleted records don't reappear, chances are that you told Visual FoxPro to remove deleted records from the table. Accordingly, Visual FoxPro rewrote the table, excluding the deleted records. In that case, you've lost the records and can't recover them.

You Got .AND. and .OR. Mixed Up

Two of the most confusing operators in Visual FoxPro are the `.AND.` and `.OR.` operators. Sometimes, I use the `.OR.` operator when I should use the `.AND.` operator and come out with the wrong result.

The `.AND.` and `.OR.` operators are called *logical operators* because they result in an answer of true or false. Visual FoxPro uses `.T.` for true and `.F.` for false. You can use these values in an `IF..ENDIF` statement if you decide to venture into programming Visual FoxPro; the `IF..ENDIF` statement causes Visual FoxPro to make a decision. (Check the online help system for more information about programming and the `IF..ENDIF` statement.)

The `.AND.` and `.OR.` operators compare the results of other logical operators. Here's an example:

```
54 > 33
```

This logical expression tells Visual FoxPro to determine whether 54 is greater than 33. If so, the program returns a true value.

Here's another logical expression:

```
76 < 100
```

This expression asks Visual FoxPro to determine whether 76 is less than 100. If so, the program returns a true value.

You also can ask Visual FoxPro to determine whether both expressions are true. Use the `.AND.` operator to combine the two preceding expressions in one expression, as follows:

```
54 > 33 .AND. 76 < 100
```

The `.AND.` operator tells Visual FoxPro to return a true value if both the first expression (`54 > 33`) *and* the second expression (`76 < 100`) are true. If both expressions aren't true, the program returns a false value.

Now change the expression to use the `.OR.` operator so that the program returns a true value if either the first expression *or* the second expression is true. Here's the expression to use:

```
54 > 33 .OR. 100 < 76
```

You Forgot a Field in a Table

Just when you think that you've designed the perfect table, you discover that you left out a field. Don't blame yourself; simply fix the problem by inserting the missing field into the table.

Here's how you do it:

1. **Choose File⇨Open to display the Open dialog box.**

2. **Choose the database that contains the table you want to use and click OK.**

   The Database Designer dialog box appears.

3. **In the Database Designer, double-click the table box that contains the field you want to add.**

   Visual FoxPro displays the records.

4. **Choose Table⇨Properties to display the Work Area Properties dialog box.**

5. **Click the Modify button to display the Table Designer dialog box.**

6. **Insert the field by using the technique that I show you in Chapter 1.**

7. **Click OK to return to the Work Area Properties dialog box.**

8. **Click OK to save your changes.**

   You return to the Database Designer.

9. **Click OK to close the Database Designer.**

You Can't Search a Remote Database

A nice feature of Visual FoxPro is its capability to search databases located on other computers — *remote databases*. (A remote database does not have to be a Visual FoxPro database.) The advantage of the feature loses its thrill, however, when you can't access the remote database.

You may have difficulty with a remote database for two common reasons:

✔ **You left out a step in the login procedure.** My suggestion: Call the system administrator who is responsible for the remote database and have that person walk you through the connection process.

✔ **The remote database isn't compatible with the Microsoft Open Database Connectivity protocol (ODBC).** In this case, you cannot use Visual FoxPro to connect to the remote database.

You Can't Run the Visual FoxPro Search Page for Your Web Site

Building a search page for your Internet Web site is easy when you have Visual FoxPro. If you discover that the search page doesn't work, though, don't go pulling out your hair. The most common reason for the failure of a search page lies in the server used to host your Web site. The search page and related files work only on Windows NT Server or the Internet Information Server; further, the server must be running Visual FoxPro Version 3.0b or later.

Ask your Internet Service Provider (ISP) whether the site's server has the proper server software and whether Visual FoxPro is on the server. If not, ask the ISP whether the software can be loaded onto the server. If the ISP won't load the software, consider moving your Web site to a more cooperative provider.

Color in Reports Doesn't Match Color On-Screen

You can spend hours designing a report and applying colors to data, only to find that the colors are different when the report is printed.

There's no guarantee that on-screen colors will match the colors generated by the printer because two separate machines are involved. The color match is usually close enough for typical applications but not commercial applications, such as advertisements.

If the colors in the printed report are drastically different from the colors on-screen, the printer's printing cartridges may be misaligned. Re-align the cartridges, using the software provided by the printer manufacturer for that purpose. Your color problem should be solved.

Chapter 23
Ten Places to Find Help

In This Chapter

▶ Online help

▶ Technical support lines

▶ Training companies

*T*his book covers everything that a normal person needs to know about Visual FoxPro. Overachievers, however, may desire more help — or at least want to know where to find additional information about Visual FoxPro. In this chapter, I discuss several places where you can go for help. You should find these places to be good sources of information.

Online Help

Visual FoxPro is ready and willing to give you assistance at a moment's notice. All you need to do is press the F1 key. Visual FoxPro is smart and can practically guess the kind of help you require from the situation that you're in when you press F1 because help is context-sensitive. *Context-sensitive* means that Visual FoxPro sees what you're doing when you ask for help and then displays the appropriate help text.

Suppose that you display the Expression Builder dialog box (see Chapter 2). The dialog box contains options that I don't cover in the book because you normally don't use these features. But if you want to know more about building an expression with the Expression Builder dialog box, press the F1 key. Visual FoxPro displays the help topic that shows you detailed information on how to use that dialog box.

Pressing F1 is much easier than using the Help menu because when you press F1, Visual FoxPro automatically displays the help topic that you need. You don't have to search through the online documentation that the Help menu provides.

Online Documentation

At one time or another, you'll be unsure how to use a feature of Visual FoxPro. I know, because it happens to the best of us. Nobody can know everything about Visual FoxPro — including the people who work for Microsoft. So when I'm unsure about something, I immediately call up the Visual FoxPro online documentation from the Help menu.

Rather than show you a single help topic, Visual FoxPro opens the online documentation so that you can review the contents.

You can review keywords in the online documentation by choosing Help⇨Index. A list of keywords appears. Scroll down the list of keywords or type the keyword in the text box; then double-click the keyword to see the topics that discuss it in detail.

Suppose that you want to find help by using the index. Follow these steps:

1. **Choose Help⇨Index.**

   A list of keywords appears.

2. **In the text box, type the word that you want to find help on or scroll down the list of keywords until you find the word.**

3. **Double-click the word.**

   If you chose print, for example, Visual FoxPro shows you all the ways that you can print, one of which is printing from a report.

Visual FoxPro Manuals

You can find a comprehensive — and rather nerdy — presentation of all features available in Visual FoxPro by reviewing the Visual FoxPro manuals, which are similar to the owner's manual that you receive when you purchase a VCR.

Visual FoxPro has two sets of manuals: on paper and on disk.

The paper version of the manual is the four books that come in the Visual FoxPro box. Although these books are perfect for putting you to sleep within the first ten pages, they do contain valuable information about every facet of Visual FoxPro that you could ever dream of using.

The online version of the manual, however, is super. Unless you loaded the customized version of Visual FoxPro on your hard disk, you have to insert the floppy disk or CD-ROM that contains the documentation into your computer before you can read the manual. When the disk is in place, choose Help➪Documentation. Visual FoxPro goes out to the disk and displays the table of contents for the manuals.

Finding your way through the manuals is easy, although the contents at times may seem to be written in a foreign language. Don't feel that you have to grasp everything. No one knows everything about Visual FoxPro — and you don't need to worry about final exams!

Visual FoxPro Technical Support Lines

If the online help and documentation are too confusing, pick up your telephone and give Bill Gates' people a call. Excellent support technicians are ready and able to answer your question, no matter how bizarre it is.

You can talk to a human, listen to answers to common questions from a machine, or receive your answers via fax. You also can e-mail your questions to technical support; someone will get back to you within about 24 hours. TDD and Text Telephone services are available for individuals with hearing impairments. You can get all the pertinent telephone numbers by choosing Help➪Technical Support.

Microsoft's telephone technical support is free for a limited time, after which you're charged per call. The amount of free support can change. You're told about the current support policy whenever you call the technical-support staff, and you're told whenever you're charged for the service. (You always need to pay for the phone call yourself.)

Community Colleges

You probably can receive hands-on help with Visual FoxPro by attending a course at your local community college. For the names and numbers of schools near you, check the Colleges listings in the Yellow Pages of your telephone directory.

Don't let the term college keep you from calling; most community colleges don't require you to take an entrance test or submit high-school grades just to take a course on Visual FoxPro. And don't be intimidated if you find the Visual FoxPro course listed in the college catalog under the heading Computer Science. Courses on Visual FoxPro normally are not designed for whiz kids; they're designed for people like you.

Training Companies

Commercial training companies are good sources of help. Some companies retrain computer professionals; others set out to train service technicians. Stay away from these training companies because they'll confuse you more than they'll help you. Instead, look for a training company that specializes in helping students who want to master the personal-computer software that's used in a typical office. No doubt you'll find Visual FoxPro offered among the courses.

Be prepared to pay for the course. Visual FoxPro courses have no set prices or required curricula, so shop around before you register for a course offered by a training company. Make sure that you're satisfied with:

- The topics that will be taught
- The facilities
- The class size
- The price
- The time of day when the course is given

Computer Stores

Your local computer store is more than a place to purchase expensive hardware and software. The computer store is also a gathering place for all sorts of people who are interested in computer topics, including Visual FoxPro.

Stop by your local computer store and ask the salespeople whether they (or anyone else who works at the store) use Visual FoxPro. You may be surprised by the answer. Chances are good that someone who works for the store is a few steps ahead of you in using Visual FoxPro.

There's also a good chance that the store manager encourages the staff to answer your Visual FoxPro questions — especially if you ask questions at off-peak times and make purchases in the store.

User Groups

Visual FoxPro is a widely used product that has many user groups through-out the country. I strongly suggest that you get together with other Visual FoxPro users in your area so that you can exchange experiences and help one another out of tough spots in using the program.

Don't try to look up local Visual FoxPro user groups in your telephone book because it lists few user groups. Instead, visit your friends at your local computer store and ask whether they know of a local group. Also contact your local community college or other training facilities and ask whether someone can put you in touch with a Visual FoxPro user group. The best place to call, however, is Microsoft, which may have a list of user groups around the country.

Consultants

If you're in a real bind and are willing to pay some bucks to get the answers to your questions, consider paying a consultant to help you. Don't rush to find a consultant, however, because the other suggestions in this chapter are better sources of help. But if you're really stuck, a consultant may be the answer.

Visual FoxPro is professional-grade software and is used by people who make their living writing Visual FoxPro programs. (You can become one of those professionals, too, after you master Visual FoxPro.) Many Visual FoxPro consultants work for a firm for a few months and then move on to another company that needs their services. Consultants may receive $40 to $150 an hour for their expertise.

To find a consultant, check the Computers or Consultants listings in the Yellow Pages of your telephone directory.

Be careful: Visual FoxPro consultants probably aren't licensed and may not have any kind of certificate or degree. Therefore, you must check a consultant's references — and record at the Better Business Bureau — before you agree to work with that person.

The Internet

You can find a wealth of information about Visual FoxPro on the World Wide Web.

If you subscribe to CompuServe, be sure to visit the FoxForum, where you can find a community of Visual FoxPro users. The forum has areas on various topics for various skill levels. You can swap Visual FoxPro tips throughout the electronic neighborhood. This forum is a great way to make new friends who are also trying to master Visual FoxPro.

Also check out *CompuServe For Dummies,* by Wallace Wang (IDG Books Worldwide, Inc.) to have the same kind of pleasurable, lighthearted experience with CompuServe that you have in the FoxForum.

If you don't have CompuServe but are connected to the Internet, stop by the Microsoft Web site at www.microsoft.com. You can find information about all of Microsoft's products, including Visual FoxPro. For more information on the Internet, check out *The Internet For Dummies,* 4th Edition, by John R. Levine, Carol Baroudi, and Margaret Levine Young (IDG Books Worldwide, Inc.).

Chapter 24
Ten Best Keyboard Shortcuts

● ●

● ●

*Y*ou'll probably get tired of choosing menu after menu by the time you create your tenth database. A more productive way to use Visual FoxPro is to press the correct shortcut keys.

Some Visual FoxPro users feel that pointing and clicking the mouse is the most efficient way to use Visual FoxPro. I disagree, at least in situations such as cutting and pasting text. The fastest method is using the shortcut keys.

This chapter presents ten useful shortcut keys that I've discovered in my years of working with Visual FoxPro. (You can find other shortcut keys listed in the online help system.)

Esc (The Universal Go-Away Key)

The fastest way to quit whatever you're doing is to press the Esc key. You can close most windows by pressing Esc rather than clicking a button. The Esc key has the same effect as clicking the Cancel button in a dialog box, so you lose any changes that you entered in the dialog box.

Ctrl+Z (To Undo the Last Change)

You may find yourself making errors such as placing the wrong label in a form. If you catch the error right away, you can undo it by pressing Ctrl+Z. The trick is to press Ctrl+Z before you do anything else because the short-cut key reverses only the last thing that you did.

Ctrl+C (To Copy)

You can copy objects (such as labels and text boxes) and text to the Clipboard by selecting the object or text and then pressing Ctrl+C. Visual FoxPro replicates the object or text and places it in the Clipboard, from which you can paste it someplace else, such as in another form.

The Clipboard is a place in memory shared by all Windows programs. You can use Ctrl+C to copy text from practically any Windows program, such as Microsoft Word, and then paste the text into a control in a Visual FoxPro form. Simply select the object or text that you want to copy; then press Ctrl+C. Visual FoxPro copies whatever you selected to the Clipboard.

Ctrl+V (To Paste)

A fast way to paste objects (such as controls) or text from the Clipboard to a form or report is to press Ctrl+V. You must cut or copy an object or text to the Clipboard, of course, before you can use Ctrl+V to paste it from the Clipboard.

Click the place in the form or report where you want the object or text to appear; then press Ctrl+V. Visual FoxPro pastes the object or text where you clicked.

Ctrl+X (To Cut)

You sometimes need to remove an object or text from a form or report and place it in another form or report. Try pressing Ctrl+X, which is a convenient way to cut an object or text from a form or a report.

Select the object or text in the form or report; then press Ctrl+X. Visual FoxPro cuts the object or text from the form or report and places it in the Clipboard. Then you can press Ctrl+V (refer to the preceding shortcut) to place the object or text in the new form.

Ctrl+Y (To Add a Record)

Whenever you're browsing a table, you can insert a new record at the end of the table quickly by pressing Ctrl+Y. This shortcut key appends a blank record to the table. When the blank record is in place in the table, you can enter data in the fields of the table the way that I show you in Chapter 1. Here's how it's done:

1. **Open the database.**

   You see the tables associated with the database in the Database Designer.

2. **Double-click the table box of the table to which you want to add a record.**

3. **Press Ctrl+Y to enter a blank record at the end of the table.**

4. **Enter new data in the fields.**

5. **Click the Close button in the upper-right corner of the window to close the table and the Database Designer.**

Ctrl+T (To Mark a Record for Deletion)

A fast way to mark a record for deletion whenever you are browsing records of a table is to press Ctrl+T. Visual FoxPro marks the current record for deletion by darkening the first column of the record.

Here's what you do:

1. **Double-click the table box of the table in which you want to mark a record for deletion.**

2. **Press the up- and down-arrow keys to move to the record that you want to mark for deletion.**

3. **Press Ctrl+T.**

   Visual FoxPro places the deletion mark in the record. (If you press Ctrl+T again, Visual FoxPro removes the deletion mark from the record.)

Ctrl+F4 (To Close the Current Window)

When you create databases, tables, forms, and reports, your screen usually becomes cluttered with windows. A quick way to close windows is to press Ctrl+F4. Visual FoxPro closes the current window, leaving one fewer window to clutter the screen.

Click the window that you want to close to make it the current window; then press Ctrl+F4. Visual FoxPro removes that window from the screen.

Ctrl+F2 (To Open the Command Window)

Entering commands in the Command Window is much faster than making your way through a series of menus and dialog boxes. I show you the most useful commands in Chapter 23.

You must display the Command Window before you can enter commands. To display the window quickly, press Ctrl+F2.

F1 (To Get Online Help)

Whenever you get stuck while using a feature of Visual FoxPro, click the panic button, which is F1. This button displays the online help topic that you need. Visual FoxPro determines the help topic based on what feature you're using when you press F1.

Suppose that you're working in the Database Designer, and you aren't sure what to do next. Simply press F1. Visual FoxPro displays the topic that discusses all the features of the Database Designer. After you find the information that you need, press the Esc key to remove the help topic from the screen and return to the Database Designer.

Chapter 25

Ten Features to Explore Someday

● ●

In This Chapter

▶ Using the spell checker

▶ Importing and exporting your stuff

▶ Doing the whole programming thing

● ●

*V*isual FoxPro has many features for you to explore — when you get the time. This chapter discusses features that you may find interesting and worth your attention whenever you're looking for something to do.

Keep these features in mind after you get your feet wet using Visual FoxPro and are ready to embark on new challenges.

Using the Spell Checker

Authors are thankful for two assistants — a computer program's spell checker and a sharp copy editor who catches words that even the spell checker misses — that ensure that readers can understand every word of the text.

Fortunately for everyone, Visual FoxPro has a built-in spell checker. Make sure that you use the spell checker whenever you enter captions for controls or need to proofread text that you placed on-screen.

To use the spell checker, choose Tools⇨Spelling. All the features that you expect in a spell checker are in the Visual FoxPro spell checker, so if you're familiar with Windows, you'll feel at home using this tool.

Using Those Other Things in the Expression Builder

The Expression Builder has many features that I don't cover in this book because those features may confuse you right now. But the dialog box does have powerful capabilities. You can create sophisticated expressions by combining the expression-building techniques that I show you in Chapter 2 with the powerful functions that are available in the Expression Builder dialog box.

To unleash the true power of Visual FoxPro, spend a few hours exploring all the facets of the Expression Builder with the aid of the online help system.

Importing and Exporting Your Stuff

Sometimes, you want to share your data with friends or colleagues who don't own a copy of Visual FoxPro. Suppose that you want to exchange tables with someone who has a Paradox, Access, or Sybase database. You can easily do so by using the importing and exporting features of Visual FoxPro.

Exchanging data isn't complicated. Choose File⇔Import and Export, choose the appropriate feature, and the rest is self-explanatory. A wizard can walk you through the process of importing data into your tables, in case you want to take the easy approach to importing data.

Getting Organized By Using a Project File

As you explore databases, tables, forms, reports, and other objects, you soon realize that many kinds of files are used to create a typical Visual FoxPro application, such as one that tracks employees for your company. You're sure to lose track of the files required for your application on your disk, simply because you need so many files. But you can have Visual FoxPro keep tabs on the files by creating a project file.

A project file is like a project manager that records the files required for a project. To create a project file, follow these steps:

1. **Choose File➪New to display the New dialog box.**

2. **Select the Project radio button.**

3. **Click the New file button.**

   Visual FoxPro creates a project file for you. The rest of the process is self-explanatory.

Doing the Whole Programming Thing

Visual FoxPro is more than a database program — it's also a full-fledged programming language that professional programmers use to develop commercial applications for business and government. (I give you a taste of programming in Chapter 13, where I explain how to add functionality to objects, such as command buttons in a form.) You can build powerful applications if you know the proper commands to give the Visual FoxPro and how to give those commands in the proper order.

Programming is like doing a jigsaw puzzle. After you find one piece, you're hooked. Try getting one command to work, and you'll be hooked on programming Visual FoxPro. Who knows? Maybe you'll find a new career, earning big bucks as a Visual FoxPro programmer.

Finding Data Phonetically

A great feature that you can build into all your Visual FoxPro applications is called Soundex( ). This feature helps people who use your database find information even if they don't know how to spell.

Suppose that you're looking for a person by her first name, but you're not sure whether she spells her first name *Cathy* or *Kathy*. Visual FoxPro requires you to know at least the first letter of the name if you're using a typical index with the table that contains the first name.

If you use Soundex( ), however, you need only spell the name phonetically because Soundex( ) searches for a name based on how the name sounds. So Soundex( ) will find *Cathy* or *Kathy*.

Using the SQL Language

You can quiz Visual FoxPro about the information that you store in a database by using many techniques, one of which is using the SQL language.

SQL is short for *Standard Query Language,* which is a standard way of accessing information in practically any database program, such as Paradox, Sybase, and, of course, Visual FoxPro. So if you understand SQL and can use it to query your Visual FoxPro databases, you can query other popular database programs without having to develop new skills.

Using the Debugger

No matter how hard you try, some things always seem to go wrong. Don't think that you'll have any better success with Visual FoxPro. Unlike the rest of your life, however, Visual FoxPro is ready with tools that can help you solve practically any problem.

The primary problem-solving tool is called the Debugger, which gets its name from removing bugs from your Visual FoxPro application. *Bug* is a nerd term for something that doesn't work properly. Therefore, a debugger is like a bug zapper (without noise). Make sure that you spend a few moments exploring how to use the Visual FoxPro Debugger; you'll find this tool to be a life-saver. To display the Debugger, choose Tools⇨Debugger.

Using the Setup Wizard

After spending countless hours creating a database and tables, building forms, and assembling reports, you may want to give a copy of your work to a friend. And when you become proficient with Visual FoxPro, you may want to sell your work to a customer for money.

Fortunately, friends and customers don't need a copy of Visual FoxPro to run your database application; all they need is a compiled version of your program on a disk that can be installed on their computers. I don't go into the nerdy details of compiling because all you really need to know is how to use the Setup Wizard. This wizard can take all your files and stuff them onto a disk so that they can be installed on another computer.

Using OLE

Object linking and embedding (*OLE*) is the wave of the future, and you can incorporate it into your Visual FoxPro applications today. OLE enables you to take a spreadsheet from Microsoft Excel, for example, and link the spreadsheet to a form in your Visual FoxPro application. When someone changes the Excel spreadsheet, the change is reflected in your Visual FoxPro form automatically. Both programs must have access to the same file, either on the same computer or on the same network server.

You can perform similar techniques for many Windows programs, such as word processors and graphical programs.

I give you a glimpse of OLE in Chapter 15, which shows you how to insert a graph into a form. You can make your Visual FoxPro application super-cool if you spend a few moments exploring OLE.

Appendix

Tips on Installing Visual FoxPro

*W*hen I received my copy of Visual FoxPro, I couldn't wait to rip open the shrink-wrapped box and sift through all the manuals and other stuff to find the Visual FoxPro CD.

After breaking the sealed CD packet, which made me legally bound by the terms of the license (although some lawyers would differ with that opinion), I placed the CD in my computer and started it up.

I share with you what happened next so you don't make any of the same mistakes that I did while loading Visual FoxPro.

Check Out the Facts Before Starting the Installation

Microsoft designed Visual FoxPro to run on a computer that has a certain minimum amount of memory; a specific amount of space available on the hard drive; and a minimum CPU requirement, such as a 486, Pentium, and so on.

Check the requirements in the next section before you buy Visual FoxPro — otherwise, you could be making a very expensive mistake.

Do you have the right equipment?

Here's what you need to install and run Visual FoxPro:

- ✔ An IBM-compatible computer
- ✔ A 486 50MHz processor or higher
- ✔ Windows 95 (Visual FoxPro also runs on Windows NT 3.51, but because most readers run Windows 95, I leave it up to you to ask the salesperson in your computer store for requirements for running Visual FoxPro on Windows NT.)
- ✔ 10MB RAM
- ✔ 15MB of hard drive space for running Visual FoxPro on a laptop computer
- ✔ 100MB of hard drive space for running Visual FoxPro for the typical installation on a desktop computer
- ✔ 240MB of hard drive space for running Visual FoxPro for the maximum installation on a desktop computer

If you don't have the right equipment

Make sure your computer has the right outfit to run Visual FoxPro before you remove the shrink-wrap that is around the Visual FoxPro box. Avoid the situation my friend found himself in after purchasing Visual FoxPro.

My buddy was running Windows 3.1 and an older version of FoxPro and felt it was time to move up to the latest version of FoxPro, which is Visual FoxPro. He opened the Visual FoxPro box and tried to install Visual FoxPro, only to learn Visual FoxPro won't run under Windows 3.1.

Discovering that he couldn't install Visual FoxPro on his computer was just the beginning of his troubles. He attempted to return the open copy of Visual FoxPro to the computer store only to be turned away. The shrink-wrap was broken and there was nothing wrong with the Visual FoxPro CD — therefore, he couldn't return Visual FoxPro.

Rather than eat the cost of Visual FoxPro, my friend decided to break down and purchase Windows 95. He thought the installation process would run smoothly once he installed Windows 95. Let's just say he wasn't having a streak of luck. Turns out his computer came with 8MB of memory, while Visual FoxPro requires 10MB. Back to the store for a memory upgrade kit. Eventually, he was able to install Visual FoxPro.

Installing Visual FoxPro

Installing Visual FoxPro isn't complicated. In fact, the process is rather straightforward. However, there are prompts during the installation that force you to make a few decisions. So, I take the time here to walk you through the process and help you make those decisions to complete the installation.

Once you have Visual FoxPro up and running, you may need to add new pieces of Visual FoxPro that are not included in the basic installation. I'm talking about pieces like online documentation, which is sometimes nice to have but takes up a lot of space on your hard drive and not required to run Visual FoxPro.

You may also want to remove infrequently used features of Visual FoxPro, such as online documentation, to free up disk space. You add and remove pieces of Visual FoxPro in the section called "Adding and removing components."

The basic installation

Here's how to install Visual FoxPro:

1. **Place the Visual FoxPro CD in your CD-ROM drive.**

2. **Click the Windows 95 Start button and then click <u>R</u>un.**

   The Run dialog box appears.

3. **Type** d:\setup **in the space provided.**

   Be sure you replace the letter *d* with the letter that represents your CD-ROM drive.

4. **Click OK.**

   The Visual FoxPro setup program displays a Welcome message and a reminder to read the licensing agreement.

5. **Click Continue**

   The Name and Organization Information dialog box appears. You can change the default name and organization. The setup program reads the name and organization from Windows 95. Changes to the default name and organization affect only Visual FoxPro and do not alter the name and organization that Windows 95 uses.

6. Click OK.

Visual FoxPro asks you to confirm the name and organization information.

7. Click OK.

The setup program prompts you to enter the 10-digit CD key, which you find on the Visual FoxPro CD case. If you can't find the CD key, then you need to call Microsoft. More information about contacting Microsoft appears in your owner's documentation.

8. Enter the 10-digit key number.

9. Click OK.

Your Visual FoxPro product ID number shows up on the screen. You need to have this number handy whenever you call Microsoft for product support.

10. Click OK.

The setup program searches your hard drive to determine if you already have Visual FoxPro installed. If you do, then the setup program determines if the files on your Visual FoxPro CD should overwrite the existing files.

11. Click OK to accept the name of the default directory on your hard drive.

The setup program recommends c:\vfp.

12. Click OK.

13. Click Complete, Custom, or Laptop installation.

I suggest you click Complete if you are installing Visual FoxPro on a desktop computer or Laptop if you are installing Visual FoxPro on a laptop computer.

The Choose Program Group dialog box appears.

Accept the default group by clicking Continue when the Choose Program Group dialog box appears.

14. Click Continue.

The Install Help File on hard drive dialog box appears.

15. Click Yes.

I suggest you install the help files so you'll always have help available when you click Help. If you don't, then you'll need to use the Visual FoxPro CD any time you want to use Help. The Choose Program Group dialog box appears again.

16. Click <u>C</u>ontinue.

Accept the default group for the ODBC (see the sidebar titled "All about ODBC" for information you really don't need to know).

The setup program determines if you have sufficient hard drive space. If there isn't enough space, then Visual FoxPro prompts you to remove files and reinstall Visual FoxPro. If there is sufficient space on your hard drive, then the setup program installs Visual FoxPro. The setup program displays a message telling you that you need to restart Windows to complete the installation.

 You may receive a message on the screen that Visual FoxPro cannot complete the installation because a file that Visual FoxPro shares with other Microsoft products currently is in use. You're asked if you want to Abort or Retry. Before making a choice, exit all other Microsoft software that you are running. For example, you'll receive the "cannot complete installation" message if you're running Microsoft Word as you install Visual FoxPro. Once you exit the other Microsoft software, click Retry and the installation of Visual FoxPro will continue.

17. Choose <u>R</u>estart Windows.

The setup program restarts Windows. When Windows restarts you can start Visual FoxPro by clicking Start, then choosing <u>P</u>rograms⇨ Microsoft Visual FoxPro⇨Microsoft Visual FoxPro 5.0.

Adding and removing components

A component is a feature of Visual FoxPro that you don't really need to run Visual FoxPro, such as online help. When you install Visual FoxPro, you can choose to have the setup program install all the components, some of the components, or just the minimum files that you'll need to perform the most common tasks.

Each component you choose to install requires drive space. Sometimes you may not have sufficient space on your drive for all the components, such as online help. Visual FoxPro tells you if you have enough space on your drive when you run the setup program.

If you have insufficient drive space, you can decide not to load the components when you install Visual FoxPro. Instead, you can load the components later on after you free up disk space by deleting files you no longer need.

If you are short on drive space after loading a component, you can delete the component from the drive without removing key Visual FoxPro files.

Here's how to add and remove components:

1. **Click the Start button.**

   The Start menu appears.

2. **Click Programs.**

   A list of programs on your hard drive appears.

3. **Click Microsoft Visual FoxPro.**

   The Visual FoxPro program group is displayed.

4. **Click Microsoft Visual FoxPro Setup.**

   The Setup program runs and examines your drive for the install components; then it displays the Visual FoxPro Setup dialog box.

5. **Click Add/Remove from the Setup dialog box.**

   You can begin installing Visual FoxPro from scratch by clicking Reinstall, or removing Visual FoxPro from your drive entirely by choosing Remove All. You'll rarely need to use either option, but you can read about how to use them in your Visual FoxPro documentation. One scenario where you would use the Remove All option is if you sell your computer and you want to remove all your files from your hard drive.

   When you Click Add/Remove, the setup program displays the Maintenance Installation dialog box.

6. **Click the option that you want to install.**

   The Options list contains the names of the Visual FoxPro options and the amount of drive space each component requires. Each option contains a number of components:

   • A dark check mark means you want the option installed. Click an option that is clear to check the box. The number of thousand bytes (kilobytes) in the Space Required On section increases by the number of thousand bytes of drive space the option requires. The number in the Components to Add section increases by the number of components contained in the option.

   • A grayed check mark means only part of the option will be installed. The remaining part, such as online documentation, is available directly from your CD. Some of the documentation is available in online help, while you can access other parts of the documentation from your CD by using the Help menu.

- A clear box means you want the option removed. Click an option that is checked to clear the box. The number of thousand bytes (kilobytes) in the Space Required On section decreases by the number of thousand bytes of drive space the option requires. The number in the Components to Remove section increases by the number of components that are in the option.

7. **Highlight the name of an option and click Change Option.**

   The Options list changes to show the list of components that comprise the option.

8. **To clear the box, click the name of the component you don't want installed.**

   By default, all the components to be installed are checked. The number of thousand bytes (kilobytes) in the Space Required On section decreases by the number of thousand bytes of drive space the option requires. The number in the Components to Remove section increases by one.

9. **Click OK to return to the full options list.**

   Repeat Steps 7 and 8 until you have chosen those options and components you want to install and remove.

10. **Be sure the Visual FoxPro CD is in your CD drive and then click <u>C</u>ontinue.**

    Visual FoxPro displays a message prompting you to confirm that you want to remove one or more components, if you decided to remove a component. If you didn't ask to remove a component, then no prompt appears.

11. **Click <u>Y</u>es.**

    The setup program adds and removes Visual FoxPro components and displays a message telling you the installation is complete.

12. **Click OK.**

    The setup program ends.

What to do when Visual FoxPro doesn't work

After spending a few minutes installing Visual FoxPro, you're ready to start the engine and jump into building your first Visual FoxPro application. Then, suddenly, disaster strikes. Visual FoxPro doesn't work.

All about ODBC

You can use the queries, forms, reports, and other features covered in this book with information you store in Visual FoxPro databases and tables. Sometimes you need to work with information located in a different kind of file, such as data stored in a:

> Microsoft Access database
>
> Microsoft Excel file
>
> Microsoft dBase database
>
> Paradox database

You may also need to connect to one of the enterprise databases located on fancy computers called servers (sometimes called SQL servers) like those corporations use.

Before you can use Visual FoxPro with a non-Visual FoxPro database or file, Visual FoxPro must learn how to use the non-Visual FoxPro database or file. Fortunately, you can locate all the instructions to access the non-Visual FoxPro database or file in a special kind of file called an *ODBC driver*. ODBC stands for Open Database Connectivity, which is a fancy term that describes how Visual FoxPro communicates with databases, tables, and files other than those that Visual FoxPro creates.

There are a number of ODBC drivers that you can load when you install Visual FoxPro. You won't use most of the ODBC drivers because you are unlikely to use information stored in many other databases or files. Databases or files that you might use, such as Excel, are loaded as the default ODBC driver selection.

Don't worry too much about loading too many ODBC drivers. If you make a mistake and load ODBC drivers that you won't need, you can still run Visual FoxPro. The only drawback for loading unneeded ODBC drivers is that each ODBC driver takes up space on your hard drive, and that space could be used for your other programs and files.

If you loaded too many ODBC drivers by mistake, you can always remove them (see the preceding section, "Adding and removing components").

Here's what to do after you've spoken a few choice words and wished you never bought Visual FoxPro:

- **Stay calm.** This sounds like your teacher speaking, but the first step to solving the problem is to think clearly, which you can't do if you panic. Remember, computers do only what they are told to do. Somehow, the computer has been instructed to do something wrong and your job is to correct the problem.

- **Determine how you know something is wrong.** There are two common symptoms to look for:

  - Visual FoxPro displays a message telling you why Visual FoxPro can't work. You'll see the message appear in a dialog box. Along with the message is usually a tip on how to fix the problem.

- Nothing appears on the screen. You simply have no clue as to what went wrong.

✔ **If Visual FoxPro displays a message that identifies the problem, then follow the remedy given in the message.** Many times the source of the problem is a component that you failed to install. The message tells you which component is missing; then you can add the component (see "Adding and removing components" earlier in this chapter).

Another common problem is that you have insufficient drive space on your hard drive for Visual FoxPro to write one of the various files that Visual FoxPro needs to work. You have to delete old files you don't need anymore from your drive. If you need all the files or can't stand the pain of deleting them, then remove Visual FoxPro components such as ODBC drivers or online documentation that you don't use frequently.

✔ **If Visual FoxPro doesn't appear on your screen, then chances are your computer cannot run Visual FoxPro.** Common problems are in the computer's ROM BIOS (a program found on a chip in your computer that makes your computer work) or the Windows video driver (the program used to display Visual FoxPro on your screen).

Your best bet is to bring the make and model number of your computer to your local computer store. Ask the store's technician if it is economical to upgrade your computer to meet Visual FoxPro's requirements. You can spend half the price of a new computer to upgrade your old computer to run Visual FoxPro.

Configuring Visual FoxPro

You can have Visual FoxPro work the way you like to work by changing the default configuration. Configuration is a term the generally used to describe how the makers of Visual FoxPro thought you'd like to use Visual FoxPro.

Sometimes you'd like to change the way Visual FoxPro handles decimals. You may want to see three decimal places and Visual FoxPro shows you only two. You may want to use commas instead of periods to represent a decimal, as is the style in some European countries. You may even want to change the buttons that appear on the Visual FoxPro toolbar.

You can change many features of Visual FoxPro and I show you how to make these changes in this section.

Setting up the Visual FoxPro environment

The term Visual FoxPro environment describes the various settings in Visual FoxPro, such as whether or not you see grid lines in the Form Designer (see Chapter 11), or if the last project you worked on (see Chapter 19) automatically opens when you start up Visual FoxPro.

By changing settings in the Visual FoxPro environment, you can customize to some degree how Visual FoxPro works. The new settings can exist for the current session of Visual FoxPro and last until you exit Visual FoxPro, or you can set them as the default settings.

Here's how to customize the Visual FoxPro Environment. I exclude options that you don't need to change:

1. **Choose Tools⇨Options.**

   The Options display box appears.

2. **Click the View tab.**

   The View options appear.

3. **Click the settings you want to change.**

   You turn on a setting by clicking on a clear box. You turn off a setting by clicking on a box that contains a check mark.

   - **Status Bar:** Displays the status bar at the bottom of the main Visual FoxPro window. You won't need to change this setting.

   - **Clock:** Displays your computer's clock in the status bar at the bottom of the main Visual FoxPro window. You may not need to change this setting because Windows 95 usually displays the clock in the lower corner of the screen anyway.

   - **Command Results:** Displays the results of certain commands entered in the Visual FoxPro Command Window. You won't need to change this setting.

   - **Systems Messages:** Displays certain messages from Visual FoxPro on the status bar at the bottom of the main Visual FoxPro window. You won't need to change this setting.

   - **Recently used project list:** Displays the last four projects you used when you click File. You won't need to change this setting because this feature is turned on by default.

   - **Open last project on startup:** Automatically opens the last project you worked on when Visual FoxPro starts. Consider changing this setting if you don't always want to work on the last project all the time.

4. Click the General tab.

The General options are displayed.

5. Click the settings you want to change.

You turn on a setting by clicking on a clear box. You turn off a setting by clicking on a box that contains a check mark.

- **Warning Sound Off:** Doesn't make a sound when you make an error.

- **Warning Sound Default:** Beeps when you make an error.

- **Warning Sound Play:** Plays a sound file called a .WAV file when you make an error. If you have a SoundBlaster card or similar card in your computer, you can use a microphone to record your own voice or sounds and save them onto your hard drive as a .WAV file. You can also purchase previously recorded .WAV files from your local computer store and copy them onto your hard drive. Type the name of the .WAV file, and include the full path (drive letter and directory) in the text box to the right of the Play setting.

- **Programming settings:** You won't need to change any of these settings.

- **dBASE compatibility:** You won't need to change this setting.

- **Use Visual FoxPro color palette:** You won't need to change this setting.

- **Confirm file replacement:** Don't change this setting. If you turn off the Confirm file replacement setting, then Visual FoxPro won't ask you if you're sure you want to overwrite an existing file. You could accidentally lose information in your tables.

- **Browse IME control:** You won't need to change this setting.

- **Data Entry Navigation keys:** You won't need to change this setting.

- **Data Entry Fill new records with current values:** You won't need to change this setting.

- **Data Entry Enter or tab to exit fields:** You won't need to change this setting.

6. Click the Regional tab.

The Regional options appear.

7. Click the settings you want to change.

You turn on a setting by clicking on a clear box. You turn off a setting by clicking on a box that contains a check mark.

- **Use System Settings:** You won't need to change this setting.

- **Date and Time Date Format:** Displays the date and time in the format customary to each country. Choose from the list of countries displayed when you select the Date Format combo box.

- **Date and Time Date Separator:** Choose the character used to separate components of the date — by default, the slash (/) is the separator. Click Date Separator and then enter the character you want used as the separator in the text box that appears to the right of the Date Separator.

- **Date and Time Century:** By default, two digits represent the century (97). Click Century, and four digits are used to represent the century (1997). You probably want to use four digits to represent the century as the year 2000 approaches because you could confuse dates if you have information dated in 1900 and the year 2000 (both centuries appear as 00 if you use two digits to represent the century).

- **Date and Time 12-Hour and 24-Hour:** The default is 12-hours, so you'll see time represented as AM or PM. Otherwise, time is represented as a 24-hour clock where 1 AM is 1300 hours.

- **Date and Time Seconds:** The default is set to display seconds; otherwise, seconds are not displayed when time is displayed.

- **Currency and Numbers Currency Format:** The default is the currency system displayed to the left of the numbers; otherwise, the currency symbol appears to the right of the numbers.

- **Currency and Numbers Currency Symbol:** The default currency symbol is a dollar sign. You can enter any other currency symbol if the currency you want is not expressed in dollars. Highlight the dollar sign in the Currency Symbol setting and enter a new symbol.

- **Currency and Numbers 1000 Separator:** The default 1000 separator is a comma. Every third digit left of the decimal separator is a comma. You can enter any character you normally use as a 1000 separator — such as a period, used in some European countries — by highlighting the comma in the 1000 Separator setting and entering a new separator.

- **Currency and Numbers Decimal Separator:** The default decimal separator is a period. You can enter any character you normally use as a decimal separator — such as a comma, used in some European countries — by highlighting the period in the decimal separator setting and entering a new separator.

- **Currency and Numbers Decimal Digits:** The default number of decimal places is two. You can change the number of decimal places by using the arrows on the spinner or by highlighting the number of decimal places and then typing the new number of decimals you want to see.

- **Week Starts on:** By default, the first day of the week is Sunday. You probably won't have to change this setting.

- **First Week of Year:** You won't have to change this setting.

Choose Set As Default if you want your changes to become the default settings.

Set As Default enables Visual FoxPro to use the settings you changed whenever Visual FoxPro runs. If you don't choose Set As Default, then the settings you changed will return to the original default setting the next time you run Visual FoxPro.

9. **Click OK.**

I purposely did not discuss the other tabs on the Options dialog box because you rarely will need to change the default settings for those options. Refer to your owner's documentation for more information about those tabs.

When you click OK, the Options dialog box disappears from the screen, and those settings you changed are active.

Customizing the Visual FoxPro toolbar

Visual FoxPro displays a toolbar under the menu when starting up. Buttons on the toolbar represent functions that you can execute by clicking on the button, such as Undo or Print.

You can change the functions that appear on the toolbar by customizing the toolbar. You can remove any of the default functions or add new functions to the toolbar. You may want to add a function to the toolbar whenever you frequently use a function that doesn't appear on the toolbar.

Here's how you customize the toolbar:

1. Choose View⇨Toolbars.

The Toolbars dialog box appears.

2. Click in the check box of the toolbar you want to customize.

Visual FoxPro has several different toolbars that it uses in different parts of the program. For example, the toolbar you see when you design forms is different from the toolbar you see when you design queries.

3. Click Customize.

4. Highlight the category that contains the function you want to add to the toolbar.

The functions associated with the selected category appear as buttons in the Button section of the dialog box.

5. Click the button that represents the function you want to add to the toolbar.

A description of the button appears in the Description section of the dialog box. Click another button if the description is the not the function you want to add to the toolbar.

6. Point to the button you want to add, hold down the left mouse button, drag the button you want to add to the toolbar, and release the mouse button.

Visual FoxPro automatically inserts the button into the toolbar.

7. Point to a button on the toolbar, hold down the left mouse button, and drag the button into the Customize Toolbar dialog box to remove a button from the toolbar.

Buttons, buttons, who's got the buttons?

Buttons you place on the toolbar behave like the default buttons that appear on the toolbar when you start up Visual FoxPro. You can call the function associated with the button only if the button is dark. You cannot call the function associated with the button if the button is grayed.

A button that is grayed indicates that you must do something else before you can call the function. What you need to do before calling the function depends on the function itself. For example, the copy button remains gray until you select text for copying. When you select text, Visual FoxPro darkens the copy button. Choose Help⇨Index and then enter the name of the function you want to review. Instructions appear on how to use the function.

Remember to use this step in case you make a mistake when you customize the toolbar. You can always remove a button from the toolbar.

8. Click Close.

The Customize Toolbar dialog box closes, and you return to the Toolbars dialog box.

Don't panic if you feel you've messed up the toolbar by adding or removing too many buttons. Click Reset on the Toolbars dialog box to return the toolbar to the default setting.

9. Click OK.

The Toolbars dialog box disappears.

Index

• G •

IDG BOOKS WORLDWIDE REGISTRATION CARD

RETURN THIS REGISTRATION CARD FOR FREE CATALOG

Title of this book: **Visual FoxPro™ 5 For Dummies®**

My overall rating of this book: ❑ Very good [1]   ❑ Good [2]   ❑ Satisfactory [3]   ❑ Fair [4]   ❑ Poor [5]

How I first heard about this book:

❑ Found in bookstore; name: [6]

❑ Advertisement: [8]

❑ Word of mouth; heard about book from friend, co-worker, etc.: [10]

❑ Book review: [7]

❑ Catalog: [9]

❑ Other: [11]

What I liked most about this book:

What I would change, add, delete, etc., in future editions of this book:

Other comments:

Number of computer books I purchase in a year: ❑ 1 [12]   ❑ 2-5 [13]   ❑ 6-10 [14]   ❑ More than 10 [15]

I would characterize my computer skills as: ❑ Beginner [16] ❑ Intermediate [17] ❑ Advanced [18] ❑ Professional [19]

I use ❑ DOS [20] ❑ Windows [21] ❑ OS/2 [22] ❑ Unix [23] ❑ Macintosh [24] ❑ Other: [25]_____
(please specify)

I would be interested in new books on the following subjects:
(please check all that apply, and use the spaces provided to identify specific software)

❑ Word processing: [26]

❑ Data bases: [28]

❑ File Utilities: [30]

❑ Networking: [32]

❑ Other: [34]

❑ Spreadsheets: [27]

❑ Desktop publishing: [29]

❑ Money management: [31]

❑ Programming languages: [33]

I use a PC at (please check all that apply): ❑ home [35] ❑ work [36] ❑ school [37] ❑ other: [38] _____

The disks I prefer to use are ❑ 5.25 [39] ❑ 3.5 [40] ❑ other: [41]_____

I have a CD ROM: ❑ yes [42]   ❑ no [43]

I plan to buy or upgrade computer hardware this year: ❑ yes [44]   ❑ no [45]

I plan to buy or upgrade computer software this year: ❑ yes [46]   ❑ no [47]

Name: _____ Business title: [48] _____ Type of Business: [49] _____

Address (❑ home [50] ❑ work [51]/Company name: _____)

Street/Suite# _____

City [52]/State [53]/Zipcode [54]: _____ Country [55] _____

❑ **I liked this book!** You may quote me by name in future
IDG Books Worldwide promotional materials.

My daytime phone number is _____

IDG BOOKS®

THE WORLD OF COMPUTER KNOWLEDGE

☐ **YES!**

Please keep me informed about IDG's World of Computer Knowledge.
Send me the latest IDG Books catalog.